"In taking us straight to the heart of the text, Phil Moore has served us magnificently. We so need to get into the Scriptures and let the Scriptures get into us. The fact that Phil writes so relevantly and with such submission to Biblical revelation means that we are genuinely helped to be shaped by the Bible's teaching."

– Terry Virgo

"Fresh. Solid. Simple. Really good stuff."

– R. T. Kendall

"Phil makes the deep truths of Scripture alive and accessible. If you want to grow in your understanding of each book of the Bible, then buy these books and let them change your life!"

– PJ Smyth – *GodFirst Church, Johannesburg, South Africa*

*"Most commentaries are dull. These are alive. Most commentaries are for scholars. These are for **you**!"*

– Canon Michael Green

*"These notes are amazingly good. Lots of content and depth of research, yet packed in a **Big Breakfast** that leaves the reader well fed and full. Bible notes often say too little, yet larger commentaries can be dull – missing the wood for the trees. Phil's insights are striking, original, and fresh, going straight to the heart of the text and the reader! Substantial yet succinct, they bristle with amazing insights and life applications, compelling us to read more. Bible reading will become enriched and informed with such a scintillating guide. Teachers and preachers will find nuggets of pure gold here!"*

– Greg Haslam – *Westminster Chapel, London, UK*

"The Bible is living and a are those who bear tha talking. Phil has written combination of cre

– Joel Virgo – *Le*

GW00498466

"Phil Moore's new commentaries are outstanding: biblical and passionate, clear and well-illustrated, simple and profound. God's Word comes to life as you read them, and the wonder of God shines through every page."

– **Andrew Wilson** – *Author of* Incomparable *and* If God Then What?

"Want to understand the Bible better? Don't have the time or energy to read complicated commentaries? The book you have in your hand could be the answer. Allow Phil Moore to explain and then apply God's message to your life. Think of this book as the Bible's message distilled for everyone."

– **Adrian Warnock**, *Christian blogger*

"Phil Moore presents Scripture in a dynamic, accessible and relevant way. The bite-size chunks – set in context and grounded in contemporary life – really make the make the Word become flesh and dwell among us."

– **Dr David Landrum**, *The Bible Society*

"Through a relevant, very readable, up to date storying approach, Phil Moore sets the big picture, relates God's Word to today and gives us fresh insights to increase our vision, deepen our worship, know our identity and fire our imagination. Highly recommended!"

– **Geoff Knott**, *former CEO of Wycliffe Bible Translators UK*

"What an exciting project Phil has embarked upon! These accessible and insightful books will ignite the hearts of believers, inspire the minds of preachers and help shape a new generation of men and women who are seeking to learn from God's Word."

– **David Stroud**, *Newfrontiers and ChristChurch London*

For more information about the Straight to the Heart series, please go to **www.philmoorebooks.com**.

STRAIGHT TO
THE HEART OF

1&2 Samuel

60 BITE-SIZED INSIGHTS

Phil Moore

MONARCH
BOOKS

Oxford, UK & Grand Rapids, Michigan, USA

First published in the UK in 2012 by Monarch Books
(a publishing imprint of Lion Hudson plc)
Wilkinson House, Jordan Hill Road, Oxford OX2 8DR, England
Tel: +44 (0)1865 302750 Fax: +44 (0)1865 302757
Email: monarch@lionhudson.com
www.lionhudson.com

ISBN 978 0 85721 252 8 (print)
ISBN 978 0 85721 319 8 (Kindle)
ISBN 978 0 85721 320 4 (epub)
ISBN 978 0 85721 321 1 (PDF)

Distributed by:
UK: Marston Book Services, PO Box 269, Abingdon, Oxon, OX14 4YN
USA: Kregel Publications, PO Box 2607, Grand Rapids, Michigan 49501

The text paper used in this book has been made from wood
independently certified as having come from sustainable forests.

British Library Cataloguing Data
A catalogue record for this book is available from the British Library.

Printed and bound in the UK by Clays Ltd, St Ives plc.

This book is for my friend Nick Derbridge.
May the disappointments of the past and the delays
of the present make you more and more into
the kind of person God can use.

CONTENTS

2 SAMUEL 1–10: A PERSON WHO LOVES GOD'S NAME

2 SAMUEL 11–24: A REPENTANT PERSON

About the *Straight to the Heart* Series

On his eightieth birthday, Sir Winston Churchill dismissed the compliment that he was the "lion" who had defeated Nazi Germany in World War Two. He told the Houses of Parliament that *"It was a nation and race dwelling all around the globe that had the lion's heart. I had the luck to be called upon to give the roar."*

I hope that God speaks to you very powerfully through the "roar" of the books in the *Straight to the Heart* series. I hope they help you to understand the books of the Bible and the message which the Holy Spirit inspired their authors to write. I hope that they help you to hear God's voice challenging you, and that they provide you with a springboard for further journeys into each book of Scripture for yourself.

But when you hear my "roar", I want you to know that it comes from the heart of a much bigger "lion" than me. I have been shaped by a whole host of great Christian thinkers and preachers from around the world, and I want to give due credit to at least some of them here:

Terry Virgo, David Stroud, John Hosier, Adrian Holloway, Greg Haslam, Lex Loizides and all those who lead the Newfrontiers family of churches. Friends and encouragers, such as Stef Liston, Joel Virgo, Stuart Gibbs, Scott Taylor, Nick Sharp, Nick Derbridge, Phil Whittall, and Kevin and Sarah Aires. Tony Collins, Jenny Ward and Simon Cox at Monarch Books. Malcolm Kayes and all the elders of The Coign Church, Woking. My fellow elders and church members here at Queens Road Church, Wimbledon.

My great friend Andrew Wilson – without your friendship, encouragement and example, this series would never have happened.

I would like to thank my parents, my brother Jonathan, and my in-laws, Clive and Sue Jackson. Dad – your example birthed in my heart the passion which brought this series into being. I didn't listen to all you said when I was a child, but I couldn't ignore the way you got up at five o'clock every morning to pray, read the Bible and worship, because of your radical love for God and for his Word. I'd like to thank my children – Isaac, Noah, Esther and Ethan – for keeping me sane when publishing deadlines were looming. But most of all, I'm grateful to my incredible wife, Ruth – my friend, encourager, corrector and helper.

You all have the lion's heart, and you have all developed the lion's heart in me. I count it an enormous privilege to be the one who was chosen to sound the lion's roar.

So welcome to the *Straight to the Heart* series. My prayer is that you will let this roar grip your own heart too – for the glory of the great Lion of the Tribe of Judah, the Lord Jesus Christ!

Introduction: The Kind of Person God Can Use

The Lord has sought out a man after his own heart and appointed him ruler of his people.

(1 Samuel 13:14)

If you want to understand the basic message of 1 and 2 Samuel, then you may find it helpful to think of Thomas Edison. He may not have been the original inventor of the light bulb, but he built tirelessly on the work of others to find the kind of filament which would make it an invention all the world could use.

Thomas Edison's experiments in 1879 were very much like the book of Judges, which covers the two and a half centuries leading up to the start of 1 Samuel. He passed electricity through many different filaments in the hope of finding one which burned brightly in the darkness. Many of them failed to do so – like Barak, the man God called to display his glory during a Canaanite invasion in around 1257 BC. He was so unwilling to let God use him that God had to show his power through a foreign woman instead.[1]

Other filaments shone as brightly as Thomas Edison intended, but failed to burn as long and consistently as was needed. They were like Gideon, who displayed God's saving power when he defeated the Midianites in about 1210 BC, but who quickly succumbed afterwards to the sins of idolatry and polygamy. They were like Jephthah, who shone brightly for the Lord when he routed the Ammonite army in about 1107 BC,

---

[1] Judges 4:8–9 makes it clear that this was shameful in his culture. The song of praise which follows blesses Jael, not Barak.

yet knew God so dimly that he went home and made a human sacrifice of his daughter in a misguided attempt to glorify him.

Finally, the Lord told a barren mother that she would conceive and give birth to Israel's twelfth and greatest judge so far. Samson would *"be a Nazirite, dedicated to God from the womb"* and he would *"take the lead in delivering Israel from the hands of the Philistines."*[2] He would be like the filament which Thomas Edison produced from carbonized cotton thread and which made him so excited that he filed for a patent for his light bulb at the end of 1879. Like that filament, however, Samson also proved to be as flawed as the eleven judges who had gone before. When the power of God came upon him, it revealed he was still governed by his lust and anger instead of by the Lord. Thomas Edison's cotton filament destroyed itself after only thirteen hours. He had still not found the kind of filament he could use.

Thankfully, the message of 1 and 2 Samuel is that God did not give up on his search. He was determined to reveal his glory by finding the kind of person he could use. We read in 1 Samuel 1–7 that he found *a humble person* in the form of the fourteenth and final judge, Samuel, and that he used him to do everything which Samson had failed to do. We read in 1 Samuel 8–15 that he looked for *an obedient person* and that when the first king, Saul, failed to be such a person God revealed a better candidate in a shepherd-boy named David. In 1 Samuel 16–31, we discover the lengths God went to in order to make David into *a pure person* so that he would be the kind of person God could use.

The story continues in 2 Samuel 1–10, as David begins his reign and proves himself to be *a person who loves God's name*. He is as different from Saul as Samuel was from Samson, like the filament of carbonized bamboo which Thomas Edison discovered in 1880 and which burned for over 1,200 hours,

---

[2] Judges 13:5. Unless we understand the failure of Samson, we cannot understand the success of Samuel.

marking the invention of the first commercially viable electric light bulb. God has finally found the kind of person he can use, and 1 and 2 Samuel look like they have reached a happy ending.

But they haven't. David sins, and badly. He fails the Lord more dramatically than Barak, Gideon, Jephthah, Samson and Saul put together. The story ends with 2 Samuel 11–24 telling us that God is looking for *a repentant person* who admits his sin and looks to a better, brighter Saviour than King David.[3] The Hebrew Old Testament groups 1 and 2 Samuel with the books that are known as "the Former Prophets" because the writer always intended us to receive his work as more than just a history book. He prophesies the coming of someone far greater than David, God's *anointed one* – the word in Hebrew is *messiah*. He prophesies that David's dynasty will produce a greater Son who will perfectly fulfil the message of these chapters and become the ultimate Person God can use.

1 and 2 Samuel must have been completed some time after 930 BC, since they refer repeatedly to "Israel" and "Judah" as two distinct kingdoms.[4] They must also have been completed some time before 925 BC, since they tell us that Ziklag belonged to the kings of Judah *"to this day"*, and we know that Ziklag was annexed by the Egyptians in that year.[5] This means that the readers of 1 and 2 Samuel had 400 years to wait before God gave them a commentary on its meaning after the Jews returned

---

[3] It is one story because 1 and 2 Samuel form one book in the Hebrew Old Testament. It was split into two books by the translators of the Greek Septuagint because Hebrew was written without vowels and therefore fitted more onto a scroll than Greek. Just to confuse things further, the Latin Bible labelled them "1 and 2 Kings" and labelled what we call 1 and 2 Kings "3 and 4 Kings"!

[4] 1 Samuel 11:8; 17:52; 18:16; 27:6; 2 Samuel 5:5; 24:1–9. This is one reason why it is a misinterpretation of 1 Chronicles 29:29–30 to think Samuel was the primary author (that and the fact he dies halfway through!), and a misinterpretation of 2 Samuel 23:1 to think David was the primary author.

[5] Other similar clues can be found in 1 Samuel 5:5, 6:18, 9:9 and 30:25, and 2 Samuel 4:3, 6:8 and 18:18.

from exile in Babylon. He gave them 1 and 2 Chronicles, the last book of the Hebrew Old Testament,[6] which the Greek Septuagint translation simply entitles "The Things Which Were Omitted". The author of 1 Chronicles intended his writing to serve as a supplement to 1 and 2 Samuel, and he deliberately fills in some of the blanks in order to help us understand its underlying message. He takes a selective view of the same incidents in the life of David and uses them to point to a better Messiah who will be the greatest filament of them all.

So get ready for the message of 1 and 2 Samuel, which are as much a personal biography of Samuel, Saul and David as they are a national history of Israel and Judah. If you read them and respond to their message – imitating Samuel's *humility* and David's *obedience, purity, passion for God's name* and *repentance* when he sinned – then God will enable you to take your own place in the great drama which he is still performing through Jesus, his Messiah. He will fill you with his power and make you glow brightly in this dark world to the praise of his all-surpassing glory.

Get ready to be part of God's great salvation story. Get ready to let him shape you into the kind of person he can use.

---

[6] 1 and 2 Chronicles are also one book in the Hebrew Old Testament, as are 1 and 2 Kings. The Hebrew Old Testament orders the books differently from English Bibles, placing 1 and 2 Chronicles right at the end.

1 Samuel 1–7:

A Humble Person

Why God Makes People Cry (1:1–28)

*In her deep anguish Hannah prayed to the Lord,
weeping bitterly.*

(1 Samuel 1:10)

I was recently reading the Roald Dahl novel *Charlie and the Chocolate Factory* to my young children. If you've never read it, it's the story of an eccentric chocolate manufacturer who invites five lucky children to visit his factory with a view to installing one of them as his heir. While Charlie is polite and instantly loveable, the other four children are definitely not. The greedy Augustus Gloop gets swept away by a chocolate river, the spoilt Veruca Salt gets thrown out with the garbage, and the gum-chewing Violet Beauregarde comes to an appropriately sticky end. At this point, one of my children turned to me and said, *"I really hope that Charlie is the one left at the end and not Mike Teavee."* It suddenly dawned on me that my children didn't know the unwritten storybook rule: bad things only happen to bad people, and good things only happen to good people.

I know the rule. You know the rule. But that makes the first chapter of 1 Samuel all the more surprising. It appears that, like my children, God doesn't know this unwritten rule, or if he does know then he decides to break it in this chapter and very often in our own lives too. If God is good then why does he make so many good people cry?

Think about it. Peninnah means *Pearl* or *Ruby*, but there was nothing beautiful about the second wife of Elkanah. She taunted Hannah for her infertility and made her life a misery, yet God blessed her with many sons and daughters. Hannah means *Grace*, and she lived up to her name, yet God rewarded her with trouble and a monthly cycle of disappointment. She thought she had married a godly man[1] – one of the few men in backslidden Israel who still came to worship at the Lord's Tabernacle in Shiloh[2] – yet after their wedding he embraced the same polygamy as his neighbours[3] and proved crassly insensitive towards her pain in verse 8. Even Eli, Israel's high priest and thirteenth judge,[4] accused Hannah of drunkenness and tried to throw her out of the Tabernacle. The writer wants us to react against this apparent injustice, so he shocks us twice in verses 5 and 6 by telling us that *"the Lord had closed Hannah's womb."* It wasn't chance and it wasn't the Devil. It was the Lord, and he did it for a reason.

Hannah wasn't the first woman in the Old Testament whom the Lord had made infertile. He had done the same thing to the wives of the three great patriarchs – Sarah, Rebekah and Rachel – as well as to the mother of Samson and the great-grandmother of David.[5] In fact, a straight reading of the Old Testament so far suggests that anguish and infertility are often part of the training programme God devises to create the kind of women he can use.

You see, unlike Peninnah or Elkanah, Hannah was delivered from her backslidden culture through the abject misery which she endured. It turned her into one of the great praying women

---

[1] Elkanah means *Purchased by God*, and 1 Chronicles 6:25–38 clarifies that he merely lived in Ephraim and was actually from the godly tribe of Levi.

[2] Moses' Tabernacle had been turned into a semi-permanent building at Shiloh after Joshua 18:1, which is why it is called a *temple* for the first time in 1:9 and 3:3.

[3] Even though the patriarchs took multiple wives, Genesis 2:24 declared it sinful, and one of the great themes of 1 and 2 Samuel is that polygamy always leads to trouble.

[4] 1 Samuel 4:18 makes it clear that Eli was Israel's judge as well as high priest. It says literally that he *judged* Israel, just as in Judges 4:4, 10:2–3, 12:7–14, 15:20 and 16:31.

[5] Genesis 11:30; 25:21; 29:31; Judges 13:2; Ruth 1:4–5; 4:13.

of the Old Testament, as she *poured out her soul* to the Lord in verse 15. She came to know God in verse 11 as *Yahweh Tsabāōth – the Lord of Armies, or Lord Almighty* – despite the fact that Israel had been overrun by the Philistines and the rest of her fellow Hebrews disregarded him as the weak and outdated deity of yesteryear. It caused her to pray such gritty, persistent, anguished prayers of faith that she became the perfect filament God could use to display his glory to the whole of Israel.

The chronology of the book of Judges suggests that the events described in this chapter took place at roughly the same time that Samson died as a prisoner of the Philistines. The writer wants us to notice the deliberate parallels between the baby Hannah was to conceive and the judge who had just failed. Samson had been born to a barren woman, had been called to be a Nazirite from his mother's womb[6] and had been called to lead Israel to freedom from the Philistines, but had failed. Samuel would be born to another barren woman, would be a true Nazirite and would succeed in delivering Israel from the Philistines in chapter 7. Even their names sounded similar, except that Samuel meant *Heard by God* and spoke of gratitude for prayers answered in the past and prophesied more answers to prayer in the future.[7] If Hannah had not graduated from the Lord's school of humility by learning lessons through her suffering, she would never have handed her little boy over to Eli to grow up in the Tabernacle without her.[8] Because she did so, she became the kind of person God could use.[9]

---

[6] Compare Numbers 6:1–21; Judges 13:7, 12–14; 1 Samuel 1:11, 22, 28.

[7] There is also another play on words here in Hebrew, since Hannah uses the verb which is at the root of the name *Saul* to describe her *asking* God for Samuel in verse 27 and for her *lending* him back to God in verse 28.

[8] In the Masoretic Hebrew text of verse 23, Elkanah wants *the Lord* to stick to his promise, but in the Dead Sea Scrolls Hebrew text and the Greek Septuagint he wants the Lord to make *Hannah* stick to her promise. Elkanah knew how difficult it would be for Hannah to hand over little Samuel.

[9] We are meant to understand the reference to a *three-year-old bull* in verse 24 to mean that Hannah weaned Samuel and handed him over to Eli at Shiloh

Nobody except you fully knows the sorrows in your own life, but if God has made you cry like Hannah then I hope you find comfort in the promises of this chapter. I hope it helps you trust that God's delays today are a sign that he has something far better in store for you tomorrow. I hope you notice that the writer doesn't bother to name Peninnah's sons and daughters, or the five children who were born to Hannah after she handed over Samuel in 2:21. Those children born out of ease and comfort had not been prayed for and blessed through the Lord making their mother cry. They were not like Samuel, who would become the greatest judge of Israel, the deliverer of God's People, the Lord's prophet and the kingmaker who would transition Israel from a loose confederation of tribes led by judges into a centralized monarchy. I hope this chapter helps you understand that God has made you cry because your tears are watering the earth of your life to produce a harvest of grace beyond your wildest dreams. After all, if God is big enough for you to blame in your troubles, then he is also big enough for you to trust him in the midst of them too.

If God grants you encouragement through this chapter, then follow Hannah's lead in verse 18 when she responds to Eli's blessing with faith and joy. Although nothing has changed visibly and she has only the word of God's priest to suggest that her prayer has been heard at all,[10] she dries her eyes and breaks her fast and starts worshipping the Lord.

As you worship alongside her, you will become the kind of person God can use.

---

when he was three years old.

[10] Eli's words in Hebrew in verse 17 can be translated in two ways. They can be a prayer, *"May the God of Israel grant you what you have asked of him"*, or they can be a priestly blessing that *"The God of Israel has granted you what you have asked of him."*

How to Make God Your Enemy (2:1–26)

Those who oppose the Lord will be broken. The Most High will thunder from heaven.

(1 Samuel 2:10)

Eli was probably full of high hopes for his children when his wife bore him two sons to succeed him as priests of Israel. He called one of them Hophni, which meant *Boxer*, because he hoped that he would perhaps spar for the Lord against the evil within Israel. He called the other one Phinehas after Aaron's famous grandson who fought zealously for the honour of the Lord in Numbers 25. Since the name meant *Mouth of Bronze*, it appears that Eli hoped his son would preach an unflinching message which would revive backslidden Israel. He hoped that his two sons would know the Lord as their greatest friend.

Sadly, Eli's hopes were not to be. Hophni and Phinehas grew up without the character which Hannah celebrates in her prayer of thanks in verses 1–10. She proclaims the greatness of the Lord, calling him *Yahweh* or *The God Who Really Is* nine times in just ten verses. Like Jacob and Moses, she calls him Israel's *"Rock"* in verse 2 and rejoices that he is the God who knows everything in verse 3.[1] She describes him as the one who befriends the humble and the stumbling soldier and the hungry beggar and the barren woman, yet who comes as a sworn enemy against the proud and the strong and the arrogant and the wealthy. Her prayer serves as the theme tune to the whole of these first seven chapters, but it wasn't a song which Hophni

---

[1] Genesis 49:24; Deuteronomy 32:4, 15, 18, 30, 31.

and Phinehas knew how to sing. They delighted in their own strength, and it turned God into their enemy.

Eli had used a Hebrew insult in 1:16 when he accused Hannah of being a *"daughter of Belial"*, meaning a worthless scoundrel.[2] He was as unfair towards Samuel's mother as he was indulgent towards his two sons. The writer of 1 Samuel uses the same phrase in 2:12 to tell us that *"Eli's sons were scoundrels; they had no regard for the Lord."* They were the exact opposite of the kind of people God could use.

Hophni and Phinehas loved the trappings of the priesthood, but neither of them actually knew the Lord. They didn't understand that the blood sacrifices at the Tabernacle pointed to a day when God's Messiah would die a bloody death for the forgiveness of the world. They sneered at the Lord's instruction to his priests in Leviticus 3:16 and 7:25 that all the fattiest meat belonged to him and that anyone who stole it must be cut off from his People. They abused their position to seduce the God-fearing women who came to serve the Lord at his Tabernacle in verse 22.[3] The only sparring Hophni did was with worshippers who tried to resist his attempts to plunder their sacrifices, and the only zeal which Phinehas displayed was to fill his belly and his bed. Eli had hoped that they would be like Aaron's godly sons Eleazar and Ithamar, but instead they were like his sinful sons Nadab and Abihu, who made the Lord their enemy and were struck dead in his anger at the Tabernacle in Leviticus 10.

When the Lord failed to judge them with instant death, Hophni and Phinehas assumed it meant he was their friend. They stepped up their activity, bullying worshippers mid-sacrifice into handing over their meat while it was still raw. When Eli

---

[2] The phrase *son* or *daughter of Belial* is used over twenty times in the Old Testament. The translators of the Septuagint understood it to mean *son of yokelessness*, and therefore translated it as *lawless person*.

[3] We should not understand verse 22 to mean that shrine prostitutes served at the Tabernacle. The Lord had invited godly women to come and serve him there in Exodus 38:8.

rebuked them weakly yet failed to suspend them from duty, it reinforced their view that God would no doubt prove a similar pushover when judgment day finally came. While Hannah lived out the words of her prayer by making painful annual visits to the son she had devoted to the Lord,[4] they continued *"treating the Lord's offering with contempt"* and provoked him to display his glory by waging war against them.

God is looking for humble people he can use as filaments to display the brilliance of his glory to the world. When people insist on being proud and arrogant, he still uses them as filaments, but as ones which display his glory through his holy anger and righteous opposition. The promise of 1 Timothy 2:4 that God *"wants all people to be saved and to come to a knowledge of the truth,"* must be balanced against the statement in 1 Samuel 2:25 that *"it was the Lord's will to put them to death."* When Hophni and Phinehas despised God Almighty and acted as if he was God All-Matey, he declared war against them as his sworn enemies and made them a warning for us all.[5]

That's why each of us needs to read this chapter and ask whether the Lord is truly our friend or whether our actions have turned him into our foe. It's not enough to say that we think he is on our side, for even wicked Hophni and Phinehas thought that. We need to examine our hearts to see if we are proud talkers, strong warriors, rich go-getters or spiritual beggars who walk humbly before the Lord. We need to take Hannah's prayer seriously, as well as the rest of Scripture, which warns

---

[4] The writer continues his Hebrew play on words in verse 20 by using the verb at the root of the name *Saul* to describe Hannah *asking* for a child and *lending* him back to the Lord. She could not out-give God, who gave her five more children in return.

[5] We can see this in the way Hannah uses the word *she'ol* to refer to *the grave* in verse 6, since this is the commonest Old Testament word for *hell* (e.g. in Job 24:19; Psalm 9:17; 49:14–15; 139:8; Proverbs 15:24; 23:14).

repeatedly that *"God **opposes** the proud but shows favour to the humble."*[6]

When we examine ourselves and find traces of the same pride which was the downfall of Hophni and Phinehas, Hannah tells us what we must do with our sin. She doesn't end her prayer in verse 10 with a prophecy that her son Samuel will grow up to serve God as a faithful priest and judge. She ends by prophesying that her son will point to someone else who will serve as God's perfect *King* and *Messiah*.[7] She sees that Jesus will walk the path of humility she describes, and will lay down his life as the great blood sacrifice which Hophni and Phinehas had despised.[8] He would be the one to whom people can run when they discover that their pride has made God into their enemy. *"Once you were alienated from God and were enemies in your minds because of your evil behaviour,"* Paul explains in Colossians 1:21–22. *"But now he has reconciled you by Christ's physical body through death to present you holy in his sight, without blemish and free from accusation."*

So don't read any further into 1 Samuel until you have straightened out this question. Are you the humble kind of person God can use, or are you the proud kind of person he calls his enemy? Let's kneel with Hannah as she celebrates humility and puts her faith in God's blood sacrifice. Let's look to the one who died for us when we were his enemies and who calls us to follow in his footsteps as the humble friends of God.

---

[6] Proverbs 3:34; James 4:6; 1 Peter 5:5. Jesus taught in Matthew 5:3 that God is looking for spiritual beggars.

[7] To fully understand the message of 1 and 2 Samuel, we need to grasp that the Hebrew word for *anointed one* is *messiah*. Although it often points to David, it always points beyond him to the coming of his greater Son.

[8] There is a deliberate echo of verse 26 when Luke 1:80, 2:40 and 2:52 describe the coming of Jesus the Messiah and of the Nazirite prophet who heralded his arrival. There is also a deliberate echo of Hannah's prayer when Mary sings praise to the Lord in Luke 1:46–55 for opposing the proud and helping the humble.

Lord, thank you that you have kept your hand on my life and thank you that you love me a banner! Lord help me to be more like Hannah, forgive me for any praudness, rich go getter, help me to stay humble to you. Amen ✗.

Water Flows Downhill
(2:27–36)

I will raise up for myself a faithful priest, who will do according to what is in my heart and mind.

(1 Samuel 2:35)

I hope you have never lived in a house that has been flooded. It happened to me once several years ago, and it was a pretty horrible experience. I was living in a house by the river and several weeks of heavy rain had caused the river to burst its banks. I sandbagged the door and installed an emergency water pump, but I couldn't resist the simple fact of physics: Water always flows downhill.

When unwanted water flows downhill into a house it means an insurance claim, but when it flows downhill to God's People then it always spells disaster. The writer of 1 Samuel turns from addressing the sins of Hophni and Phinehas, and starts addressing the sins of their father Eli, the thirteenth judge of Israel. He warns that the character of a leader flows downhill like a river and is replicated in the lives of those he leads. Eli had failed to be a humble filament in God's hands, and he was responsible for the way in which the whole of Israel burned very dimly.[1]

God sends a nameless prophet to confront Eli with his sin in verse 27. As the heir of the first high priest Aaron's eldest

---

[1] Although many English translations understand the Hebrew of verse 24 to mean that the *news of the sin* spread throughout Israel, the Greek Septuagint is probably more accurate when it understands the Hebrew to mean that the news it was unrestrained caused *the sin itself* to spread throughout Israel.

surviving son, Eleazar, Eli was responsible for all the blood sacrifices in the Tabernacle and for teaching the Israelites how to be the kind of people God could use. His failure to stop his sons from compromising both of those things had proved he loved them more than the Lord and had made him party to their sin.[2] His toothless rebuke in verses 23–25 had been a far cry from God's command in Deuteronomy 21:18–21 that he should stone his sons to death if they continued to lead Israel astray. The prophet's curse uses the "you plural" form of the Hebrew verb in verse 29 because Eli had grown fat on the meat which his sons had stolen from the altar and given him, which is one of the reasons why God judges him by making his fatness a direct cause of his death in 4:18. God traced the sins of Israel back to the source of the river and laid the blame there. Eli was God's appointed leader, and water always flows downhill.

It doesn't matter whether you have been entrusted with leading a church, a small group or simply your own family, you should find these verses very sobering. You should also find it sobering to read 1 Timothy 3, Titus 1 and 1 Peter 5 to find that thirty-two out of forty-five qualifications for church leadership concern the leader's character and only thirteen concern his skill. 1 Timothy 3 and Titus 1 major on how a leader manages his family, because Eli was not the first leader to infect God's People through his failure to lead his family well, and he will not be the last. If the great patriarchs Abraham, Isaac and Jacob reaped disaster through the way they led their wives and children, and if God threatened to kill Moses en route to his showdown with Pharaoh in Exodus 4:24–26 unless he dealt with the glaring issues in his own family, then we dare not grow complacent in this area.

The prophet starts singing Hannah's theme tune again in verse 30, telling Eli that God says *"Those who honour me I will*

---

[2] The Lord states this even more explicitly in 3:13. If you dare not confront, you cannot lead.

honour, but those who despise me will be disdained." Even though Eli's name meant *Exalted*, he had failed to be the kind of person God could use and had brought disgrace and disaster on his dynasty. The clan descended from Aaron's son Eleazar would be wiped out except for one lone survivor in 1 Samuel 22, and even that survivor would be sacked in disgrace in 1 Kings 2:26–27.[3] The clan descended from Aaron's other son Ithamar would take over the priesthood instead, led by Zadok, and Eli's cursed clan would be reduced to begging favours from them.[4] Hophni and Phinehas would both die on the same day in chapter 4 as a down payment which guaranteed that the rest of the curse would be paid in full. Whatever level of leadership God has entrusted you with, these words should make you take it very seriously.

But it isn't all bad. You should also find these verses very encouraging. After all, if water truly flows downhill then our task becomes much easier as leaders. We don't need to worry about how to change a small group or church or nation, but simply about how to change ourselves. Changed leaders change churches, which change communities, which in turn change nations. When Eli was replaced with Samuel, it meant that *"all the people of Israel turned back to the Lord"* in 7:2. When Samuel gave way to Saul the Israelites lost faith and were scattered in 13:6–8, but when Saul gave way to David they surged forward with a fresh shout of faith in 17:52. Water flows downhill positively as well as negatively, which means leaders God can use produce whole churches God can use simply by being themselves.

---

[3] The words for *seed* and *strong arm* are written the same way in Hebrew but with different vowel pointings. The Masoretic Hebrew text assumes that Eli's *strength* will be cut off in verse 31, but the Septuagint is probably right to assume that his *seed* – in other words his *clan* – would be cut off.

[4] 2 Samuel 8:17; 1 Kings 2:35. Astonishingly, Eli failed to discipline his sons even after a prophecy like this one. We will examine his complacency in the chapter "Act like a Little Girl".

What's more, the prophet ends by telling us some even better news. Just like Hannah, he points to the perfect leader Jesus and promises that he is the true head of the river and that his pure water flows downhill too. *"I will raise up for myself a faithful priest, who will do according to what is in my heart and mind,"* God promises, and he can't simply mean Samuel and Zadok since neither of them were able to *"minister before my messiah always."*[5] He means the one who will be both King and Great High Priest, and who promises to make God's People little *"kings and priests"* as they drink daily from his river.[6]

Eli is therefore more than a tragic lesson in what happens to leaders who sin against the Lord. He is also a reminder that Jesus has promised to let leaders drink his Holy Spirit and be changed into the kind of leaders God can use. Jesus urges us in John 7:37–39: *"'Let anyone who is thirsty come to me and drink. Whoever believes in me, as Scripture has said, rivers of living water will flow from within them.' By this he meant the Spirit, whom those who believed in him were later to receive."*

So let's drink from Jesus as the source of God's river, and let's expect him to change us and, through us, those we lead as well. Let's look at tragic Eli and give thanks to the Lord that his better High Priest's water still flows downhill to us today.

---

[5] Samuel grew estranged from King Saul, and the last priest in Zadok's line died 2,000 years ago. Hebrews 2:17 and 7:21–28 tell us that this prophecy was only completely fulfilled in Jesus our Great High Priest.

[6] Revelation 1:6; 5:10; 20:6. Some Greek manuscripts of 5:10 read *"You have made us kings and priests."*

Far Away from Witnesses
(3:1–21)

The boy Samuel ministered before the Lord under Eli.

(1 Samuel 3:1)

When Muhammad Ali told reporters, *"I am the greatest!"* in February 1964, few people could argue. The twenty-two-year-old had just beaten Sonny Liston to become the heavyweight boxing champion of the world. Everybody wanted to know his secret, and he wasn't shy in telling them: *"The fight is won or lost far away from witnesses – behind the lines, in the gym, and out there on the road, long before I dance under those lights."*

Like Muhammad Ali, Samuel was training in secret far away from witnesses. The first-century Jewish historian Josephus tells us that he was twelve years old by the time God spoke to him in 1 Samuel 3, and had been ministering before the Lord for many years in secret.[1] Except for an annual visit from his mother and father, his only witnesses were Hophni and Phinehas and the women they abused. Eli had become physically as well as spiritually blind, so no one saw Samuel's faithful years of training in the Tabernacle except for the God who looks for a person he can use.

While most Israelites thronged to the temples of their idols instead of to the Tabernacle,[2] Samuel lived and slept inside the Tabernacle. His bed was in the Holy Place, with only a curtain

---

[1] Josephus in *Antiquities of the Jews* (5.10.4).

[2] The writer literally calls the Tabernacle *the Temple* in verse 3 to remind us that Moses' mobile tent was now a semi-permanent building at Shiloh. It stood at the heart of Israel's land, but not at the heart of Israel's life.

separating him from the inner room which housed the Ark of the Covenant. While Judges 21:25 tells us this was a period where *"everyone did as they saw fit"* and cared little for what the Lord had to say, a literal translation of 1 Samuel 9:15 is that the Lord was beginning to *uncover Samuel's ear*. Eli's physical blindness was an outward marker of his failure as Israel's high priest and judge to see any visions from the Lord, because verse 1 tells us that *"in those days the word of the Lord was rare; there were not many visions."* In contrast, the twelve-year-old Samuel constantly put himself in the place where God might speak. When he least expected it, late one night, the Lord finally started speaking.

Eli had failed to repent even after the prophet came to him at the end of chapter 2, but Samuel leapt to his feet and sprang into action as soon as he heard the Lord calling his name. Verse 7 tells us that at this point *"Samuel did not yet know the Lord"*, so he rushed through to Eli's bedroom and told him he was ready to obey. Hearing God speak was so outside of Eli's frame of reference that he thought Samuel was imagining things and sent him back to bed. It was only on the third time that he grasped whose voice it was. Samuel had rested in the place where the Lord might speak, and he was about to receive the reward of those who seek God's presence in secret, far away from witnesses.

You want God to speak to you. If you didn't, you wouldn't be reading 1 Samuel or this commentary. The Lord therefore wants to encourage you to persevere when he seems silent. He wants you to keep on reading the Bible in secret when his voice seems very hard to hear, as well as when it seems easy. The great John Bunyan, author of *The Pilgrim's Progress*, confessed that

> *I have sometimes seen more in a line of the Bible than I could well tell how to stand under, and yet at another time the whole Bible hath been to me as dry as a stick; or rather, my heart hath been so dead and dry unto it that I*

could not conceive the least dram of refreshment, though I have looked it all over.[3]

Because he persisted in those hard times in the place where God might speak, Charles Spurgeon read his work and exclaimed,

Why, this man is a living Bible! Prick him anywhere; his blood is Bibline, the very essence of the Bible flows from him. He cannot speak without quoting a text, for his very soul is full of the Word of God. I commend his example to you, beloved, and, still more, the example of our Lord Jesus. If the Spirit of God be in you, he will make you love the Word of God; and, if any of you imagine that the Spirit of God will lead you to dispense with the Bible, you are under the influence of another spirit which is not the Spirit of God at all.[4]

Samuel calls back through the curtain: *"Speak, Lord, for your servant is listening."* God replies that Eli that has failed and no sacrifice can save him,[5] which places Samuel in a corner when Eli charges him with a solemn Hebrew oath to tell him what God said. Would Samuel shrink back as God's messenger, or would he tell the truth? When Samuel swallowed hard and shared what he had heard, he proved he had become the kind of person God could use.

Hearing God speak is like pulling a tissue out of a tissue box. If we act on what he gives us, we quickly hear him speaking more. If we hesitate to obey, we find he waits before he speaks again. Because Samuel kept on obeying what he heard in secret,

---

[3] John Bunyan in *Grace Abounding to the Chief of Sinners* (1666). He wrote *The Pilgrim's Progress* in 1678.

[4] Charles Spurgeon in a sermon preached at The Metropolitan Tabernacle, London, on 25th June 1882.

[5] If you find verse 14 shocking, you are safe from the danger it describes. Eli had grown so blind to his sin that God knew that even this warning would not make him repent and seek forgiveness.

verse 21 tells us that *"The Lord continued to appear at Shiloh, and there he revealed himself to Samuel through his word."* He *"let none of Samuel's words fall to the ground"*, which is a Hebrew way of saying that none of his words ever failed to hit their mark.[6] Before he knew it, the Lord declared that he was ready to dance under the lights: *"Samuel's word came to all Israel."*[7] That's what happens when we are faithful in listening to the Lord far away from any witnesses.

Last week I shared a coffee with a friend I helped lead to Christ eleven years ago. On Sunday he was appointed pastor of his church. As we marvelled at what God had done in his life in a relatively short space of time, it struck us that six years after his conversion no one would have picked him out of the crowd as a future church leader. He spent the first six years of his Christian life in quiet Bible study and prayer and worship, spending countless evenings in secret conversations with his God. When I invited him in year seven to start sharing some of what he had learned from God with others, he was instantly fruitful. He is now pastoring people who have been Christians four or five times longer than he has, because he was faithful in the early years far away from any witnesses.[8]

Muhammad Ali told the reporters what made him different from the other would-be heavyweight boxing champions. God is calling you to be faithful in the dark where no one sees you, investing hours in prayer and worship and faithful listening like the young boy Samuel. If you are faithful in the dark, far away from any witnesses, then God promises to make you the kind of person he can use.

---

[6] The same phrase is used in 1 Kings 8:56 and 2 Kings 10:10. See also 1 Samuel 9:6.

[7] Since *Dan* was the northernmost Israelite town and *Beersheba* the southernmost, the writer wants us to understand that the length and breadth of Israel recognized Samuel's authority as a prophet.

[8] Galatians 1:17–18 and Acts 9:30 and 11:25 tell us that the apostle Paul also spent a total of nine years in similar obscurity in Arabia and Tarsus before the Lord launched him into public ministry.

Act Like a Little Girl (3:18)

Then Eli said, "He is the Lord; let him do what is good in his eyes."

(1 Samuel 3:18)

In the Clint Eastwood western *Pale Rider*, a mining baron sends hired gunmen to drive out villagers who stand in the way of his plans to mine their land for gold. During an attack at the start of the movie, the dog of a little girl called Megan is shot between the eyes. As the smoke clears, the grown-up villagers begin to leave in resignation, but Megan buries her dog and starts to pray:

The Lord is my shepherd; I shall not want – **but I do want.**
He leadeth me beside still waters. He restoreth my soul – **but they killed my dog.**
Yea, though I walk through the valley of the shadow of death I shall fear no evil – **but I am afraid.**
For thou art with me; thy rod and thy staff they comfort me – **but we need a miracle.**
Thy loving kindness and mercy shall follow me all the days of my life. And I shall dwell in the house of the Lord forever – **but I'd like to get more out of this life first. If You don't help us we're all going to die. Please? Just one miracle!**[1]

---

1 *Pale Rider* (Warner Brothers, 1985). Megan is quoting from Psalm 23.

While the old men around her assume that their fate is sealed and they must surrender, Megan dares to lay hold of God and becomes the kind of person he can use. As a result of the little girl's prayers, a mysterious stranger rides into town at the very moment that her stepfather is being beaten by the gunmen and his wagon is about to be set on fire. When all hope seems lost, a bucket of water from off-camera suddenly drenches one of the gunmen and extinguishes the flames. *"You shouldn't play with matches,"* drawls Clint Eastwood before he rescues Megan's family and village single-handedly in answer to her prayer.

Eli was an old man, but God wanted him to act like a little girl. When Eli failed to repent after the prophecy at the end of chapter 2, the Lord tried to provoke him further. His prophecy through Samuel should have humbled Eli into crying out in prayer and into begging the Lord to change his mind. Instead, he responded with the pious passivity which had become the hallmark of his rule: *"He is the Lord; let him do what is good in his eyes."* Don't mistake Eli's fatalism for faith, or his spinelessness for submission. God was calling him to answer back in prayer and plead with him to change his mind. He wanted Eli to fight like a little girl named Megan, but instead he surrendered prematurely.

Megan's kind of praying is so rare among Christians today that the suggestion that God might change his mind is treated by many as if it were tantamount to blasphemy. The writer of 1 Samuel does not feel the same way, and he uses the Hebrew word *nāham* – meaning *to relent*, *to repent*, *to regret* or *to change one's mind* – twice in chapter 15 to shock us into action. He uses it in verse 29 to agree with us that the Lord never changes his mind, but he also uses it in verse 11 to tell us that the Lord nevertheless changed his mind about making Saul king. He echoes similar teaching in the Pentateuch when it uses the word *nāham* in Numbers 23:19 to tell us that God never changes his mind, but also in Exodus 32:14 to tell us that he changed his mind when Moses prayed.[2] Failure to answer God back in prayer isn't faith in his sovereignty at all. We only truly understand God's sovereignty when we grasp that he is sovereign even over how his People respond in prayer.

Eli could have acted like Megan or like Moses when the Lord threatened to destroy Israel after they worshipped the Golden Calf. He could have told the Lord that he knew him too well to accept that his words to Samuel were truly his final word on the matter. He could have reminded the Lord of his *character* and pointed out that he must not refuse to forgive a repentant sinner as he had threatened in verse 14. He could have reminded him of his *history* with Aaron and of his *promises* to Eleazar's descendants. He could have reminded him that his *purpose* was not primarily to make the ears of Israel tingle with his judgment, but with his mercy, despite what he had threatened. He could have taken words of Scripture and spoken them back to the Lord as Megan did with Psalm 23. His failure to do so marked his final failure as Israel's leader. It proved that he was not the kind of person God would use.

I live in London, a city which has known many Christian revivals in its history but which is now as backslidden as Eli and his sons. In the wake of a fresh outbreak of sin and violence on the streets last month, a well-meaning Christian lady told me that *"God has finished with London. We deserve the judgment we are getting."* What surprised me was that she genuinely thought her view was honouring to God. She couldn't see that she was aping Eli's pious resignation to a fate which wasn't meant to be God's final word.

Instead, God wanted her to answer him back like a little girl called Megan, or like the warrior Aragorn near the end of *The Lord of the Rings*. When he looks death and judgment in the

---

[2] Most English translations are so offended by this idea that they do not translate *nāham* as God *changing his mind* in Exodus 32:14 and 1 Samuel 15:11. Yet God wants us to be offended – and challenged.

face on the battlefield, he tells the shattered remnants of his army:

> Hold your ground! Hold your ground!... A day may come when the courage of men fails, when we forsake our friends and break all bonds of fellowship, but it is not this day. An hour of wolves and shattered shields, when the age of men comes crashing down, but it is not this day! This day we fight! By all that you hold dear on this good earth, I bid you stand![3]

Perhaps you suspect that God has spoken judgment over your city or nation. It is not too late for you to act like a little girl and find that he planned for you to change his mind in prayer. Perhaps he has spoken judgment over a friend or family member. If he has, he wants to use 2 Samuel 14:14 to rouse you into trying to change his mind through prayer. *"Like water spilled on the ground, which cannot be recovered, so we must die,"* he explains, *"But that is not what God desires; rather he devises ways so that a banished person does not remain banished from him."* One of the ways he has devised is for you to act like a little girl named Megan, who refused to take his judgment as his final word and dared to answer him back in prayer.

Heaven has spoken but heaven has not said its last word. It waits with bated breath to see if you will pray. It waits to see if you are the kind of person God can use.

---

[3] Aragorn says this near the end of *The Return of the King* (New Line Cinema, 2003).

Pint-Sized God (4:1–6:21)

The ark of God was captured, and Eli's two sons,
Hophni and Phinehas, died.

(1 Samuel 4:11)

Samson had failed.[1] Eli was about to fail too. The resurgent Philistines had re-invaded Israel, and all that Eli had to fight them with was his faith in a pint-sized god.[2]

Eli responded by doing nothing. He had no vision, no strategy and no direction for the nation he was called to lead. He loved the Tabernacle so much that he fell off his chair and died when he heard that the Ark of the Covenant had been captured (not that his sons had died), but he knew so little of the God whose Tabernacle it was that he let the Israelites go to war trusting in a false god who could not save them.

Their pint-sized god could not deliver them in the first battle in which 4,000 Israelite soldiers died. If Eli had showed the elders God's warning in Deuteronomy 28:15 and 25 that backsliding always results in defeat, he might have lifted their eyes to see the Living God. Instead, they thought they had God in a box and simply fetched the Ark of the Covenant from the Tabernacle at Shiloh. God would surely have to help them if his golden box was at risk of being captured. They had forgotten what the writer says about the Lord in 4:4 – that he is *Yahweh*

---

[1] Judges 16:27–30 tells us that Samson killed only a few thousand Philistines in his lifetime. This was a far cry from his calling in 13:5 to *"take the lead in delivering Israel from the hands of the Philistines"*.

[2] This chapter takes place thirty to forty years after Samson temporarily curtailed Philistine power at the end of Judges 16. Aphek was probably twelve miles north-east of Joppa and on the road to Shiloh.

Tsabāōth, which means the *Lord of Armies* or *Lord Almighty*, and that he *"is enthroned between the cherubim"*.[3] They were about to discover that their pint-sized god was an idol of their own making.

There are plenty of people like the elders of Israel in our churches today. They talk much about God but very little to God. They talk much about religion but very little about repentance. They assume that if they set things up in the right way then the Lord will have to play by their superstitious rules.[4] When Eli despatches Hophni and Phinehas with the Ark to the Israelite camp, the soldiers erupt into a worship celebration which shakes the ground. They have their pint-sized god just where they want him, but they are about to discover that God is far bigger than they think. Amen!

The Israelite soldiers return to the battlefield with the Ark as their lucky mascot, but the Lord is powerful enough to sidestep their manipulation. He has a way to protect his name and glory even when the Ark falls into uncircumcised hands, and by the time the Israelites have learned this to their horror 30,000 of them have died. Among the dead are Hophni and Phinehas as proof that Eli's house has failed and the judgment God has promised is on its way. Proud Israel is humbled and the Ark of the Covenant is captured by the Philistines.

Even in this moment of tragedy, Eli fails to rally the nation back to the Lord. He is as blind as those he is called to lead and is just as infected with a pint-sized vision of the Lord. He has grown fat on sin and self-indulgence, like some of the doddery superstition which masquerades for Christianity today. Instead of using the moment to call Israel to repentance, he throws up his hands in horror, falls off his chair and joins his sons in the

---

[3] The Lord promised to dwell between the two golden cherubim angels on the lid of the Ark of the Covenant in Exodus 25:16–22 and Numbers 7:89, but he did so as a mighty King and not as a pint-sized god.

[4] The Israelite messengers to Shiloh did not bother to consult with Samuel there, despite the fact that 3:19–21 tells us that Samuel had a proven track record of speaking God's Word very clearly to Israel.

grave. The Tabernacle at Shiloh would be destroyed and would never again re-house the Ark of the Lord. The Israelites had used it to preach a pint-sized view of God, so God breaks their box and begins to preach his glory to the nations.

The Philistines understand better than the Israelites that they are dealing with a mighty God. They remember that the Lord struck the Egyptians with ten plagues during the Exodus, and exclaim to one another in 4:8 that *"We're doomed!"*[5] When they rout Israel so completely that its army ceases to exist,[6] they revise their view of God and wonder if he might have been less powerful than their own national idol Dagon all along. They place the Ark in Dagon's temple at Ashdod as the spoils of their idol's victory. The following morning, the Lord reminds them of his greatness when they find their idol prostrate in a worship position before the Ark. When they put him back on his feet, he falls down so heavily the following night that his head and hands fall off before the Lord.[7] When they still hesitate, the Lord strikes Ashdod with one of the plagues which destroyed Egypt and makes them confess in 5:7 that *"his hand is heavy on us and on Dagon our god."*[8]

This leads to a seven-month mission trip for the Ark around the cities of the Philistines, striking Gath and Ekron with the same plague and humbling the Philistines into repentance. They cry out not just to *God* but to *the Lord* in 5:12–6:2, and they

---

[5] Since the Hebrew word *elōhīm* can mean either *gods* or *God*, it is deliberately ambiguous in 4:7–8 whether the Philistines are talking about *gods* or *God*.

[6] According to 4:10 the Israelite soldiers who survived the massacre went and hid in their own tents. The defeat was so decisive that the Israelite officers lost any chance of regrouping their men.

[7] Dagon was worshipped as an idol with the head and arms of a man but the body of a fish. All that was left of him when he fell the second time was a headless fish. Zephaniah 1:9 suggests his priests still remembered this severe humiliation centuries later.

[8] The Hebrew words *techōr* and *ōphel* refer to *itchy boils* and *swellings*. Deuteronomy 28:27 uses the word *techōr* to describe the plague of boils which struck Egypt in Exodus 9. The Septuagint adds that this plague was spread by rats, which would explain the otherwise incongruous reference to golden rats in chapter 6.

seek atonement in 6:3–5 by preparing a guilt offering which will *"give glory to Israel's God"*. They understand so little of the Gospel that they offer God gold, not knowing that only a blood sacrifice can make amends for sin, but God is gracious towards their stumbling acts of repentance and provides them with the kind of sacrifice they need. He performs a miracle by making cows which have never pulled a cart abandon their calves to run towards the Israelites in the border town of Beth Shemesh,[9] knowing that they will instinctively sacrifice the two cows as a burnt offering on wood they have plundered from the cart. The Philistines watch this from a distance and discover that the Lord has lifted the plague because of their act of repentance and faith in his blood sacrifice for sin.

Eli had failed. Israel's elders had failed. The Israelite army had failed, but the God of Israel had won. He was not a pint-sized god who could be manipulated into victory. He was strong enough to turn defeat into deliverance, and to use the pride of his chosen People to preach the Gospel to the Gentiles. He still does the same today.

Paul explains in Romans 9–11 that the Lord still saves Gentiles as part of his continuing plan to save ethnic Israel. Paul ends his explanation with an encouragement to turn our backs once and for all on Israel's pint-sized view of God:

> *Oh, the depth of the riches of the wisdom and knowledge of God! How unsearchable his judgments, and his paths beyond tracing out! "Who has known the mind of the Lord? Or who has been his counsellor?" "Who has ever given to God, that God should repay them?" For from him and through him and for him are all things! To him be the glory for ever!*[10]

---

[9] *Beth Shemesh* means *Temple of the Sun*, which hints at the Israelite city's idolatry. Since the name *Samson* came from the same word and meant *Sunlight*, it may also hint back to Samson's failure.

[10] Romans 11:33–36. Paul is quoting from Isaiah 40:13 and Job 41:11.

Thank you Lord that you are a mighty God, you shed your blood for us, so that we can be freed from sin be in your mighty family. Amen.

The Glory Has Not Departed (4:19–22)

She named the boy Ichabod, saying, "The Glory has departed from Israel" – because of the capture of the ark of God and the deaths of her father-in-law and her husband.

(1 Samuel 4:21)

The year 1948 was a terrible one for the Church in China. Mao Zedong and his Communist army swept into power and violent persecution broke out against the Christians. In the port city Wenzhou in Zhejiang province, forty-nine pastors were sent to prison camps in 1950 alone and only one of them returned. Other Christians nearby were crucified on the walls of their churches or chained to vehicles and dragged to death. Within a few years, Mao Zedong's wife was able to boast that *"Christianity in China has been confined to the history section of the museum. It is dead and buried."* A visiting delegation from the USA reported in the 1970s that *"There is not a single Christian left in China."*[1] What happened to the Church in China under Mao Zedong was a disaster of Shiloh proportions.

The widow of Phinehas was not the only person who concluded in the wake of the Philistine victory and capture of the Ark that the glory had departed from Israel. When she named her fatherless son Ichabod, meaning *No Glory*, she was merely expressing the general shock and horror which had gripped God's People. Years later, the psalmist Asaph still looked

---

[1] These events and quotations come from Brother Yun's moving book *The Heavenly Man* (2002).

back to it as a year when the Lord *"rejected Israel completely. He abandoned the tabernacle of Shiloh, the tent he had set up among humans. He sent the ark of his might into captivity, his splendour into the hands of the enemy. He gave his people over to the sword; he was furious with his inheritance."*[2] Centuries later when the Lord wanted to warn the inhabitants of Jerusalem not to treat him like a pint-sized god, he told them to *"Go now to the place in Shiloh where I first made a dwelling for my Name, and see what I did to it because of the wickedness of my people Israel... I will make this temple like Shiloh and this city a curse among all the nations of the earth."*[3] Phinehas' widow was not exaggerating. The defeat of Israel and the destruction of the Tabernacle was a calamitous disaster.

The writer of 1 Samuel wants us to grasp this, because he knows God's People will often face major setbacks at different stages in their history. The Church in the West has seen defeat in the past fifty years on a similar scale to Shiloh or to China under Mao. In my own country, the United Kingdom, the number of people in their twenties attending church dropped from 520,900 in 1985 to 230,600 in 2005. This means that for every twenty-something who attends church today, almost three times as many used to do so only twenty years ago, or to put it another way 3 per cent of British twenty-somethings go to church and 97 per cent do not.[4] You would have to be blinder than Eli to think this is not a disaster of Shiloh-sized proportions. But the writer of 1 Samuel has a surprise in store which should encourage us in days of disaster.

He wants us to understand that Phinehas' widow was wrong. She went into premature labour, gave up the will to

---

[2] Psalm 78:56–64. The Philistines sacked Moses' Tabernacle at Shiloh in about 1080 BC, and Asaph wrote this psalm after David installed his new Tabernacle on Mount Zion in about 1000 BC.

[3] Jeremiah 7:12–14; 26:4–6.

[4] Data from a UK Evangelical Alliance survey in 2009 entitled *The 18–30 Mission: The Missing Generation?*.

live and didn't even bother to look at her newborn son before she died, yet she was wrong to assume that God's glory had departed. The Lord was far wiser and mightier than her own pint-sized plans, and he was already at work on a better plan to display his glory by judging his proud People. Not only was the Ark about to go on a missionary tour and preach the Gospel to the Philistines, but Israel's darkest night would also prove to be the beginning of a new dawn.[5] With Eli and his sons out of the way, Samuel could step into the vacuum as the fourteenth judge of Israel. Defeat on the battlefield, news of what the Lord had done through the Ark in Philistia and the judgment that fell on the seventy men of Beth Shemesh who dishonoured the Ark and died, all proved to be a turning point for Israel.[6] The once-proud nation had been humbled at the same time as their new leader became the kind of person God could use. We read in 7:2 that this wasn't a day of disaster at all: *"Then all the people of Israel turned back to the Lord."*

Asaph doesn't end his psalm with the disaster which fell on Shiloh. He carries on with inspired commentary on these chapters, telling us that

> *Then the Lord awoke as from a sleep... He chose the tribe of Judah, Mount Zion, which he loved. He built his sanctuary like the heights, like the earth that he established for ever. He chose David his servant and... David shepherded them with integrity of heart; with skilful hands he led them.*[7]

---

[5] It was even a new dawn for Phinehas' widow. She had been rid of an unfaithful husband and become mother to a male heir. You can trust God that, whatever your misfortune, he is still on his throne.

[6] Most Hebrew manuscripts and the Septuagint tell us the Lord struck down *50,070* people, but the figure seems so high that many English translations prefer the few texts which read *seventy*. Others read it *"seventy men and fifty leaders of a thousand"*.

[7] Psalm 78:65–72. David placed Asaph in charge of his new Tabernacle on Mount Zion in 1 Chronicles 16.

The destruction of Moses' Tabernacle did not just pave the way for revival under Samuel, but also for the building of a new and better Tabernacle under David on Mount Zion.[8]

Nor did the Lord end his warning through Jeremiah with the disaster which fell on Shiloh. He promised a time when *"people will no longer say, 'The ark of the covenant of the Lord.' It will never enter their minds or be remembered; it will not be missed, nor will another one be made."* Instead of being enthroned between the cherubim angels on the lid of a golden box, he would be enthroned among his People, and Gentile nations would look at them and recognize them as *"The Throne of the Lord".*[9] The disaster that marked the birth of Ichabod did not mean that God had finished with his People. It meant that he was just getting started.

Xu Yongze, one of a new generation of Chinese church leaders, has a similar perspective on the years of persecution under Mao:

> *I believe God allowed the atheist government to destroy the old structure of the Chinese church so that he could rebuild it according to his own purposes. He started with little and has made it much! The simple fact that the Chinese church has grown into a force tens of million strong today is a sign not only of God's existence but also of his matchless power.*[10]

The expulsion of Western missionaries after 1948 made it look as though God's glory had departed from China, but it proved to be the dark night which cleared the way for the dawn of a massive victory.

---

[8] Moses' Tabernacle was repaired and reinstalled under Zadok at Mount Gibeon, but the Ark of the Covenant was never returned there. It was brought to David's Tabernacle. See 1 Chronicles 16:39–40; 21:29.

[9] Jeremiah 3:16–17.

[10] Also from Brother Yun's book *The Heavenly Man*.

If you live in the West, then learn this lesson and remember Hannah's song. God uses poor and broken things to display his glory – not gold boxes, gifted speakers, church denominations or methodologies. When he strips you down to size, don't think the glory has departed. He is simply turning us back into the kind of people he can use.

—Amen Lord! "

Success Where Samson Failed (7:1-17)

So the Philistines were subdued and they stopped invading Israel's territory. Throughout Samuel's lifetime, the hand of the Lord was against the Philistines.

(1 Samuel 7:13)

The grand finale to the first section of 1 Samuel is a description of what happens when God finds a person he can use.

The Israelites have been humbled by being routed by the Philistines, and they have a new and humble leader who hears and speaks the words of God. Twenty years have passed since the end of chapter 6, and it is now around 1060 BC.[1] That makes it sixty years since the tragic death of Samson, and Samuel is about to succeed where Samson failed.[2]

Samson had polluted himself with the sins of the Philistines. He was a Nazirite, but he ate food plundered from corpses, got drunk at parties, took Philistine lovers and could even be found visiting the prostitutes of Gaza.[3] In contrast, Samuel calls the Israelites to prove their claim that they have turned back to the Lord by getting rid of their Philistine and

---

[1] The Ark was in Kiriath Jearim for eighty years from around 1080 to 1000 BC, but the writer is telling us in verse 2 that it had been there for twenty years when the Philistines invaded again in chapter 7.

[2] Verses 6 and 15 use the same stock phrase as Judges to tell us literally that Samuel *judged* Israel. The rest of the chapter clearly shows that he also acted as a priest after the death of Eli.

[3] Judges 14:1-2, 9; 16:1, 4. The word *mishteh* in 14:10 means literally a *drinking-feast*.

Canaanite idols in verses 3 and 4. Baal was the god of fertility and harvest, and Ashtoreth was the goddess of love and war, so Samuel is telling the Israelites to stop worshipping money, sex and power.[4] Samuel was now in his fifties and had been serving the Lord wholeheartedly for half a century. Because the Israelites knew he was a radical worshipper of the Lord, his water flowed downhill and convinced them to throw away their own idols too.

Samson had been a loner who never got close enough to the Israelites to influence them for the Lord. When his parents threw a bachelor's party for him before his wedding, they had to find thirty strangers to celebrate with him because he had no friends. By the end of the party, he had so offended his thirty guests that they threatened to murder his bride and father-in-law, and within a few weeks he offended them so much that they did so. After he retaliated violently, he hid on his own in a cave rather than seeking refuge within his tribe.[5] It didn't matter how often the Holy Spirit came upon him, he was never close enough to anyone to influence them deeply. In contrast, Samuel assembles the Israelites and imparts something of his humble prayerfulness to the nation as a whole.[6]

There is no record of Samson ever offering a blood sacrifice, but Samuel instinctively offers a burnt offering of a lamb. The closest Samson came to repentance was a final prayer for strength so that he could take revenge, but Samuel leads the Israelites in fasting and confession that *"We have sinned against the Lord"*. He teaches them to pour out a drink offering as a promise that from now on their lives will be poured out for the

---

[4] The plural *Ashtoreths* in verse 3 appears to include Asherah, goddess of prosperity, as well. 1 Thessalonians 1:9 makes it clear that repentance means turning from idols as well as committing to the Lord.

[5] Judges 14:10–11, 15; 15:6, 8.

[6] Mizpah meant *Watchtower* or *Look-Out Post*, and it was the place where Israel had gathered to defend the purity of God's name in Judges 20:1. Samuel brought them back there to make the same commitment again.

Lord and not in rebellion as before.[7] He preaches the Gospel so clearly within the limits of his Old Covenant understanding that the Devil springs into action and stirs up the Philistines to attack.[8] Samuel isn't just the fourteenth judge of Israel, but also a priest who rallies God's People to victory through a lamb.[9] The name *Beth Kar* in verse 11 is Hebrew for *Temple of the Male Lamb*, because Samuel's prayers are offered on the basis of a slaughtered animal which prophesies God's victory over Satan through Jesus' death at Calvary. Since the Philistines believe that Baal controls the thunder clouds, the Lord routs them with deafening thunder which casts their minds back to his seven-month missionary tour and to the plagues which humbled them twenty years earlier.

The Lord had called Samson and promised in Judges 13:5 that *"he will take the lead in delivering Israel from the hands of the Philistines"*. Sadly, due to his sin, we are told in Judges 16:30 that he slaughtered fewer Philistines before he died than could fit inside a large theatre. Israel was still under the oppression of the Philistines when he died, but Samuel succeeded where Samson failed. He too was a Nazirite, the child of a barren woman, called from his mother's womb and filled with grace and power even as a child, but he had served the Lord in secret and had been prepared to fulfil Samson's failed calling.

Samson had never learned to think about the long term, and didn't think twice about throwing away a weapon that had killed 1,000 men as soon as the immediate crisis of battle was over.[10] Samuel, on the other hand, understands that victory

---

[7] Paul explains in Philippians 2:17 and 2 Timothy 4:6 that Old Covenant drink-offerings were a promise from worshippers to pour their lives out for the Lord, regardless of the cost.

[8] Note that times of revival bring more spiritual attacks, not fewer.

[9] Samuel's ancestor Korah had arrogantly tried to force his way into the priesthood instead of Aaron in Numbers 16, and died (1 Samuel 1:1–2; 1 Chronicles 6:22–35). Because of his humility, Samuel was invited to serve as priest in place of Aaron's descendants Hophni and Phinehas.

[10] Judges 15:15–17.

must be guarded. He sets up a pillar in verse 12 as a permanent reminder that they have only beaten the Philistines because they humbled themselves before the Lord.[11] Ebenezer means *Stone of Help*, and Samuel tells them that *"Thus far the Lord has helped us"* – in other words this victory must lay the foundation for a brand new lifestyle. He sets up an altar of blood sacrifice at his home town of Ramah as a replacement for the fallen Tabernacle which once stood at Shiloh, and he keeps returning there from his ministry trips around Israel in order to hold court as Israel's ruler through further sacrifice of lambs.[12] One day the Philistines would return, peace with the Canaanites would end,[13] and Samuel's sons would fail to follow in their father's footsteps, but none of this would matter if Israel remained a people focused on the blood through which the Lord works his on-going victory.

Samuel had succeeded where Samson failed. He had perfectly sung his mother's theme tune from the start of this first section of 1 Samuel. He had been the humble kind of person God can use. Now, as we end the first section, he points us back to his pillar at Ebenezer and tells us to be humble people too.

[11] According to 4:1, the Israelites were defeated at Ebenezer when they trusted in the Ark instead of in the Lord. This marker on the site of their previous disaster reminded them not to go back to the superstition of before.

[12] The Lord had forbidden the Israelites on pain of exile from offering sacrifices anywhere but the Tabernacle in Leviticus 17:8–9, but Samuel built and used this altar until the Tabernacle was restored some years later at Nob.

[13] *Amorites* in verse 14 is a generic reference to the *Canaanites*, as in Genesis 15:16, Joshua 10:5 and 2 Samuel 21:2.

1 Samuel 8–15:

An Obedient Person

The People's Choice
(8:1–22)

But the people refused to listen to Samuel. "No!"
they said. "We want a king over us. Then we shall be
like all the other nations, with a king to lead us."

(1 Samuel 8:19–20)

Israel had a talent for snatching defeat from the jaws of victory. No sooner had they learned how to be the humble kind of nation God could use, than they went and threw it all away. With Hannah's prayer as their marching song, they had routed the Philistines, but within ten years they forgot how to sing it and returned to the pride which had been the source of their nation's misery throughout the book of Judges.[1]

It wasn't that the Lord was against the idea of a monarchy. He had given clear instructions for a monarchy centuries earlier in Moses' Law because he always intended to give Israel a king who would reign in godly submission to him. Hannah had prayed that *"There is no one besides you; there is no Rock like our God... He will give strength to his king and exalt the horn of his messiah."* The issue was not that the Israelites wanted a king, but that they wanted the wrong sort of king. They wanted a human rock in whom they could place their confidence instead of in the Lord. They wanted *"a king to lead us and to go out before us and fight our battles"* because they had forgotten that the Lord *"is enthroned between the cherubim"*, as we were reminded in 4:4.

---

[1] Events in 1 Samuel are not easy to date, but we know from 1 Kings 6:1 that David must have reigned from 1010 to 970 BC, and from Acts 13:21 that Saul must have therefore reigned from 1050 to 1010 BC.

A humble nation needed no other king but God. Their request was not for a king *under* the Lord, but for a king *besides* the Lord, and they would very quickly turn him into a king *instead* of the Lord.

The writer of 1 Samuel fills this chapter with clues that the Israelites' request was fuelled by *sinful pride*. For a start, this confrontation takes place at Ramah, the town where Samuel had built an altar of blood sacrifice so that Israel could continue to worship the one who had granted them victory at the *Temple of the Male Lamb*. The writer concedes that Samuel is growing older in verse 1, but he is still only sixty-five and has a further thirty-seven years of active ministry.[2] The issue was not that Samuel was too old or weak, but that the Israelites had begun to place their faith in human strength once again. We learn in 12:12 that this request was triggered by their knowledge that King Nahash of the Ammonites was about to march against them, and their fear that an aged prophet and his slaughtered lamb would not be enough to save them. When Samuel tells them to leave Ramah and go back to their own towns in verse 22, he is passing a spiritual verdict over Israel. Their request means they have rejected the Lamb who brought them victory through humility.

The writer also fills this chapter with clues that the Israelites' request was fuelled by *disobedience*. They were not looking for a king who would help them to walk humbly before the Lord, but one who would serve as an expression of their words in verse 19: *"No! We want...!"* Never mind that the Lord had chosen Israel to be different, telling them in Exodus 19:5–6 that *"Out of all nations you will be my treasured possession. Although the whole earth is mine, you will be for me a kingdom of priests and a holy nation."* They were not looking for the sort of king the Lord had described in Deuteronomy 17, who would

---

[2] Even after Saul became king, Samuel continued to serve as Israel's fourteenth judge until his death in about 1013 BC. See 7:15 and 25:1.

write out Scripture and study it to help him lead the Israelites in obedience to the Lord. They tell Samuel that *"We want a king over us. Then we shall be like all the other nations."*[3] Pride and disobedience go together as surely as humility and obedience.[4] The Israelites were telling the Lord that they refused to be the humble kind of people he could use.

That's why the writer also tells us that the Israelites' request was fuelled by a desire for *independence* from the Lord. Israel already had a King, about whom Moses had sung in Exodus 15:18 literally, *"The Lord will reign as King for ever and ever."* Israel was already ruled by the one Jephthah had worshipped in Judges 11:27 as *"the Lord, the Judge"*, and for whom the fourteen judges had simply been custodians of his rule. God's very first instruction about Israel's king in Deuteronomy 17 had been that he alone must choose him, but it is clear from verse 18 that the Israelites want a king of their own choosing. *"It is not you they have rejected, but they have rejected me as their king"* God tells Samuel in verse 7.[5] They will get their Saul – a man whose name means *Asked For* or *Demanded* – but they will quickly discover that we shouldn't always press God into giving us what we ask for.[6] David was about to be born in Bethlehem ten years later in 1040 BC, and their premature request would bring disaster on their nation and delay the start of his reign.

Samuel therefore warns the Israelites what will happen as a result of their refusal to be the kind of people God can use.

---

[3] Ezekiel 20:32 tells us that when we desire to be like unbelievers, we are guilty of idolatry.

[4] Since the Hebrew word *shāma'* means both *to listen* and *to obey*, there is a deliberate double meaning when the Lord tells Samuel to *listen* to the Israelites and consent to their disobedience in verses 7, 9 and 22.

[5] Christian leaders need to remember this and do the same as Samuel in verses 6 and 21. Do not stew over criticism and unruliness in those you lead. Take it to the Lord in prayer.

[6] Psalm 106:15 agrees with this chapter that there is something far worse than ungranted prayers. It is demanding something so rebelliously that the Lord grants our request in order to judge us.

Since they refused the reign of the Lord who had served them as king like a loving father, they would be given a king as proud as themselves who would force them to serve him as his soldiers, staff and slaves. Since they refused to be ruled by the generous God who had given them everything that they needed, they would be given a new king who would plunder them in order to line his pockets and those of his courtiers with the best produce of their land. Since they refused to follow the Lord to victory on the battlefield, they would be given a king who would lead them to defeat in fulfilment of the warnings in Hannah's marching song. If they had not yet learned that a hereditary monarchy spelt disaster from what had happened with Gideon's son, Eli's two sons, or Samuel's two sons, then they would learn it at their leisure in years to come.[7] They were about to learn in chapters 8 to 15 not to rebel against the Lord.

So get ready for this second section of 1 Samuel, which records the start of the disastrous reign of King Saul. Get ready to learn that God spells humility o-b-e-d-i-e-n-c-e, and that he is looking for obedient men and women as the kind of people he can use.

---

[7] Verse 1 tells us literally that Samuel made his two sons *judges* under him. Like Eli, he must have had high hopes for them when he named them Joel, which means *The Lord is God*, and Abijah, which means *My Father Is The Lord*. Like Eli, his hopes were to be sorely disappointed.

What Humility Is and Isn't
(9:1–10:27)

When all those who had formerly known him saw him prophesying with the prophets, they asked each other, "What is this that has happened to the son of Kish?"

(1 Samuel 10:11)

Many people find the life of Saul confusing. They see him as a wise and humble ruler in his early days, who failed to live up to his early potential. As he rides into the story at the start of chapter 9, it's important that we grasp that this isn't a right view of Saul at all. The writer of 1 Samuel wants us to understand what humility is and isn't.

Saul has all the outward trappings of humility. Even though we read in 9:2 that he was *handsome, young* and *a head taller* than the other Israelites – the perfect candidate for their trust in man when they faced Nahash in battle – Saul was attractively unaware of his natural gifting and abilities. *"Am I not a Benjamite, from the smallest tribe of Israel, and is not my clan the least of all the clans of the tribe of Benjamin?"* he objects in 9:21.[1] Saul is so aware of his limitations that he hides from his new subjects behind a pile of supplies in 10:22, but the writer urges us to dig a little deeper because a sober view of self is only half of true

---

[1] God had humbled sinful Benjamin when all but 600 of its men were wiped out in Judges 20–21, but he was gracious to the survivors. Benjamin produced a judge in Ehud, a king in Saul and an apostle in Paul (Judges 3:15; Philippians 3:5).

humility. The other half is a sober view of God's great glory, and here we discover that Saul is not as humble as he seems.

First, he displays an astonishing ignorance about the judge God has called to lead his nation. Saul is led on a wild donkey chase to Zuph, a town made famous as the birthplace of God's prophet Samuel.[2] Saul is not only unaware of this, but seems unaware of Samuel's ministry altogether. He fails to recognize him when he stops him in the street to ask directions in 9:18, despite the fact that he has led a great spiritual revival of Israel in Saul's own lifetime. Being aware of our own inadequacies is not humility unless it is coupled with awareness of God's great purposes and power.

Second, Saul displays a surprising disregard for what God has to say. When he grasps that his own strength has failed him in his donkey chase, he immediately gives up and tells his servant they should go home. His servant needs to persuade him it is worth seeking a man who can speak the word of God to him instead. Saul has used up all his resources in feeding his own strength, but his servant has held back enough to be able to lay hold of the Lord as the answer to their need. While the writer tells us literally in 9:15 that the Lord *"uncovered Samuel's ear"*, he will never tell us anything similar about Saul. In fact, 1 Chronicles 13:3 will tell us after Saul's death that he barely enquired of the Lord at all. True humility means more than simply giving up on our own strength. It means running to the Lord to be strengthened by the words he has to say.

Third, Saul is very slow to obey the Lord's commands. God is exceptionally gracious towards him, since he tells Samuel to anoint him in 9:16 as heir to the promise which he gave to Samson and to Samuel – *"He will deliver them from the hand of the Philistines"* – and since Samuel reconvenes the Israelites at Mizpah to link Saul's rule back to the great revival and victory of chapter 7. Even though Saul's name means *Asked For* or

---

[2] 1 Samuel 1:1.

Demanded and he is described in 8:18 as *"the king **you** have chosen"*, Samuel declares in 10:24 that he is also *"the man **the Lord** has chosen"*. He even gives Saul carte blanche to go and fulfil God's mission, telling him in 10:7–8 to *"do whatever your hand finds to do, for God is with you... but you must wait seven days until I come to you and tell you what you are to do."*

Saul had no problem waiting seven days, although that wouldn't always be the case.[3] What he struggled to do was gain the proper view of God which always results in courageous action. He dismisses Israel's army in 13:2 without ever using it to attack the Philistines, and he hides in fear in 14:2 when the Philistines overrun the land. God gives him a valiant entourage of warriors in 10:26, but instead of leading them into battle with the Philistines he leads them home and goes back to his ploughing in 11:5! Don't mistake Saul's reticence for his being the humble kind of person God can use. The writer wants us to understand that he hid in fear because he had too low a view of God.

Fourth, Saul cared too little for God's power. Much of our confusion about the life of Saul comes from our assumption that he must have been a true believer since the Holy Spirit came on him in 10:10. We fail to spot that this phrase which means literally that the Spirit *rushed* on him, or even *pounced* on him, is the same phrase which was used for the disobedient Samson throughout Judges.[4] We also fail to spot Samuel's loaded comment in 10:6 that if Saul ever co-operates with God's power then *"you will be changed into a different person"*, and the incredulous reaction of his friends to his experience of the Spirit when they ask in 10:11, *"What is this that has happened to the son of Kish?"* Saul has no idea how to handle a group of Spirit-

[3] See 1 Samuel 13:7–14. Humility means both waiting for the Lord and being ready to act when he comes.

[4] Judges 14:6, 19; 15:14. The phrase is also used for the young David in 16:13, but it is particularly used of Saul in 10:6, 10:10 and 11:6 to hint that he was far more like Samson than Samuel.

filled warriors in 10:26, and would prove too jealous to handle men like Jonathan and David in years to come. Humility means far more than confessing that our own power is insufficient. It means crying out for the power of God, which Saul never learned to do.

Fifth, Saul shared the Israelites' refusal to submit to the Lord as the true King of Israel. They had requested a *melek* in chapter 8, using the Hebrew word for *king* which up until that time had been reserved for the Lord alone.[5] When the Lord calls Saul, he refers to him in 9:16 as a *nāgīd*, the first time the word is used in the Old Testament and which was used to describe a lesser *viceroy* or *deputy*.[6] The Lord tells Samuel in 9:17 that Saul must not *reign* as king, but simply *govern* God's People for him.[7] Samuel tells this to Saul in 10:1, with a reminder that Israel is God's inheritance and not his own. He writes down the commands of Deuteronomy 17 for him in 10:25, which the writer describes literally as *the justice of the kingdom*, or *the right way to be a judge in the kingdom*.[8] Yet despite all this, Saul fails to rebuke his new subjects when they hail him as their *melek* in 10:24. Let's not fail to spot the danger signs in these two chapters which lead to his building a monument in his own honour as king in 15:12.

So don't be over-impressed by Saul's discretion in 10:16 and 10:27, or by his superficial show of humility as he hides behind a pile of supplies. The writer of 1 Samuel wants us to be wise where Saul was foolish. He wants us to grasp what humility is and isn't.

---

[5] Abimelek had laid a sinful claim to the title of *melek* in Judges 9 and had died under God's curse.

[6] 1 Chronicles 13:1 demonstrates this when it uses the word *nāgīd* for David's captains.

[7] The Hebrew verb *'ātzar* means literally to *restrain*, and appears to form a deliberate contrast with Judges 21:25.

[8] Deuteronomy 17:18–20 told kings to write out and study Scripture too, but there is no evidence that Saul did so. He did not share David's delight in God's Law as expressed in Psalm 19.

Advertisement for Obedience (11:1–15)

Saul said, "No one will be put to death today, for this day the Lord has rescued Israel."

(1 Samuel 11:13)

The Lord had changed Saul's heart in 10:9 in order to produce a great advertisement for obedience. For just one chapter, he shows Saul and Israel what their national story can be like if they become the obedient kind of people he can use. It's still a great advertisement for you and me today.

Obedient people have a *vision of God's glory*. The men of Jabesh Gilead had no such vision when King Nahash laid siege to their city on the eastern frontier of Israel.[1] Instinctively, they sent ambassadors to surrender since they had grown so accustomed to disappointment and defeat that it barely crossed their mind to appeal to God's newly anointed messiah. Nahash shows us what happens when we attempt to compromise with Satan, as he exploits their weakness to cripple them beyond repair. Only when they are threatened with blindness do the men of Jabesh Gilead finally begin to see. At last, they cry out to God's messiah for salvation.

Saul has been given an obedient heart to offer him a brief advertisement for what his life might yet be. Consequently, he

---

[1] Jabesh Gilead was east of the River Jordan near the border with Ammon. It had failed to take God seriously in judging Benjamin in Judges 21:8 so its women had been captured to provide descendants for the Benjamites. They were rewarded, since one of these was Saul, and they expressed their gratitude by rescuing his defiled corpse in 1 Samuel 31:11–13. David therefore blessed their once-cursed city in 2 Samuel 2:4–7.

has twenty-twenty vision of what is going on under the surface in terms of God's perfect plan. The name Nahash means *Snake*, and Saul sees clearly that the Ammonite king has been sent by the great serpent Satan to plunder, kill and destroy God's holy People.[2] Gouging out their right eyes was not merely an attempt to stop them from using a bow or having the depth perception swordsmen need. It was birthed from a venomous desire to bring disgrace on Israel's God. Saul is like Sherlock Holmes, who could look out of his window on the crime of Victorian London and see the hand of the arch-villain Moriarty behind it all:

> *He is the Napoleon of crime, Watson. He is the organiser of half that is evil and of nearly all that is undetected in this great city. He is a genius, a philosopher, an abstract thinker. He has a brain of the first order. He sits motionless, like a spider in the centre of its web, but that web has a thousand radiations, and he knows well every quiver of each of them.*[3]

Saul could do the same when he looked at Nahash and saw Satan.

Obedient people are *ready for action*. When Satan's rule is left unchallenged, anger becomes a virtue and calmness a vice. Saul is shaken from his complacent ploughing and steps up to take the role God has given him at the head of Israel's army. Like Samuel at Mizpah, he instinctively turns to a blood sacrifice as the action which will save his nation. He cuts his oxen in twelve pieces and sends them to the twelve tribes of Israel with a threat that, in a similar way, he will destroy the livelihood of

---

[2] John 10:10. Satan also wants to blind Christians to God's promises so that they become useless on the battlefield and a reproach to the God they serve.

[3] Spoken by Holmes in Arthur Conan Doyle's short story *The Final Problem* (1893).

anyone who fails to rally to the God of Israel's cause.[4] The result is astonishing, and soon Saul is commanding one of the largest ancient armies.[5]

Obedient people set about the Lord's work *with great urgency*. Saul can no longer linger in the cornfields, for he knows that he and his soldiers belong on the battlefield. He sends messengers to the men of Jabesh Gilead with a promise that they will be delivered by noon the following day. His urgency is infectious, and they trust him at his word, rejoicing as they send word to Nahash that they will surrender if their messiah has failed to rescue them within twenty-four hours. The kind of person God can use knows that delayed obedience is simply disobedience today. Saul stakes everything on immediate victory and leads his men across the River Jordan without delay.

Obedient people are *never satisfied* with the ground they gain today. Saul divides his army into three divisions and attacks the besieging Ammonites while it is still dark. He slaughters them until midday, refusing to take rest until they have been slaughtered or else scattered so completely that they will never be able to regroup and threaten Israel again.[6] Having done so, he then thinks of how he can safeguard victory for the future, and refuses the suggestion that he should execute those who criticized him in 10:27. He acts like Winston Churchill when he became prime minister and forgave his bitter opponents for the sake of the greater goal of winning the war with Germany, saying, *"Of this I am quite sure, that if we open a quarrel between the past and the present, we shall find that we have lost the*

---

[4] He threatens to do this to their oxen, not to them. Compare Saul's actions to those of the Levite who rallied Israel against Saul's hometown of Gibeah in Judges 19:14–30. The parallel is probably intended.

[5] Army sizes in 1 and 2 Samuel are so large that some scholars refuse to credit them here and elsewhere. They point out that *thousand* also meant *military unit* in Hebrew, so this may simply refer to 330 units.

[6] The Ammonites were descended from Lot's incest with his daughter in Genesis 19:36–38. They had troubled Israel in the time of Ehud and Jephthah. Saul broke their power and David finished the job in 2 Samuel 10 and 12.

future."[7] The proud and disobedient man cannot suffer people detracting from his glory, <u>but the obedient man lives for a far greater glory than his own.</u>

Finally, obedient people *give glory to the Lord.* Although he loved to be hailed as a *melek* next to God in 10:24, Saul has lost his self-assertive pride. He submits to the Lord's prophet and his purposes this one and only time in verse 7 when he musters Israel to *"follow Saul and Samuel"*. When he defeats Nahash, he tells his subjects that *"the Lord has rescued Israel"*, not him. Although the word for king in verses 14–15 is still *melek*, there is something different about this reaffirmation of Saul as king. It takes place at Gilgal, the place where the Israelites had consecrated themselves to the Lord before entering the Promised Land in Joshua 4:19–5:10, and Saul is made king to the sound of worship *"in the presence of the Lord"* surrounded by blood sacrifices which proclaim that Israel's true hope is in a far greater King who is yet to come.

I used to work in the advertising industry, so I know the power of a brief commercial to change the habits of a nation. The change God makes to Saul's heart in chapter 11 is more compelling than any advertisement I have ever seen, yet incredibly he fails to use it to change his nation's habits at all. In the very next chapter, Samuel is forced to preach judgment against them for returning to their faith in human power, and in the chapter after that Saul sends his troops home and returns to a lifestyle of hiding from the Philistines and from obedience to God's Word.

The Lord had given Saul a brief break in his life story so that he could watch an advertisement for obedience. Saul filtered it out and paid the penalty, so let's not do the same. <u>Let's allow it to turn us into the obedient kind of people God can use.</u>

---

[7] Churchill spoke this on 18th June 1940 in a speech entitled "Their Finest Hour".

How to Persuade People to Obey (12:1-25)

So all the people stood in awe of the Lord and of Samuel.

(1 Samuel 12:18)

The American writer and broadcaster Garrison Keillor gives his frank assessment of the way most church leaders try to inspire their congregations to obey the Lord:

> *Most of the sermons I have ever heard in my life could easily have been dispensed with and the congregation would have been better for it. The sermon is, I think, one of the terrible failings of the church. And they're doing it to their own people. They're punishing the faithful with this querulous exercise in piety, the terrible harangues that nobody is entitled to deliver.[1]*

Perhaps you agree with Garrison Keillor. Perhaps you don't. But at least we can all agree that if God is looking for people with humble obedience he can use, then church leaders need to encourage people to develop it. They have a primetime opportunity every Sunday when they preach a sermon, and the state of most congregations suggests that they could do with a little help. Perhaps that's why chapter 12 records for us in detail the final sermon preached by Samuel as an example for us all.

---

[1] Spoken in an interview with W. Dale Brown in his book *Of Fiction and Faith* (1997).

In verses 1–5, Samuel's sermon shows us the importance of a preacher's *lifestyle* in persuading people. The world is full of fine-sounding rhetoric, but only those who walk the talk can hope to persuade people to obey God. Samuel emphasizes this by using an unusual Hebrew phrase twice in verse 2 to describe the role of Israel's leader. He says literally that he has *"walked before you from my youth to this day"*.[2] He isn't pleading with them to be the obedient kind of people God can use because he thinks it is a good idea in theory. He is pleading with them because he has lived out his message over the course of many decades, and he gets some audience participation in order to force his hearers to confess the integrity of what he says.[3] The nineteenth-century Scottish essayist Thomas Carlyle rejected the Christian faith of his parents based on the character of its preachers. *"Let him who would move and convince others, be first moved and convinced himself,"* he complained. *"Be true if you would be believed."*[4] Only after forcing the Israelites to confess the obedience of his own life did Samuel feel ready to confront the disobedience of theirs.

In verses 6–11, Samuel's sermon shows us the importance of *connecting* with the people we wish to persuade. He takes his hearers on a tour of Israel's history in order to persuade them that the Lord has always worked through weak people who obeyed him and cried out to him in prayer. God used the tongue-tied ex-murderer Moses to deliver the Israelites from slavery in Egypt when they cried out to him for help. After God settled them in the Promised Land, they only lost it to the Canaanites and Philistines and Moabites because they disobeyed him. Whenever they repented and cried out to him

---

[2] Eli had died when Samuel was thirty-five years old, so Samuel had only been a *youth* in Hebrew eyes.

[3] Paul does something very similar in Acts 20:33–35 and 1 Thessalonians 2:10. So must we.

[4] Thomas Carlyle in his *Critical and Miscellaneous Essays*, Volume One (1838).

in prayer, he restored their fortunes through weak but obedient men, like Gideon who hid or Barak who proved more fearful than the women God provided to support him.[5] Samuel gets the Israelites nodding that God uses weak yet obedient people, before he challenges them to imitate the character they have just admired.

In verses 12–15, Samuel's sermon shows us the importance of *confronting* our hearers. He does not do so clumsily, before he has prepared the ground, but he does so forcefully and without mincing any of his words. He tells the Israelites that despite their noisy worship songs at Gilgal, they have turned their backs on the Lord as the true King of Israel, just like their rebellious ancestors throughout the period of the Judges. Despite the Lord's brief advertisement for obedience in the previous chapter, they have not shed their proud confidence in man instead of God.[6] Samuel does not use the word *nāgīd* or *viceroy* in this sermon, but only *melek* or *king*. He does not speak about his *governing*, but only about his *reigning*. Samuel leaves the Israelites in no doubt that they are still rebelling against the Lord, and that unless they and their human king respond to God's advertisement with lasting change, they will experience the same foreign invasions as their ancestors and worse.

In verses 16–18, Samuel's sermon shows us the importance of *signs and wonders* in persuading our hearers to obey God. Many of us live in church situations where miracles are few and far between. Since they are also situations where Christians do not wholeheartedly obey the Lord, we need to take this seriously and not consign it to another place and time. The wheat harvest was standing in the fields, so Samuel brings

---

[5] Jerub-Baal was Gideon's other name. The Hebrew text refers to *Bedan* instead of *Barak*, but since there is no one of that name in Judges most English translators follow the majority Septuagint reading.

[6] Samuel was still grieved even though the celebrations at Gilgal were more positive than those at Mizpah. He is not afraid to use the word *Saul* to mean *asked for* in verse 17, though Saul was probably standing there.

disaster on their economy by asking the Lord to destroy it with a freak thunderstorm as a price worth paying for repentance. Since Paul shares in Romans 15:18–19 his successful strategy for *"leading the Gentiles to obey God by what I have said and done – by the power of signs and wonders, through the power of the Spirit of God"*, we must also cry out to God for miracles of healing and of judgment if we want to persuade people to become the obedient kind of people God can use.[7]

Samuel's sermon is successful and his hearers become so afraid of the Lord and his prophet that they think they will surely die. They confess they have sinned in asking for a king and ask Samuel to pray for their salvation. This enables Samuel to show us one more thing which we must include in our messages if we hope to persuade people to obey.

In verses 19–25, Samuel's sermon shows us the importance of *making a clear appeal*. We are not called to deliver sermons but to deliver people. He presents the Israelites with a clear response that they must make (to obey God and throw away their idols), and he gives them a clear description of what will happen to them if they refuse (they will die). He gives them reasons for faith (the Lord will not reject Israel because he still has plans to work through them), and assures them that he is on their side (he will continue to pray for them and teach them).[8] He demonstrates that obedience to the Lord is too important for preachers to end their sermons with mere generalities. He tells us to do the preaching equivalent of grabbing our hearers by their lapels and pleading with them to change.

It was said that *"When Cicero spoke, people marvelled, but when Caesar spoke people marched."* The writer of 1 Samuel has shown us how to preach so that our listeners march obediently towards becoming the kind of people God can use.

---

[7] Samuel had preached a similar sermon in chapter 8 without any miracles, and the people had not repented.

[8] We find similar appeals at the end of sermons in Deuteronomy 30:15–20, Haggai 2:18–19 and Joshua 24:14–27.

As for me, far be it from me that I should sin against the Lord by failing to pray for you.

(1 Samuel 12:23)

"He's the angriest man you'll ever meet. He's like a man with a fork in a world of soup."[1] Noel Gallagher's famous description of his brother, the Oasis frontman Liam, stands in contrast to what the writer of 1 Samuel has to say to us in this verse. He tells us that our problem is not that we get angry, but that we don't get angry enough at the sin and disobedience all around us. He warns us that unless we learn to feel God's righteous anger, then we will end up sinning without doing anything.

Saul would later become an expert in the unrighteous anger of jealousy, frustration and rage, but we mustn't forget that he didn't start out that way.[2] When the Holy Spirit came upon him powerfully in 11:6, *"he burned with anger"* because the Spirit enabled him to see the world with heaven's eyes. The Lord gets angry over the work of Satan in the world through people's sin and disobedience,[3] and he tells us in 28:18 that it is actually sinful for us to remain calm in the face of what angers him. *"Don't make me angry. You wouldn't like me when I'm angry,"*

---

[1] Noel Gallagher said this during an interview for the April 2009 edition of Q magazine.

[2] 1 Samuel 18:8, 10–11; 19:9–10; 20:30–33. It is this fleshly anger which James 1:20 condemns.

[3] See 2 Samuel 6:7; 22:8; 24:1. Jesus demonstrates this in John 11:33 and 38 when he looks at Satan's work in the life of Lazarus and the Greek tells us literally that he *snorted with anger*.

warns the Incredible Hulk repeatedly in Marvel Comics, but the writer of 1 Samuel tells us that the Lord really likes it when we get angry about the right things. It is one of the things which makes us the kind of people he can use.

The Danish church leader and playwright Kaj Munk was one of the leaders of the resistance against the Nazi occupation of his country. He encouraged Danish Christians to share God's anger at the injustice which was being perpetrated in their land, and to stand up to the work of Satan which was stealing their Jewish neighbours' lives. Before he was executed by the Gestapo in January 1944, he warned:

> *What we Christians lack is not psychology or literature... We lack a holy rage – the recklessness which comes from the knowledge of God and humanity. The ability to rage when justice lies prostrate on the streets, and when the lie rages across the face of the earth... a holy anger about the things that are wrong in the world. To rage against the ravaging of God's earth, and the destruction of God's world. To rage when little children must die of hunger, when the tables of the rich are sagging with food. To rage at the senseless killing of so many, and against the madness of militaries. To rage at the lie that calls the threat of death and the strategy of destruction peace. To rage against complacency. To restlessly seek that recklessness that will challenge and seek to change human history until it conforms to the norms of the Kingdom of God. And remember the signs of the Christian Church have been the lion, the lamb, the dove and the fish... but never the chameleon.*[4]

Feeling righteous anger isn't enough, however. We can get angry at the things which anger God yet still sin without doing

---

[4] Quoted by Shane Claiborne in *The Irresistible Revolution* (2006).

anything. Samuel makes that clear when he tells the Israelites in 12:23, *"Far be it from me that I should sin against the Lord by failing to pray for you."* Samuel would remain Israel's judge until he died in around 1013 BC in 25:1, thirty-seven years into King Saul's reign, but most of his work in the final quarter century of his life would be in the form of getting angry and turning that anger into prayer.[5] We are told in 15:11 that *"Samuel was angry, and he cried out to the Lord all that night"*, and the writer wants to stir us here with that same anger so that we will also cry out to the Lord in prayer. Samuel saw Israel as God saw it and cried out for him to revive the nation because of his *purposes* for Israel (12:22b), his *history* with Israel (12:24), his *promises* to Israel (15:29) and *his passion to be glorified* through Israel (12:22a).[6] Even though Samuel dies less than halfway through 1 and 2 Samuel, the two books rightly bear his name. The blessings which God brought on Israel through David were the direct result of Samuel's indignant prayers.

We desperately need to take this message to heart if we are to be the kind of people God can use. When we treat calmness in the face of sin as virtue instead of vice, we fall into the same trap which will snare complacent Saul in the next few chapters. He is about to sin without doing anything, while David is about to please the Lord through sharing his anger over spiritual pride, sin and injustice.[7] Let's not grow complacent over such things and regard our calmness as a virtue. Let's listen to Eugene Peterson when he points out that

---

[5] Samuel's withdrawal from public leadership didn't make his ministry any less active. In fact, Acts 6:4 tells us that one of the principal tasks of public church leaders is to give themselves to private prayer.

[6] David will show us in 2 Samuel 7:25 that God's promises should cause us to pray *more*, not less. God's great promises make David pray all the more for him to *"Do as you promised"*. See also Daniel 9:2–3.

[7] David's anger in 2 Samuel 1:14–15 corresponds to God's anger in 6:7, and his anger in 2 Samuel 12:5 and 13:21 corresponds to God's anger in 22:8 and 24:1.

With the vastness of the heavenly invasion and the urgency of the faith decision rolling into our consciousness like thunder and lightning, we cannot stand around on Sunday morning filling the time with pretentious small talk on how bad the world is and how wonderful this new stewardship campaign is going to be.[8]

Instead, let's be angered by what angers God and let's allow that anger to launch us into battle for the world in prayer.

The fifth-century church leader Augustine of Hippo taught that *"Hope has two beautiful daughters; their names are Anger and Courage. Anger that things are the way they are, and Courage to see that they do not remain as they are."* As Samuel finishes his final sermon to Israel and prepares to take a more background role in the story, he urges us to embrace both of Hope's beautiful daughters. He tells us to get angry at the way the world is, and to combine it with the courage to remind God of his promises, purposes and passion to be glorified in the world. He tells us not to sin by failing to lay hold of God in prayer.

He tells us not to be guilty of sinning without doing anything. He tells us to be the angry, courageous, praying kind of people that God has always used to change the world.

71

Dear God,
Thank you that you keep me on your paths. Help me to be obedient to you Lord. Help me to not become complacent with Sin but to stir an righteous anger within me against the sin that causes me to urgently pray for a change! Thank you, Lord that you love despite our disobedience!
Love
Miriam, Amen

---

[8] Eugene Peterson in *The Contemplative Pastor* (1989).

How to Disobey in Five Easy Steps (13:1–22)

*The Lord has sought out a man after his own heart
and appointed him ruler of his people, because you
have not kept the Lord's command.*

(1 Samuel 13:14)

The advertising break is well and truly over. Even as his subjects
pledge their continued obedience to Samuel, King Saul slips
instinctively back into his old disobedient ways. He is barely
two years into his reign, but already he forfeits his throne in this
chapter through five easy steps by which he disobeys the Lord.

First, Saul shows that disobedience begins with *too small
a vision of the Lord*. He has an army of 330,000 men at his
disposal, buoyed by victory over the Ammonites and ready for
a showdown with the Philistines. This is the moment where
Samson's flawed first steps and Samuel's mighty sequel should
reach their great crescendo in Saul's fulfilment of God's promise
to him in 9:16 and the final destruction of Israel's bitter enemy.
Yet sadly, Saul has lost the grand vision of God which he was
given when his heart was changed temporarily in 10:9. He
dismisses his whole army except for 3,000 men and makes
no attempt to use them to follow up his eastern victory over
Ammon with a similar western victory over the Philistines.

When Helen Keller was asked *"What could be worse than
being born blind?"*, she replied *"To have sight without vision."*
Saul might as well have been as blind as Eli for all his pint-sized
vision of God. The Lord had told the kings of Israel to study
Scripture and commit it to memory in Deuteronomy 17 because

this is the only way any of us can obtain the God-sized vision which permanently changes a person's heart.

Second, Saul shows that small vision fosters disobedience by causing us to *abdicate our God-given responsibility*. The rumour spreads through Israel in verse 4 that Saul has attacked a Philistine outpost, but it is not true. He has left it to his teenaged son Jonathan[1] to take the initiative using a unit of soldiers which is only half the size of his father's. Saul only blows the trumpet to rally back his army from their homes when he realizes that this means his policy of appeasement towards the Philistine invaders has been scuppered by his son.[2] Even when his troops return, he fails to take responsibility to lead them into battle. Armies quickly lose morale when they are left idling in the camp without orders, just as churches start shrinking when too little is asked of them, and in the absence of any strong lead from Saul his soldiers scatter to hide in caves and holes in the ground, or else flee across the Jordan to the green fields where the Ammonite raiders no longer roam. Saul forgets that delayed obedience is simply disobedience today, and before he knows it his mighty army has been whittled down to 600 in verse 15 – even smaller than in verse 2![3] If we find that our own churches are shrinking, then we must learn from the mistakes of Saul.

Third, Saul shows that these two mistakes spring from a heart which *fails to seek God*. 1 Chronicles 10:13–14 tells us that

---

[1] Only the Septuagint text tells us in verse 1 that Saul was *thirty*, and the corrupted Hebrew text should probably read that he began to reign at *forty* and had reigned for *two years* so far. Nevertheless, since Jonathan became friends with David, he must have been a teenager when he attacked the outpost at Geba.

[2] Geba was a city in Benjamin (1 Chronicles 6:60), so Saul had not only failed to invade Philistine territory but had even come to tolerate their raiders camping in his own tribal land.

[3] The leader who relies on his own authority cannot restrain God's People as we read he must in 9:17. Unlike the leader who submits to God, he has only his own authority to fall back on. David could gather as many soldiers as an outlaw in 23:13 as Saul could gather as king in verse 15.

"Saul died because he... did not enquire of the Lord", and there is no mention in this chapter of his seeking guidance through Scripture or prayer. If he had, he might have learned that the Lord had routed far bigger foreign armies than this one through the humble men and women who cried out to him throughout the book of Judges. Because he fails to meditate on "Judges theology", he falls victim to the "cave theology" of the man-made leader who swaggers in peacetime yet crumbles in a crisis. He abandons his last stronghold in the Benjamite city of Michmash in the time it takes us to read from verses 2 to 5. As an act of mercy, Samuel promises to come within a week and offer blood sacrifices to help Saul remember that a better Messiah than himself can save him, yet Saul is unwilling to wait that long and usurps the role of priest because he views blood sacrifice as little more than a crowd-pleasing piece of superstition to boost Israel's morale.[4] He has tried to play the part of *melek*, which is the Lord's alone to play, so it is only a small step for him to try to play the part of priest instead of Samuel too.

Fourth, Saul shows that disobedience prospers in an atmosphere of *blame-shifting instead of repentance*. When Samuel confronts him in verse 11 with the question *"What have you done?"*, he has a perfect opportunity to confess that he has sinned out of desperation and that he now needs to throw himself on the Lord for forgiveness and deliverance.[5] Instead, he blames his soldiers for scattering and Samuel for delaying, while painting his own actions in the best possible light as part of his overzealous thirst for the Lord's favour. *"I forced myself to sacrifice the burnt offering,"* he says literally in verse 12, but Samuel corrects him firmly in verses 13–14 by saying that in fact he has disobeyed the Lord. As a result, God has found another

---

[4] The issue was not that Samuel was late, since he arrived just as Saul finished sacrificing. The issue was that Saul despised the Lord's priesthood and blood sacrifice too much to wait for him.

[5] Samuel's question is not a request for information but a call to repent, like the one in Genesis 3:9.

man *"because you have not kept the Lord's command"*, and that man will happily serve as *nāgīd* or *viceroy* over God's People because he is *"a man after his own heart"*. Paul paraphrases this verse loosely in Acts 13:22 to explain that the principal difference between Saul and David was that Saul took these five easy steps towards disobeying the Lord: *"I have found David son of Jesse, a man after my own heart; he will do everything I want him to do."*

Fifth, Saul shows that fully grown disobedience expresses itself in *compromise with the enemy*. Having forfeited God's help, Saul is reduced in verses 16–22 to letting the Philistines raid his land and confiscate every weapon which the Israelites might someday use against them. A similar compromise takes place today when Christians let go of their faith in the Bible, their experience of the Holy Spirit and their belief in the uniqueness of the Christian Gospel in order to curry favour within a culture which has effectively been conquered by the values of unbelievers.[6] Instead of gaining ground through this disobedience, they simply pour the Church's resources into the coffers of the world and settle for using domesticated tools instead. Chapter 13 ends with Israel being as shamed and routed through disobedience as they were honoured and victorious at the end of chapter 11 through obedience. This should serve as a terrible warning for us all that we must not have any share in these five easy steps towards disobeying the Lord.

But all is not lost. God has found a new messiah in David. Our man-made messiahs will fail us every time, but God has a messiah in the wings who will obey at each point where Saul failed.

---

[6] Shockingly, 14:21 tells us that such Christians are turncoats who switch sides in the heat of battle.

Perhaps (14:1–15)

Perhaps the Lord will act on our behalf. Nothing can hinder the Lord from saving, whether by many or by few.

(1 Samuel 14:6)

Niccolò Polo was a man with an impressive thirst for danger and adventure. The father of the famous Marco Polo had been smitten by the vast wealth of the east, and he travelled from Venice to the other side of the world in order to make his fortune through foreign trade. He became one of the first white men to stand at the court of Kublai Khan in what is present-day Beijing, and he returned to Italy in 1269 with an astonishing invitation. The great emperor had learned about a man called Jesus Christ, who was God, and he wanted 100 of his followers to come and preach his message in China. If Niccolò Polo could bring back 100 missionaries from Europe, Kublai Khan promised that he and his subjects would become Christians.

Sadly, Europe's Christians had less ambition for their Messiah than Niccolò Polo had for his money. It took two years for the Catholic Church to receive the emperor's messenger, and when the Pope finally read his letter he could only muster two missionaries. Both of those two missionaries deserted Niccolò and Marco Polo en route to China due to the hardships of their journey and an increased sense of fear as they contemplated preaching Christ in pagan lands. Marco Polo returned to Italy after twenty-four years of service in China for the sake of a massive fortune. Not one single European Christian paid the same price for the sake of China's massive population. The Polo family were thirsty for danger and adventure. The Christian family were decidedly not.[1]

King Saul was much more like a the Pope and his cardinals than like Niccolò and Marco Polo. He bore God's promise to Samuel that he would deliver Israel from the Philistines. He still remembered God's advertisement for obedience when he had crushed the Ammonites. He was accompanied by the high priest Ahijah, Eli's great-grandson and heir, who bore the ephod through which Saul could receive up-to-the-minute instructions from the Lord.[2] Saul was a head taller than the other Israelites, better armed than any of them, and still had command of 600 loyal troops with which to attack the invading Philistines. He simply needed to remember the Lord's promises and take risks to obey them. But he didn't. He hid with his men under a pomegranate tree and waited while the Philistines laid waste the Promised Land.

His teenaged son Jonathan, however, was like Niccolò and Marco Polo.[3] Instead of focusing on the reasons to fear the Philistines, he remembered how God delivered Israel through the Judges. He tells his armour-bearer that *"Nothing can hinder the Lord from saving, whether by many or by few,"* and doesn't let the fact that they only have one sword between them deter his battle plan.[4] He has caught a vision of God's greatness and sees the Philistines as nothing more than *"uncircumcised men"* in verse 6. He is more consumed with the thought that God's plans

---

[1] Marco Polo and Rustichello da Pisa tell this tragic story in *The Travels of Marco Polo* (c.1300 AD).

[2] Ahijah meant *My Brother Is the Lord* and his other name Ahimelek meant *My Brother Is the King*, which hints he grasped that Yahweh was the true King of Israel. The ephod was the priest's clothing which had a pocket for the Urim and Thummim, through which the Lord gave guidance (Exodus 28:30).

[3] Jonathan's name means *Gift From the Lord*, and he was God's gift to show Saul what he might yet become.

[4] Jonathan evidently gave his sword to his armour-bearer and used his staff to fell them (verse 27) so that his armour-bearer could stab them. Even though he was a royal prince, he took greater risks than those he led.

are defied, God's name is defiled and God's People are despoiled than he is with protecting his own skin. While his father sees the dangers of action, like the European Christians who rejected Kublai Khan's plea for missionaries, Jonathan sees the dangers of disobedience instead.

Jonathan has no personal promise from the Lord to expect victory, as far as we can tell. The writer of 1 Samuel tells us in verse 1 that he launches the attack on *"one day"* like any other because he trusts that *"perhaps"* the Lord will use him if he obeys. He may well be thinking back to the example of Caleb in Joshua 14:12, since Caleb used this same Hebrew word when he attacked a group of giants on the basis that *"perhaps"* the Lord might help him.[5] Notice the progression of events in these verses: Jonathan does not tell his father of his plans because he knows that Saul will try to stop him.[6] He shares his plans with another teenager, and the two of them lay down the simplest of fleeces to obtain some guidance from the Lord.[7] When it suggests that they should bet everything on launching a suicide attack upon the garrison, Jonathan embraces it as a sign that *"the Lord has given them into the hand of Israel"*.[8] He leaps up to fell the Philistines with his staff so that his armour-bearer can follow and stab the fallen enemy with his sword. While Saul debates the dangers with his disobedient generals, Jonathan and his armour-bearer become the kind of people God can use.

Jonathan's obedience is highly contagious. While his father is deserted by all but 600 of his men, Jonathan's armour-bearer swears that *"I am with you heart and soul"*, and proves it by

---

[5] Caleb uses this same Hebrew word *'ūlay* when he says *"if the Lord is with me"*.

[6] It is only two years into Saul's reign yet the Lord is forced to deliver Israel despite him, not through him.

[7] These two crags are called Bozez, which means *Glistening White*, and Seneh, which means *Thorny*. Jonathan launched his attack in an arid, sun-scorched, vicious desert land.

[8] Jonathan's faith is obedient, not reckless. He gives the Lord space to guide him not to act if necessary.

obeying the Lord with him.[9] When news spreads throughout the Philistines that twenty of their comrades have been killed by just two Israelites, they are gripped by *"a panic sent by God"* and start fleeing for the border. They get so confused that they start killing one another in verse 20, and so demoralized that even Saul can chase them back home to Philistia. That's what happens when God finds a person he can use – someone who dares to say *"perhaps"* and take the battle to the enemy.

A young English shoemaker named William Carey behaved like Jonathan when he refused to let older and more experienced church leaders stop him from travelling to India to preach the Gospel message to its unreached millions. *"Expect great things from God; attempt great things for God,"* he urged a complacent English Church,[10] and stirred so many to follow him that he is known as "the father of modern missions". By the time he died, there were half a million Christians in his part of India.

An English medical student named Hudson Taylor behaved like Jonathan when he took up Kublai Khan's challenge to preach the Gospel throughout China five and a half centuries after the European Church had failed. Despite discouragement from senior Christians, despite the odds stacked against him, and despite the dangers it entailed, he sailed for China in belief that

> *Want of trust is at the root of almost all our sins and all our weaknesses; and how shall we escape it but by looking to Him and observing His faithfulness?... All God's giants have been weak men, who did great things for God because they reckoned on His being with them... Oh! beloved friends, if there is a living God, faithful and*

---

[9] He says literally that *"I am with you like your own heart"*, using the same Hebrew phrase which the Lord used to describe David's loyal obedience in 13:14.

[10] Carey repeated this line several times while preaching in Nottingham from Isaiah 54:2–3 on 30th May 1792, before sailing as a pioneer missionary to India the following year.

true, let us hold His faithfulness... Let us not give Him a partial trust, but daily, hourly serve Him, counting on His faithfulness.[11]

Like Jonathan and William Carey, his pioneering act of obedience caused a whole army of missionaries to emulate his death-defying faith.[12]

So don't be like Saul and list reasons why you dare not obey God. Be like Jonathan or William Carey or Hudson Taylor, and obey. Perhaps the Lord will act on your behalf. Perhaps he will see you as the kind of person he can use.

---

[11] Writing in the November 1875 edition of his magazine *China's Millions*.
[12] 14:14–22 and 17:51–52 promise that one person with faith can cause the whole Church to surge forward.

Too Busy to Listen
(14:16–52)

> *While Saul was talking to the priest, the tumult in the Philistine camp increased more and more. So Saul said to the priest, "Withdraw your hand."*
>
> (1 Samuel 14:19)

Even though the Duke of Wellington confessed after winning the Battle of Waterloo that it had been *"the nearest run thing you ever saw in your life"*, he had no idea how close he had come that day to disaster. Only later did it come to light that the Prussian army which turned the battle in his favour would have been slaughtered had General d'Erlon simply listened to Napoleon's order to cut off its retreat when it was defeated two days earlier at Ligny. Only later did he discover that Marshal Grouchy might have turned the battle the other way if he had responded to the sound of Napoleon's cannons calling him to march his troops to Waterloo. The Duke of Wellington only succeeded because two of Napoleon's officers were too busy fighting to listen to his orders.

Saul's unwillingness to listen to the Lord in this chapter makes General d'Erlon and Marshal Grouchy seem very attentive to their emperor in comparison. Jonathan has won a mighty victory that morning, and God has sent such a panic into the Philistine army that they start scattering in all directions and killing one another in confusion. Thousands of Hebrew soldiers who defected to the Philistines or hid in the hills start to return to Saul. All he has to do is hear from the Lord how to lead them in pursuit of the Philistines in order to break their power once and for all.

Saul knows this. He still remembers Samuel's instruction

that he must govern as the Lord's obedient viceroy instead of trying to reign as an independent king. He tries to consult the Lord, but he has neglected him for so long that he doesn't know how to do so. He tells the high priest to bring *"the ark of God"*, when what he really means is the ephod[1] (the priestly robe with a pocket containing the Urim and Thummim[2]). The Lord had given his priests these two stones as a way of revealing his will, but Saul gets frustrated by the length of time it takes Ahijah to reach into his pocket and draw out one of the stones. The noise in the Philistine camp grows so loud that he abandons the attempt to hear God's voice and rushes into battle with all the wisdom of General d'Erlon and Marshal Grouchy.

In the absence of the Lord's guidance, Saul decides to reassert his reputation as a dangerous warrior after months of shameful hiding from the Philistines. He does not mention the Lord's name at all as he curses his troops if they eat any food before he has finished wreaking his royal vengeance on his enemies. All this achieves is to make his men so weary from their hot pursuit that they give up before they have truly broken the power of the retreating Philistines, and so famished that they break the Law of Moses by devouring their plunder without first draining the meat of blood. Verse 33 suggests that Saul knows so little of Scripture that one of his men has to point out that Leviticus 17:10–12 forbade this on pain of being exiled from God's People. Saul decides to erect an altar as a tactical concession to the Lord, even though he still despises God's blood sacrifices (the writer tells us *"it was the first time he had done this"* so far during his entire reign). Thinking that the Lord

[1] Since 1 Chronicles 13:3–7 tells us that Saul ignored the Ark at Kiriath Jearim throughout his reign, Saul must be so unfamiliar with seeking God that he mixes up his words when he tries to do so. The translators of the Septuagint corrected Saul's mistake to read *ephod* instead of *ark*, based on verse 3.

[2] Exodus 28:30. The words Urim and Thummim begin with the first and last letters of the Hebrew alphabet and mean *Lights* and *Perfections*. It appears that whichever of the two stones the priest drew out of his pocket enlightened him to be able to declare God's perfect will for any situation.

is appeased by such tactical concessions, he begins to gather his troops to renew the pursuit.[3]

Before we judge Saul too harshly, let's recognize that this is exactly how many Christians act towards God today. We assume that good things (like Saul's national fast) must be in accordance with God's will, and we press on without clarifying with him first in prayer. When we are unfruitful, we find fresh strategies and convince ourselves that these are what were lacking the first time. We return to our furious but fruitless church activity and repeat the cycle again. Saul's example warns us that being too busy to listen to God actually turns victory into defeat and devotion into sin. If Ahijah had not stopped Saul by urging him, *"Let us enquire of God here"*, the Philistines would have been able to reverse by night the mighty victory which Jonathan had won during the day.[4] Christian leaders must warn their followers not to act like General d'Erlon and Marshal Grouchy. They must warn them not to be too busy to listen to God.

Saul is in for a shock because this time the Lord isn't willing to talk to him. He is so disgusted with Saul's independent spirit as a human king that he refuses to answer his disobedient viceroy even when he slows down enough to listen. He forces Saul to wait as the priest draws the Urim and Thummim to reveal that Israel cannot conquer because of Saul's rash oath that morning. Jonathan had not heard the oath and had eaten forbidden honey as he chased the enemy through a wood, and the Lord uses Saul's precious son and heir to humble him into repenting for not listening earlier.[5] Astonishingly, Saul would

---

[3] The writer hints that Saul's disdain for God's blood sacrifice resulted in the death of his son years later. The soldiers literally *ransom* Jonathan's life by force in verse 45, but because Saul does not pay the ransom price for his sin by following up with blood sacrifice he still goes on to die.

[4] The Hebrew means literally *"Let us draw near to God here."* This was precisely what Saul felt too busy to do.

[5] Jonathan submits to the Lord, telling his father literally in verse 43, *"Here I am. I will die."* Instead of listening to him, Saul should have listened to God and repented in order to lift the curse off his son.

rather execute Jonathan than repent, and orders his death despite the fact he did not hear an oath which should never have been uttered anyway![6] Saul's soldiers are forced to step in and side with Jonathan, leaving Saul so hurt and angry that he gives up on the idea of a night-time pursuit of the Philistines after all.[7] What began as a day of victory through Jonathan's faith ends with a night of failure through Saul's busyness.

The Duke of Wellington wrote a letter home on the evening of his victory at Waterloo. He mourned that *"My heart is broken by the terrible loss I have sustained in my old friends and companions and my poor soldiers. Believe me, nothing except a battle lost can be half so melancholy as a battle won."*[8] The Lord wants us to see that there is nothing more melancholy than the defeat which comes to a person who is too busy to listen to God's Word. Because Saul let the tumult of the day stop him from listening to Israel's true King, he became like General d'Erlon and Marshal Grouchy. He would needlessly spend the rest of his reign in bitter warfare with the Philistines.[9]

So let's not be too busy to spend time listening to the Lord's commands. Let's draw near to God through Bible study, worship, prayer and fellowship with other Christians. However loud the tumult of activity which is facing us today, let's never be too busy to listen for the voice of God.

AN OBEDIENT PERSON

84

---

[6] In fact, he utters two more rash oaths in verses 39 and 44, which result in Jonathan and him dying a few years later at the Battle of Gilboa in 31:1–6.

[7] Note the difference between leading through democracy and leading through hearing God. Although Saul's soldiers tell him twice in verses 36 and 40 to *"Do whatever seems best to you"*, they actually mean *"Guess what seems right to us."* As soon as he misjudges their mood, he has no authority left with which to lead. Those who lead through hearing God retain their authority even when their decisions are unpopular.

[8] Quoted by Sir Edward Shepherd Creasy in *Fifteen Decisive Battles of the World* (1851).

[9] Moab, Ammon, Edom and Zobah in verse 47 were all to the east of Israel and affected by Saul's obedient campaign in chapter 11. They hint at what Saul might have achieved had he been equally obedient on the western front in chapter 14.

Dear Lord, thank you that you have chosen me, help me to listen to your words, to not be so busy that I don't. Amen!

Rejected (15:1–35)

Because you have rejected the word of the Lord, he has rejected you as king.

(1 Samuel 15:23)

Saul had been drinking in the last-chance saloon for far too long. He was about to drink one cup of disobedience too many. In chapter 15, the Lord sends Samuel for a final showdown with the king and to call last orders on the disobedient reign of Saul.[1]

Given Saul's failure to obey the Lord in chapters 13 and 14, it comes as quite a surprise that Samuel's message is not a rebuke but a fresh and gracious call to wholehearted obedience. God deliberately takes Saul back to his advertisement for obedience in chapter 11 several years before. Then, Saul had obeyed the Lord and won an impressive victory over Nahash, king of the Ammonite enemies of Israel, who were descended from Lot's shameful act of incest with his daughter. Now, the Lord sends him to fight Agag, king of the Amalekite enemies of Israel, who were descended from Esau's grandson Amalek and who had been persistently hostile towards Israel from the time they came up out of Egypt and throughout the period of the Judges.[2] Samuel tells Saul that the Lord has decided to use him to fulfil the promise of Exodus 17:16 and the command of

---

[1] The writer tells us in 1 Samuel 28:18 that this act of disobedience was what forfeited Saul the monarchy and turned the Lord from acting as his friend to acting as his foe.

[2] Genesis 36:12; Exodus 17:8–16; Numbers 24:20; Deuteronomy 25:17–19; Judges 6:3.

Deuteronomy 25:17–19.[3] Despite his consistent disobedience so far, the Lord has decided to give Saul a final opportunity to be the kind of person he can use.

At first, Saul is as obedient as he was against the Ammonites. He musters 210,000 soldiers in the name of the Lord – compared to the 600 he was able to muster in his own name in chapter 14 – and he leads them into battle on behalf of the Lord. Although Samuel acknowledges in verses 1 and 17 that Saul is reigning as a *melek* over Israel instead of governing as a *nāgīd* under God, Saul remembers that this campaign is not about his gaining territory or fame, but about avenging the Lord's glory.[4] He remembers that the Kenites are the descendants of Moses' brother-in-law Hobab, who joined the Israelites at the Exodus and became their loyal scout across the desert.[5] Since they lived in the same southern part of Israel as the Amalekites, he warns them to flee because he dares not overstep his mandate from the Lord. Saul is transformed from the coward who hid under the pomegranate tree in chapter 14 back into the obedient warrior of chapter 11. All is going smoothly until Saul's eye catches the plunder.

The Lord had specifically commanded the king of Israel in Deuteronomy 17 not to amass large amounts of livestock and treasure, or to *"consider himself better than his fellow Israelites"*. Saul has no problem slaughtering the rank-and-file Amalekites, but his failure to carry out the Lord's command completely betrays the true state of his heart.[6] He spares King Agag on the

---

[3] The Amalekites attacked their Hebrew cousins in *c.*1446 BC in Exodus 17, yet the Lord still remembers their sin here in *c.*1040 BC. Do not fool yourself that God will forget sin with the passage of time.

[4] The Hebrew word *hāram* in verse 3 means *to devote to the Lord through destruction*. This attack was not to be a royal power-grab, but an act of obedient worship.

[5] Numbers 10:29–32; Judges 4:11. Jael the Kenite was also a woman God had used to deliver Israel from Canaanite invaders in Judges 4:21.

[6] When we are repulsed that God should order the destruction of a people group, it reveals the true state of our own hearts too. Samuel shows us in verse

basis that they are fellow kings bound by a common royal code, and he spares the sheep and cows according to the ancient laws of royal plunder. The Lord could have anything which was weak and surplus to his royal requirements, but he couldn't take the king's share. Don't be shocked that Saul erected a monument to his own glory after the victory in verse 12. He had been living for his own glory for so long that the Lord was about to call last orders on his reign.

The Hebrew word which God uses in verse 11 to tell Samuel that he *regrets* making Saul king is the same word *nāham* which we looked at in the chapter "Act like a Little Girl". He tells Samuel that he has *changed his mind* about Saul being king of Israel after all, although he also uses the same word again in verse 29 to clarify that Saul's disobedience hasn't taken him by surprise. He never actually changes his mind, but knew all along that he would change his mind at this point when Saul failed in his last chance to be the kind of person he could use. Samuel is angry with Saul for despising his calling and cries out to the Lord all night for him before going down to Gilgal – the place where he had confirmed him as Israel's king in chapter 11 – in order to confront him with his sin and tell him that his dynasty is dead.

True to form, Saul responds to the rebuke with flat denial instead of repentance. He insists that he has carried out the Lord's instructions to the letter, and if livestock has been spared then it is either due to his soldiers' disobedience or due to his own devotion to the Lord.[7] He pretends that he cares so much for God's blood sacrifices that he spared the animals to make a bloodbath of them later on the altar of the Lord. Yet even as he makes his sorry excuses, he betrays in verse 21 that he has not

---

11 that it is right to get angry over wickedness, and warns in verse 3 that it can sometimes be a sin to show compassion. As if to emphasize this, verse 33 tells us literally that Samuel *hacked Agag to pieces before the Lord*. God takes sin very seriously, and so must we.

[7] Blaming his men was no excuse anyway, since his calling in 9:17 had been literally to *restrain* God's People under God's rule.

served the Lord throughout his reign by telling Samuel that he is merely *"the Lord your God"*. Samuel responds by telling Saul about the kind of person God can use – not a smooth-talking king who worships him on his own terms, but a humble and obedient viceroy who does not try to modify the Lord's instructions.[8] *"Because you have rejected the word of the Lord,"* Samuel tells him, *"he has rejected you as king."* The Lord has found a better man to rule as his viceroy instead. He has found the kind of person he can use.

Saul comes the closest in his life to repenting at this news, but note the clues the writer gives us that his heart has not fundamentally changed. He still blames his soldiers for his own sin in verse 24, and he still calls God *"the Lord your God"* in verse 30. He is far more interested in whether Samuel will honour him before the elders of Israel than in the fact that he has offended the honour of the Lord, the *"Glory of Israel"*. He still leaves the task of executing King Agag to Samuel, the judge's last public act of ministry. Samuel departs to Ramah, never to return,[9] yet Saul neither follows him to Ramah nor goes to Kiriath Jearim to bring back the Ark of the Covenant instead. As the second section of 1 Samuel draws to a close, Saul still prefers to be a rejected king than a repentant viceroy.

Saul's incomplete obedience meant that God allowed a small remnant of Amalekites to raid and plunder Israel throughout the rest of his reign. Even after David destroyed this remnant, God allowed an Amalekite descendant of Agag named Haman to survive and launch a plot to annihilate the Jews in the time of Esther.[10] He did this to warn us that disobedience

---

[8] The Hebrew word for arrogance in verse 23 means literally *pushiness*. What we call self-assertiveness, God calls witchcraft and idolatry because it seeks to assert our own will above God's will, just like Saul.

[9] Samuel refused to talk to Saul even in 19:24. He simply grieved and prayed privately as promised in 12:23.

[10] 1 Samuel 30; Esther 3:1. Other than Haman, the last Amalekites were slaughtered by the Simeonites at the time of King Hezekiah in 1 Chronicles 4:38–43, completely fulfilling God's prophecy against them.

always has a terrible price to pay. As the curtain falls on the second section of 1 Samuel, God calls us to surrender our lives to him and become the obedient kind of people he can use.

Lord thank you we are able to read your word and be reminded that we must obey you Lord. Help me to be more obedient to you, to follow your words throughout all that I do. Amen :)

1 Samuel 16–31:

A Pure Person

Skin-Deep Isn't Deep Enough (16:1–13)

The Lord does not look at the things people look at. People look at the outward appearance, but the Lord looks at the heart.

(1 Samuel 16:7)

There is a reason why *Shrek* struck a chord with moviegoers of all ages around the world. We live in an age when people make superficial judgments based on outward appearances, and *Shrek* refuses to play by those rules. An ugly ogre is the hero, the damsel in distress can fight like a ninja, and it is a stupid and annoying donkey whose loyalty finally saves the day. The posters for *Shrek* summed up the reason for its appeal: *"The Prince isn't charming. The Princess isn't sleeping. The sidekick isn't helping. The ogre is the hero. Fairy tales will never be the same again."*

The third section of 1 Samuel has more surprises than *Shrek*, as the Lord corrects our shallow thinking about the kind of person he can use. After sections one and two, we might have assumed that he is looking for somebody stronger than Saul – someone with the common sense and natural gifting which Saul so sorely lacked. Alternatively, we might assume that he is looking for somebody weaker than Saul – someone who has more cause than the tall and good-looking Saul to be humble and obedient. The opening verses of this third section inform us that both of these views fail to go deep enough beneath the story. God is not looking at outward appearances at all. He is looking at the heart to find the kind of person he can use.

Several years have passed since the end of chapter 15, but Samuel is still mourning for Saul's failed reign at Ramah.[1] When the Lord finally commands him to go and anoint a new king who will succeed where Saul has failed,[2] Samuel points out that Saul has not forgotten his warning that God has found another ruler and will view this act as treason. The Lord's solution is to command him to offer a sacrifice on the altar at Bethlehem as the perfect cover for visiting Jesse, the great-grandson of Boaz and Ruth, and to anoint one of his sons as the new king.[3]

Jesse parades his seven sons before Samuel, hoping that one of them will be the kind of person God can use. His eldest son Eliab is so impressive that Samuel assumes he has found his messiah, but he remembers that the Lord was insistent in verse 1 that this time he will do the choosing. He senses God telling him, *"Do not consider his appearance or his height, for I have rejected him. The Lord does not look at the things people look at. People look at the outward appearance, but the Lord looks at the heart."* He senses the same about Jesse's other six sons, and Samuel asks him in confusion if he is sure he has no other sons. Jesse confesses that there is an eighth and youngest son, but he is so unimpressive that his father did not even bother to invite him to the party.[4]

If David's brothers had been puny and David had been strong, then it would mean that Saul's problem was that he was too weak for God to use. If David had been puny and his brothers had been strong, then it would mean that Saul's problem was that

---

[1] Since David was born in 1040 BC, the same time as the events of chapter 15, Samuel may have mourned for fifteen years or more.

[2] Although the Lord uses the word *melek* to describe this new *king* in verse 1, we learn in 2 Samuel 5:2 that Samuel prophesied as he anointed him that he must govern Israel as God's obedient *nāgīd*, or *viceroy*.

[3] Jesse and David are mentioned at the very end of the book of Ruth. This sacrifice was more than just a ruse, since 20:6 tells us that there was an important altar in Bethlehem.

[4] Like Abraham's servant in Genesis 24, Samuel refuses to sit down to eat the sacrifice until he has completed his God-given mission.

he was too strong for God to use. However, David's brothers are strong and impressive, and verse 12 tells us David *"was glowing with health and had a fine appearance and handsome features"* too.[5] The difference between David and Saul was nothing to do with outward appearances at all. The theme of this third section is that God looks for a person who is pure in heart.

Eliab, Abinadab and Shammah had led such untroubled lives that their hearts were unrefined. They could gladly serve in Saul's army because they grasped God's character as little as he did and shared his fear when the Philistine giant Goliath blasphemed the Lord's name by his pagan gods. David, on the other hand, had been despised and dismissed all his life as the youngest and least important son of the aged Jesse.[6] He had been forced to tend the family's flock of sheep – a job so menial and dirty that the Egyptians viewed shepherds as the lowest of the low[7] – and had spent many hours alone with no other company but God. His spirit had been purified through many trials which had taught him to surrender his whole heart to the Lord.

Shrek developed his loveable character in the harsh school of prejudice and rejection in his swamp. He tells Donkey that *"People take one look at me and go, 'Aargh! Help! Run! A big, stupid, ugly ogre!' They judge me before they even know me. That's why I'm better off alone."*[8] In the same way, David had learned humility and obedience through the many difficulties of his childhood as he herded sheep alone. Psalm 132 tells us that David vowed to restore God's fallen Tabernacle during the many nights he spent sleeping in the fields between Bethlehem

---

[5] The Hebrew word for *glowing with health* means literally *reddish*. David may have had red hair like Esau in Genesis 25:25, but it is more likely that he had the fair skin colour which is praised in Song of Songs 5:10.

[6] 17:12 tells us that Jesse was very old by the time he had his eighth son – possibly as an afterthought.

[7] Genesis 46:33–34. Shepherds poured out their lives for dirty sheep and slept under the stars like paupers.

[8] *Shrek* (Dreamworks Pictures, 2001).

and nearby Kiriath Jearim.[9] While Saul neglected the Ark of the Covenant which was housed there, David meditated on God's purposes and vowed to restore his dwelling place in Israel.

Eliab had not learned this passion for God's glory, or the faithfulness which David learned far away from witnesses among the sheep. He despises them in 17:28 as *"those few sheep in the wilderness"*, but Psalm 78 tells us that *"David shepherded them with integrity of heart; with skilful hands he led them,"* and that this was why God *"chose David his servant and took him from the sheepfolds; from tending the sheep he brought him to be the shepherd of his people Jacob."* David had developed a pure and obedient heart as a shepherd-boy. When Samuel stepped into his life, he discovered that it had made him the kind of person God could use.

British people spent £143 million on cosmetics and beauty products in the year that *Shrek* was released. In the eight years which followed, that figure rose more than eightfold to £1.2 billion. It appears we like the message of *Shrek* in theory, but we have taken it to heart no more than Eliab or Abinadab or Shammah.

So let's get ready for the message of this third section of 1 Samuel. In a world where people judge one another based on what they look like on the outside, and where people prefer outward comfort to the inner training school of trials, the Lord warns us that he looks at the heart. He is looking for the pure-hearted kind of person he can use.

---

[9] *Ephrathah* in Psalm 132:6 is the ancient name for Bethlehem. The Hebrew word translated *Jaar* in many English Bibles is probably a variant of Kiriath *Jearim*, only eight miles from Bethlehem.

Spirit-Filled? (16:13–23)

From that day on the Spirit of the Lord came
powerfully upon David.

(1 Samuel 16:13)

A PURE PERSON

When I became a Christian, I was discipled by well-meaning people who told me that I must receive the Holy Spirit as a one-off experience and that I would know it had happened if I spoke in tongues or prophesied. They were right to tell me that I needed to be filled with the Holy Spirit, but the more I read this passage the more I am convinced that they were wrong about the rest. The writer wants to show us how the Lord changes a person on the inside through his Holy Spirit, and he gives us a very different definition from the one which I was given of what it means for us to be Spirit-filled.

Saul had received the Holy Spirit as a one-off experience and he had prophesied as a result. Chapter 10 tells us that God even changed Saul's heart through the experience so that he became a different person.[1] He was an early poster boy, therefore, for the kind of charismatic thunderbolt from heaven which I was told to ask for. However, chapter 16 is at pains to convince us that this is not enough to make anyone the kind of person God can use. Saul received all this, yet by verse 14 *"the Spirit of the Lord had departed from Saul, and an evil spirit from the Lord tormented him."*[2] The writer wants us to see from David's life that the Holy Spirit has a character, and the

---

[1] 1 Samuel 10:6–13.

[2] Since the Lord is sovereign over everything, even demons are subject to his command. In this sense the demon came *"from the Lord"* in 16:14, 18:10 and 19:9. Compare also 2 Samuel 24:1 with 1 Chronicles 21:1.

primary evidence of us being filled with the Spirit is that we start displaying it too.[3]

The Holy Spirit is *the Spirit of humility*. He came upon Jesus at his baptism as a gentle dove, not as a violent bird of prey.[4] Although the same Hebrew phrase is used for the Spirit coming on David in verse 13 as was used for him coming on Samson and Saul, the Spirit didn't come to help him force his way onto the throne. He gave him contentment with his life as he continued to tend sheep and run errands for his father. When Saul summoned him to the palace and told him to serve as a minstrel in a throne room which should now be his, the Spirit gave him grace to play the lyre and polish Saul's shield as his armour-bearer, when he should have been wearing his crown as king.

The Holy Spirit is *the Spirit of obedience.* We saw in section two that Saul's great undoing was his refusal to obey God, and as a result the Spirit abandons him in this passage and hands him over to his sin.[5] Saul was disobedient over little things and therefore lost everything, but David submits to the Spirit and is obedient in little things.[6] Even though Saul is simply piggy-backing on David's obedience as a way to preserve the power of the Spirit without having to surrender to the Spirit's will, he is forced to admit that he is pleased with the obedient new addition to his court, and his servants are forced to confess that *"the Lord is with him"*.

The Holy Spirit is *the Spirit of courage*. That's why Paul contrasts him in 2 Timothy 1:7 with a spirit of timidity or cowardice instead. We tend to forget, like Saul hiding under the pomegranate tree, that the Lord prizes this virtue so highly

---

[3] Paul makes this same point in Galatians 5:22–25.

[4] John 1:32. John stresses that the Spirit *remained* on Jesus, the very opposite of what happened with Saul.

[5] This is a frightening example of what Paul warns about in Romans 1:24, 26 and 28.

[6] Like Noah or Moses in Genesis 6:22 and Exodus 40:16, David does exactly as he is commanded in 17:20.

that he throws the cowardly into hell alongside the unbelieving and the vile in Revelation 21:8. The Spirit-filled David was so brave that he single-handedly fought off lions and bears which attacked his father's flock.[7] His exploits were so remarkable that news of the teenager's reputation as *"a brave man and a warrior"* had even reached Saul's servants in verse 18. When the invitation came from Saul's palace, it took similar courage to accept it, since David knew as well as Samuel in verse 2 that Saul was insanely jealous of any potential rival. He might have heard about David's anointing and be luring him into a trap, yet David had the courage to trust in God and go to his palace all the same.

The writer of 1 Samuel therefore wants to demonstrate that the true sign of whether or not we have been filled with the Spirit is not a one-off experience or tongues or prophecy, but *a passion for these three things which please the Spirit.*[8]

Humility gave David a passion for God's greatness, and caused him to pass his time in worship on the lyre while his sheep grazed. One day he would be able to fulfil his dream of Psalm 132 by building a new worship Tabernacle for the Israelites, but this only happened because he first learned to worship the Lord on his own, far away from witnesses, through the Holy Spirit.

Obedience gave David a passion for the honour of God's name. Those who hold their Master's glory lightly in their own lives will never be used to call a nation back to God. Those who deal with personal sin when no one else is watching, however, become those who can sense the shame a nation brings to God's reputation when it sins. Like David in 17:26 and 44–47, God uses them to face down giants which dare to defy his great name.

---

[7] 1 Samuel 17:34–37. 10:26 tells us that whenever God touches a person's heart they become courageous.

[8] If we display this *fruit* of the Spirit, then God will be able to entrust us with more *gifts* of the Spirit too.

Courage gave David a passion for the extension of God's rule. While Saul abused the kingship and lost the ability to prophesy altogether in 28:6, those who knew David confessed that *"he speaks well"* in verse 18, and never better than when he was speaking about his God. David possessed the same primary sign of being filled with the Spirit which Martyn Lloyd-Jones saw in the life of the eighteenth-century Welsh revivalist Howell Harris:

> *This is the only explanation of this man. This is what created within him a compassion for the lost. This is what urged him to go out and to tell the people about their condition and do something about them... Is not this the crucial test which we must apply to those who claim to have received the baptism of the Spirit?... It does not lead to an inward looking, self-indulgent, church movement that turns in on itself and spends its time reciting and even boasting at times of experiences. It always leads to this concern for others. There have been movements in the church claiming great things for themselves, as there are certain similar movements at this present time, but they have had to admit that the evangelistic concern has not been prominent among them. The baptism of or with the Spirit, however, shows itself primarily by giving its recipients a great evangelistic concern.*[9]

So let's seek the gifts of tongues and prophecy, but let's not view them as the ultimate sign that we have been filled with the Spirit. Let's expect a moment of initial filling, but let's not let that become a substitute for fresh infillings day by day. Let's grasp that the Holy Spirit is a person with a character, and that he wants to develop that same character in us. He wants us to co-operate with him to become the pure-hearted kind of people God can use.

---

[9] Martyn Lloyd-Jones in *The Puritans: Their Origins and Successors* (1987).

Don't Try to Be a Hero
(17:1–58)

When the Philistines saw that their hero was dead,
they turned and ran. Then the men of Israel and
Judah surged forward with a shout and pursued the
Philistines.

(1 Samuel 17:51–52)

If I had a pound for every sermon I have heard on 1 Samuel 17 which told me I should dare to face up to my giants like David, I would be able to retire and live in style. Frankly, I'm sick of hearing that message and I honestly believe that God is too. It's the exact opposite message to the one which he wants us to take from this chapter and from the whole third section of 1 Samuel.

Let me point out the obvious in this chapter. This isn't a story about how we can become heroes, but a story which reminds us that we *can't* beat the giants in our lives. The writer stressed twice in 9:2 and 10:23 that Saul was a head taller than the other Israelites, but even he cannot defeat the three-metre-tall Goliath.[1] In case we put this down to his cowardice, let's remember that Jonathan was also a commander in Saul's army. Even the one who had engineered the great victory of chapter 14 was not able to take on a Philistine this size. Saul's general Abner was such a skilled fighter that he later killed one of David's best warriors with ease, yet even he was no match for Goliath.[2]

---

[1] Goliath was one of the last surviving Anakite giants left over from the slaughter in Joshua 11:21–22. His armour alone weighed as much as a normal man, and his name meant either *Raw Splendour* or *Naked Exile*.

[2] 2 Samuel 2:18–23. Abner was Saul's cousin but he had earned his rank by merit and not just nepotism.

As for the rest of Saul's army, David's impressive older brother Eliab confesses that none of them is up to a battle with this giant. He and his fellow Israelite soldiers *"all fled from him in great fear"*. Even the promise of riches, a royal wedding and exemption from paying taxes is not enough to convince any of them to try to be a hero, even though Goliath gives them forty days in which to volunteer.[3] This isn't a story about our need to trust in our own ability. God used Goliath to teach Israel to confess their own lack of power, so that they would cry out for him to provide them with a hero who would come from another place and save them from their foe.

David was more than just the kind of person God could use. He was also a picture of the perfect Saviour who would come from his family line. Jonathan Edwards writes that

> *God wrought many lesser salvations and deliverances for His church and people before Christ came. These salvations were all but so many images and forerunners of the great salvation Christ was to work out when He came... David being the ancestor and great type of Christ... may in some respects be looked on as an anointing of Christ Himself.*[4]

He was God's messiah, born in Bethlehem, and who served as the good shepherd. His name means *The Beloved One* and he was filled with the Holy Spirit to proclaim the message of God's Kingdom.[5]

With this in mind, we cannot view this story as a call for us

---

[3] The Hebrew word for *camp* in verse 20 means literally *entrenchment*. Instead of spending the forty days preparing to fight Goliath, they had spent their time digging a trench to avoid having to do so.

[4] Jonathan Edwards in *A History of the Work of Redemption* (preached in 1739, published in 1773).

[5] We also find him humbling himself in verses 17–20 in order to serve his father for the sake of his brothers. Unlike the hired hand in John 10:12–13, he also cared enough for his sheep to risk his life to save them.

to try to be spiritual heroes, but rather as a call to get out of the way so that Jesus can be the Hero who delivers us instead. Eliab represents confidence in human strength, so he is furious at the idea that he needs to humble himself and admit his weakness so that David can take centre stage. Saul represents our desire to rule instead of God, so he tries to make David wear the same royal armour which he has worn during his own disobedient reign. He tries to discourage David in verse 33 that the enemy is too strong and that his foolish weapons are too weak. When Goliath looks at David's sling and stones yet accuses him of coming to fight him with mere *"sticks"*, there may even be an unwitting hint towards the foolishness of Jesus' cross in 1 Corinthians 1:18. This story is full of people who laugh at the foolishness of God's chosen Saviour and his weapons. It is an invitation to kneel down at Jesus' cross and stop pretending that we can play the hero.

Isaiah 53 prophesied the arrival of Jesus the Messiah on our life's battlefield:

> *He had no beauty or majesty to attract us to him, nothing in his appearance that we should desire him. He was despised and rejected by mankind, a man of suffering and familiar with pain. Like one from whom people hide their faces he was despised, and we held him in low esteem.*

Those words might just as easily serve as a description of David as he steps forward to fight Goliath with nothing but a sling and five smooth stones. *"I will give him a portion among the great, and he will divide the spoils with the strong,"* Isaiah continues. Just as David succeeded in killing Goliath, Jesus will always win the battle when we admit that we cannot.

Note what happens in verses 51–53 when the Israelites stop pretending they are heroes and let God's messiah be their hero instead. David fells the mighty giant, then leads the rest of the army in routing and plundering the defeated enemy.

Suddenly soldiers who have cowered in the trenches for forty days are empowered to conquer and plunder through their messiah's victory. *"Then the men of Israel and Judah surged forward with a shout and pursued the Philistines to the entrance of Gath and to the gates of Ekron... When the Israelites returned from chasing the Philistines, they plundered their camp."*

Perhaps you need forgiveness and deliverance from a sense of guilt which looms large like a giant on your conscience. Don't try to be a hero and make your own amends with God. Praise him that another has stepped onto the battlefield for your soul so that his blood can eradicate your sin and deliver you from the winepress of God's righteous judgment.[6]

Perhaps you need deliverance from a sin from which you know you are forgiven, yet which still wields continued power like a giant in your daily life. Don't try to be a hero and resist sin through willpower alone. Praise God that another has chopped off Goliath's head so you don't have to, then surge forward with a shout of faith to use the sword of his word to tell sin you're not a slave to it any more.

Perhaps you need healing or provision or some other breakthrough. Don't try to be a hero and scheme your own way to God's blessing. Speak out the authority which has been given you through Jesus' name, and plunder Satan's camp through faith. As you do, you bring glory to God through your faith in Jesus the mighty Hero.

For we have not been called to be heroes who achieve great things *for* Christ in our own strength, but who receive great things *from* Christ in his. When we shift our attention onto him like the Israelites in this chapter, he enables us to rise up with a shout and press our Hero's victory home.

---

[6] Ephes Dammim in verse 1 means *End of Blood*, while Gath and Ekron in verse 52 mean *Winepress* and *Eradication*. Isaiah goes on to describe Jesus' victory in these terms in Isaiah 63:1–7.

Lions, Bears and Philistines
(17:32–37)

The Lord who rescued me from the paw of the lion
and the paw of the bear will rescue me from the hand
of this Philistine.

(1 Samuel 17:37)

You've got to love the first few weeks of the TV series *The X Factor*. It's the time when every wannabe performer gets a chance to convince the world that they know how to sing. I don't know which I love more, the moment when a superstar is discovered or the moment of toe-curling embarrassment when ambition is cut short by total lack of talent. But I have learned to tell which one of the two a performer is going to be before they start to sing. When they are asked why they want to win *The X Factor*, if they say they want to be rich or famous then I know they will never make it. If they say that they just love to sing, however, then it's possible that a future superstar has just taken the stage.

David was a man who loved to sing. I know most people treat his battle with Goliath as the start of his ministry and view it as a sudden strike of good fortune, like landing on the right square in Snakes and Ladders, but the writer of 1 Samuel litters this chapter with clues which tell us that David's victory began many years before. He was not interested in fame or fortune or any of the things which Saul offers him in verse 25. He was simply a man who loved to sing about the Lord, and it made him the kind of person God could use when a giant came his way.

David had developed *a passion for God's name* far away

from any witnesses in the lonely fields around Bethlehem. The main theme of this chapter isn't that Israel needed victory on the battlefield, but that the Lord's name needed to be rescued from disgrace in the eyes of the nations. Goliath had called out eighty times in forty days, *"I defy the armies of Israel."*[1] Men like Saul and Eliab, who loved fame and fortune, were able to tolerate such blasphemy, but David sees immediately in verse 26 that Goliath is an uncircumcised Gentile who must be killed to *"remove this disgrace from Israel"*. Because of who David had become in private, he sees this Philistine very differently from the rest of Israel in public.

They compared him to themselves and found him far too big to fight, but David compared him to the Lord and found him far too big to miss. He tells Saul confidently in verse 36 that Goliath will surely fall to him *"because he has defied the armies of the living God"*. When Goliath curses him in the name of Dagon in verse 43, he knows the giant will fall on his face before him like Dagon in chapter 5. He sees Goliath as the perfect candidate to prove in verse 47 that *"It is not by sword or spear that the Lord saves; for the battle is the Lord's."*

William Booth led a revival in nineteenth-century London which spread throughout the world, but his victory over the enemy did not begin with chasing fame and fortune in the East End. Before he could revive a nation, he was first revived himself by the Holy Spirit convicting him as a fifteen-year-old boy of stealing a silver pencil case from his friends. He remembered later that

> *Merely to have returned the gift would have been easy, but to confess the deception I had practised upon them was a humiliation to which, for some days I could not bring myself... I remember, as it were but yesterday,*

---

[1] The Hebrew word *hāraph*, which is translated *defy*, can mean literally *to blaspheme*.

the spot in the corner of the chapel [where God gave me strength], the resolution to end the matter rising up, the rushing forth, the finding of the young fellows I had chiefly wronged, the acknowledgement of my sin, the return of the pencil case – the instant rolling away from my heart of the guilty burden, the peace that came in its place, and the going forth to serve my God and my generation from that hour.[2]

Like David, his heart had been purified in private before he won his victories in public.

David had developed *courage to confront giants* as a faithful shepherd for his father.[3] Lions and bears were such an ever-present danger for Israelite farmers that most of them simply put up with losing a few sheep as the cost of doing business. Not David. With astonishing courage, he would chase the bear or lion to grab it by its mane or fur and kill it so the frightened sheep could be saved.[4] While Saul fears Goliath as a *warrior* in verse 33, David knows that God has also made him a *warrior* in 16:18.[5] While Saul tells David that *"you are not able"* in verse 33, David tells Goliath literally in verse 46 that *"I **have** struck you down and I **have** cut off your head."*

William Booth had learned to fight the equivalent of lions and bears when he worked as a pawnbroker's assistant at the age of twenty-one. When his boss told him that he must work on Sundays, he refused, even though his Christian friends warned

---

[2] Quoted by Roy Hattersley in *Blood and Fire: William and Catherine Booth and Their Salvation Army* (1999).

[3] Note how he refuses to leave his sheep in verse 20 until another faithful shepherd comes to care for them.

[4] Samson had also been able to kill lions through the power of the Holy Spirit in Judges 14, but it appears from rest of this chapter that David first stunned them with a slingshot before closing in to finish the job.

[5] The phrase in Hebrew is the same in both verses. 17:11–12 also offers a contrast by telling us literally that *"Saul and all the Israelites were dismayed and terrified, but David…"*

him not to risk losing his job and the lodgings it provided him above the shop. He told his boss that *"Not one hour or one minute of Sunday will I work for you or all your money."*[6] He was duly fired, but could laugh at death threats and angry mobs later on in public because, like David, he had first learned to stand up to lions, bears and bosses in private.[7]

David had developed *a willingness to die* which eluded Saul. Cowardice is when somebody preserves their life at too great a cost, but David had learned that some things are worth dying for. Having run after lions for the sake of sheep, he thought nothing of going to meet a Philistine for the sake of the Lord's name. There is no mention of God speaking an encouragement to David, but he *"ran quickly towards the battle line to meet him"* in verse 48. He runs as quickly towards Goliath as the rest of the Israelites had run away.

William Booth was asked in an interview towards the end of his life to give the secret of his successful ministry. He replied:

> *I will tell you the secret. God has had all there was of me. There have been men with greater opportunities; but from the day I got the poor of London on my heart, and a vision of what Jesus Christ could do with the poor of London, I made up my mind that God would have all of William Booth there was. And if there is anything of power in The Salvation Army today, it is because God has all the adoration of my heart, all the power of my will, and all the influence of my life.*

His interviewer concluded that *"I learned from William Booth that the greatness of a man's power is the measure of his*

---

[6] Quoted by Helen Hosier in *William and Catherine Booth* (1999).

[7] David probably prayed for the Lord to stop the lions and bears from attacking his sheep. The Lord did not grant his request because those trials would turn him into the kind of person God could use.

surrender. It is not a question of who you are or of what you are, but of whether God controls you." [8]

David learned through encounters with lions and bears in private to fight Philistines in public. He didn't fix his eyes on fame or fortune, but on singing about God's name and about courage and about willingness to die. If we do the same then, like David or William Booth, we will become the kind of people God can use.

Amen! Links to John Groves talk on prayer dated 15/9/13.

---

[8] Quoted by Charles Bateman in *The Life of General Booth* (1912).

Back to Where It All Began
(17:54)

*David took the Philistine's head and brought it to
Jerusalem; he put the Philistine's weapons in his
own tent.*

(1 Samuel 17:54)

Sadly, the text of 1 and 2 Samuel is missing from one of the
oldest copies of the Greek Septuagint. To his horror in 1844,
the German Bible scholar Count von Tischendorf discovered it
had been burned by monks to keep themselves warm. Although
he rescued most of what we now know as the fourth-century
Codex Sinaiticus from the basket of firewood at St Catherine's
Monastery on Mount Sinai, these two books had already been
burned. Now, it's not that those papers didn't make good
firelighters. It's just that lighting fires was not what they had
originally been intended for.

Saul's reign had been a time of treating what was sacred
as irreverently as the monks of Mount Sinai. It had been the
culmination of three centuries of forgetting what the Lord had
saved Israel for under the Judges. They still talked about the
Lord, used the name of the Lord and expected the Lord to bless
them in the Promised Land. It was just that they had completely
forgotten the purpose for which he had brought them out of
Egypt in the first place.

David was a person God could use because, while the
rest of the Israelites forgot where their story had all begun,
he still remembered. We have seen what Psalm 132 tells us he
learned as a young teenager tending his father's flocks in the

fields around Bethlehem. As he looked at the lights coming from Kiriath Jearim and thought about the Ark of the Covenant which lay neglected in Abinadab's living room at the top of the hill, he remembered why the Lord had rescued Israel from Egypt. It wasn't just to free them from slavery, to give them the Promised Land or to bring judgment on the Philistines. The Lord had told the Israelites in Exodus 29:46 that he *"brought them out of Egypt* **so that I might dwell among them.** *"* David remembered that God was looking for a dwelling place among his People.

The Israelites had forgotten this. At least under the Judges the few remaining worshippers of Yahweh had gone to the Tabernacle at Shiloh to worship him at the tent which housed his Ark. Even during the backslidden days of Eli, the Israelites had recognized Moses' Tabernacle as *"the house of the Lord"* and had brought God's Ark to help them when they were defeated by the Philistines. In Saul's day, however, no one sought the Ark at all, including Saul himself. David would have to urge the Israelites when he ascended to the throne, *"Let us bring the ark of our God back to us, for we did not enquire of it during the reign of Saul."*[1] Psalm 132 tells us that David *"swore an oath to the Lord, he made a vow to the Mighty One of Jacob: I will not enter my house or go to my bed, I will allow no sleep to my eyes or slumber to my eyelids, till I find a place for the Lord, a dwelling for the Mighty One of Jacob."* David had started longing to lead Israel back to where their salvation history had begun.

Unless we grasp this, we will miss the significance of two comments which the writer makes in verse 54. We will treat them as throwaway comments, when in fact they hold the key to understanding the early actions of David's reign.

First, we are told that *"David took the Philistine's head and brought it to Jerusalem."* Don't rush over that comment, because it's actually pretty weird. The city of Jerusalem was not yet the

---

[1] 1 Chronicles 13:3. In light of Exodus 29:46, Saul's neglect was as serious as that of the monks at Sinai.

capital of Israel, and it was still in the hands of the Jebusites.[2] David didn't take Goliath's head to Jerusalem because his house was there or because there was a temple on Mount Zion. He did so in order to put Goliath's head on a spike as a statement that he would be back to do to the city what he had just done to the Philistines.

Did David understand that Jerusalem stood on Mount Moriah, the mountain where the Lord had provided a sacrificial lamb to save the life of Isaac in Genesis 22? Almost certainly. Did he understand what Abraham had meant when he predicted that one day *"On the mountain of the Lord it will be provided"*? Quite possibly, since he was a prophet. Did he understand that Melchizedek, king of Jerusalem, had been a picture of that coming Saviour in Genesis 14:18–20? Probably, since he wrote a song in praise of the coming Messiah in Psalm 110 which rejoiced that *"The Lord will extend your mighty sceptre from Zion... You are a priest for ever in the order of Melchizedek."*[3] David's first two acts as king would be to capture Jerusalem and to bring up the Ark to a new Tabernacle on Mount Zion. Even as he returned from defeating Goliath, he resolved that when God gave him the throne he would bring Israel back to where it all began.

Second, we are told that David *"put the Philistine's weapons in his tent"*.[4] Don't rush over that comment either, because it's also pretty weird. David was a teenager who lived with his father and had only come on a day's errand to the battlefield. He didn't need a tent in Bethlehem or in the army camp, and no shepherd used a tent while guarding the sheep since he needed to be on the look-out all night for danger.

---

[2] Jerusalem had been captured by the Israelites in Joshua 12:1 and 10 and by the men of Judah in Judges 1:8, but Judges 1:21 tells us that the Jebusites had retaken the city and reinforced their position.

[3] Since few of the psalms are dated, we are left guessing at what stage in his life David grasped these things.

[4] Some English translations say *"his own tent"*, but the Hebrew simply says *"his tent"*.

The Hebrew word for *tent* is the word which is often translated *tabernacle*. It's possible David had set up a little tabernacle of his own as a personal praise tent for worshipping God. More likely, however, is that he took Goliath's weapons to what remained of Moses' Tabernacle at the town of Nob after its destruction at Shiloh.[5] If *"his tent"* means *"David's tent"*, then it shows that he worshipped the Lord at his own mini-tabernacle for years before God enabled him to lead the whole of Israel into worshipping at his great new Tabernacle on Mount Zion.[6] If *"his tent"* means *"God's tent"*, then it means he brought Goliath's weapons to Moses' re-erected Tabernacle to declare that all the glory for his victory belonged to the Lord.[7]

Whichever tent the writer is referring to as David returns from taking Goliath's head to Jerusalem in verse 54, the basic story stays the same. David had remembered that God's primary goal in bringing the Israelites out of Egypt was to dwell among them, and he pledged to devote his reign to bringing Israel back to where it all began.[8]

---

[5] Since David retrieves Goliath's sword from the Tabernacle at Nob in 21:8–9, this second option is more likely. 22:15 tells us David was a regular visitor to Moses' Tabernacle. Nob was on a ridge of land in Benjamin which overlooked Jerusalem (Isaiah 10:32), so he could look out from there onto Zion and Moriah.

[6] This would remind us that leaders can only lead their people as far as they have gone themselves.

[7] We can see from 31:10 that this was the normal ancient way of giving worship to a god for victory. Contrast this with Saul building a monument to his own honour after a victory in 15:12.

[8] Don't be confused by the way Saul fails to recognize David in verses 55–58. He knows David by sight but now feels he should enquire into his parentage, since he has become a potential son-in-law (17:25) and a possible candidate for Samuel's rival king (15:28).

The School of Purity
(18:1–19:24)

*Saul became still more afraid of him, and he
remained his enemy for the rest of his days.*

(1 Samuel 18:29)

Universities love to boast about how many applications they
receive per place. God's university has very few applicants and
even fewer graduates. To become the kind of person God can
use is painful, as David was about to discover.

His anointing by Samuel did not result in instant
promotion, but in instant enrolment in God's school of purity.
The more the Lord intends to do through a person's life, the
more he needs to deal with the last vestiges of sin which lurk
within their heart. Many people drop out of God's school
because they find the curriculum too hard, but David was
determined to let God refine him until he finally graduated.

In chapters 18 and 19, the Lord deals with *the last vestiges
of pride* in David's heart. A whole new world opens up to the
architect of Israel's victory over Goliath, and David has to learn
how to live according to Hannah's prayer. David becomes the
favoured friend of Jonathan, Saul's son and heir, and gets to wear
Jonathan's royal clothes.[1] He becomes a part of Saul's family and
should have received Saul's eldest daughter Merab in marriage
to fulfil the promise of 17:25. His life as a humble shepherd and
armour-bearer is over, and his new life tests his character in

---

[1] Since Jonathan was at least a teenager in chapter 14, he was over twenty
years older than David. Nevertheless, they became devoted friends. See also
20:17 and 2 Samuel 1:26.

new ways. *"Do you think it is a small matter to become the king's son-in-law?"* he asks in 18:23, as he passes this first test with flying colours. *"I'm only a poor man and little known."*[2]

That soon changes, as David is promoted to a high rank in the army and becomes famous for his military successes.[3] The Israelite women sing songs in praise of David, which make no mention of the God who granted him victory: *"Saul has slain his thousands, and David his tens of thousands."* David is sorely tempted to let success go to his head like Saul when he built a monument to his own glory after defeating the Amalekites in 15:12, but he passes this next test in God's school of purity too. Few temptations are as subtle or as dangerous as that of pride. The Lord needed to refine David before he could entrust him with a throne.

In these two chapters, the Lord also deals with *the last vestiges of self-pity* in David's heart. *"Now what have I done? Can't I even speak?"* he complained to Eliab in 17:29, with the indignant sense of injustice which all younger brothers know. When Saul becomes jealous of his success, he treats David more unjustly than his seven older brothers put together. He reneges on his promise to give him his daughter Merab in marriage,[4] and he tries to kill him by pretending to send him to *"fight the battles of the Lord"* while caring nothing for God's glory and everything for ending David's life prematurely on the point of a Philistine sword. Finally, Saul's jealousy and hatred boil over into three occasions when he throws a javelin at David in order to impale him to the wall.[5] How easy it would have been for him

---

[2] The words are similar to Saul's in 9:21, but unlike Saul his heart lines up with what he says. Because David does not seek fame, the Lord makes him famous anyway in 18:30. See 1 Peter 5:5–6.

[3] We can read about two of his successes during this period in 2 Samuel 23:9–12.

[4] The Lord cursed her treacherous marriage and judged it in 2 Samuel 21:8–9.

[5] Saul's continued disobedience makes his demonic oppression increase to a state where even David's lyre playing no longer makes the demon leave him.

to pull the javelin out of the wall and throw it back to seize Saul's throne, but David passes this next test in God's school of purity by refusing to succumb to self-pity.

As David's position in Saul's court grows increasingly perilous, he learns to rely increasingly on the Lord. Saul vows in 19:6 never to harm him, but spends the next few verses plotting to take his life,[6] and even when he gives him his younger daughter Michal in marriage, he refuses him the love and trust which a royal son-in-law deserves. When David finally flees from his court and adopts the lonely life of an outlaw, he does not run to those who will nurse his wronged sense of entitlement, but to the prophet of the Lord.[7] He avoids those who might tempt him to take his claim to kingship into his own hands, and makes straight for Samuel's home at Ramah. He accompanies the elderly judge on a school trip to the academy of prophets he is training at Naioth. The Lord is so pleased with David's school report that he saves his life by making his Spirit fall on Saul as he arrives in Naioth so that he joins the academy of prophets for a short season too.[8] If Hebrews 5:8–9 tells us that even Jesus *"learned obedience from what he suffered and, once made perfect, he became the source of eternal salvation for all who obey him"*, and if David had to walk that same path to become the kind of person God could use, then we cannot be surprised if God tests us in the same way too. We must ask God for grace to pass each test as well as David did.

In these two chapters, the Lord also deals with *the last vestiges of disobedience* in David's heart. When he becomes best

David passes God's test but Saul fails completely.

[6] Since Saul resists the Holy Spirit, the only one who can bring about true repentance in our hearts, he perpetually makes resolutions which he cannot keep. See also 24:16–20, 26:21 and 28:23.

[7] He wrote Psalm 59 just before he fled, telling the Lord that he is the true refuge to which he is fleeing.

[8] As ever, Saul refuses to be changed long-term by this experience. Although he has been called to restrain God's People, his disobedience even loses him control of the hearts of his son Jonathan and daughter Michal.

friends with Saul's heir Jonathan, will he forget the prophecy that he himself is God's chosen royal heir? When he is given high rank in Saul's army will he forget that the Lord is the true King of Israel? When he marries Saul's daughter, will he adopt the character of the man he now calls father? The writer hints that Michal is an idolater who scorns the worship of the Living God which her husband learned in the fields of Bethlehem. She professes love for him but is unwilling to go with him as an outlaw, maligns him to her father and quickly remarries once he is gone.[9] Will David pick up his wife's character and learn the disobedience which proved the downfall of Saul's dynasty? Yet again, David passes each new test in God's school of purity. Saul's attempts to kill David only succeed in killing the little Saul which lurked in David's heart.

Even though David ends chapter 19 as a fugitive, his decision to flee Saul's court is in fact a triumphant end to his first year in God's school. He has God's anointing, Samuel's prophecy, a track record of military victories and the adulation of the Israelites, so he is perfectly positioned to launch a bid to seize Saul's throne. Yet he honours the Lord too much as King to grieve him by splitting his kingdom, and he honours the Lord's sovereign choice and timing too much to decide for himself when he must reign. Jesus returned from his testings in the wilderness and was able to say in Matthew 11:29 that *"I am gentle and humble in heart."* David is able to say the same thing as he embarks on his own testings in the wilderness.

C. T. Studd, the great missionary to China, India and Africa, told those who wished to emulate his success that *"What I would have you gather is that God does not deal with you until you are wholly given up to Him, and then He will tell you what He would have you do."*[10] The writer of 1 Samuel would have you gather the same thing. He invites you to enrol in God's school of purity today.

---

[9] 1 Samuel 19:13, 17; 2 Samuel 3:13–16; 6:16–23.

[10] Quoted by John Pollock in *The Cambridge Seven* (1966).

Little White Lies (20:1–21:9)

David answered Ahimelek the priest, "The king sent me on a mission and said to me, 'No one is to know anything about the mission I am sending you on.'"

(1 Samuel 21:2)

Jim Devine lied and wished he hadn't. He lied about his expenses as a British MP and told the judge he only did so because it was a little white lie. He had been given a *"nod and a wink"* from a fellow MP in the House of Commons bar, which told him everyone was doing it and nobody would care. Bankrupted and vilified by the media, he tried to save himself by lying to the judge that it was all his office manager's fault anyway. *"Are you just making this up as you go along?"* asked one of the barristers. He was convicted and given a sixteen-month sentence. He exchanged his offices in Parliament for the inside of a prison cell.[1]

117

David was a star student in God's school of purity, but that didn't mean that he always got perfect test scores. When he realized that Saul had guessed he was the new king God had chosen, he got so scared that he started telling white lies like those around him. Like Jim Devine, he was convinced his untruths wouldn't really matter, but the Lord was able to use Saul's death threats to refine the character of a future king.

David didn't stay at Samuel's academy of prophets at Naioth. Instead of staying with God's seer, he rushed back to Jonathan his friend.[2] Although he uses the Lord's name to swear

---

[1] Quotes taken from a report in the British newspaper *The Independent* on 31st March 2011.

[2] We will examine this friendship in the chapter "Second Fiddle". We can tell from 20:13–15 that Jonathan knew that David was God's chosen king, so David swears to Jonathan and not the other way around.

an oath to him at the start of chapter 20, his focus is all on *"I... my... I... me"*, and his loss of perspective leads to sin. He asks Jonathan to tell a lie to his father Saul and Jonathan obliges in verses 28–29. He knows full well that David is hiding in a nearby field, but he tells his father he has gone to celebrate the new moon festival with his family in Bethlehem.[3] If David had stayed with God's prophets at Naioth, he might have given Saul time to calm down, but as it was his plan backfires and his lie inflames Saul's anger even further. Saul vents his frustration on Jonathan, first by insulting him and then by trying to kill him.[4] God wants to teach David that no lie is white or little in his eyes, and David learns this as he weeps even more than Jonathan as they say their last goodbyes in verse 41. He would only see his best friend one more time before Jonathan died on the battlefield.

Sadly, David forgets his lesson as quickly as Jim Devine when he lied in court to stop himself from being convicted of lying. David rushes to Moses' Tabernacle at Nob and stands before Ahimelek, the great-grandson of Eli and the new high priest of Israel.[5] This is the perfect place for him to confess his sin and find forgiveness by throwing himself on the mercy of the priests of God. Instead, he tries to save himself with more lies when Ahimelek grows suspicious that he has arrived unarmed and alone.[6] David assures Ahimelek that he has been sent on a top secret solo mission and is planning to rendezvous with

---

[3] Numbers 28:11–15 and Deuteronomy 12:5 tell us that the new moon sacrifices were to take place at the Tabernacle alone, but the Israelites had set up altars across the country after the fall of Shiloh.

[4] Saul is so blinded by jealousy that he calls Jonathan the Hebrew equivalent of a *bastard* or *son of a bitch*, then tries to blame him for shaming his mother! He then tries to murder his heir in order to safeguard his dynasty!

[5] This high priest had two names – Ahijah and Ahimelek – which meant *My Brother Is the Lord* and *My Brother is the King* (14:3). His two names were a declaration that Yahweh was the true King of Israel.

[6] Some readers try to argue from Matthew 12:3–4 that David was sinless here and only lied to shield the priests from being blamed by Saul. This fails to take into account the judgment he reaps in chapter 22.

Saul's soldiers later. He even lies that this mission somehow makes him holier than usual, instead of confessing that he is guiltier than ever. The high priest trustingly gives him the bread from the Holy Place[7] along with Goliath's sword which David placed there as part of his vow to bring the Israelites back to God's original plan.[8] Like Jim Devine, David thinks he has got away with his deception, but he is about to learn again that lies are never white and never little.

Saul's chief shepherd, Doeg, is at the Tabernacle and witnesses David's deception. He is an Edomite toying with conversion to Israel's God, but he lives up to his name which means *Fearful One* by deciding to side with the disobedient king instead of with the Lord. Lured on by the promise of wealth and promotion which Saul offers in return for loyalty in 22:7, Doeg lusts after the brief pleasures of rebellion instead of God's eternal reward and thinks nothing of slaughtering the eighty-five priests who serve at Nob.[9] The Lord fulfils his curse on Eli's family in chapters 2–3 as only one of his descendants escapes to carry on as priest for David. Worst of all, the Tabernacle falls into disuse again. David's lies have brought about the destruction of what he holds most dear.

David eventually learned his lesson from failing God's lie detector test in these two chapters. He wrote Psalm 52 in the wake of Doeg's slaughter and expressed renewed hatred for *"falsehood rather than speaking the truth"* and for the *"deceitful tongue"*. He learned to pray later that *"I know, my God, that you*

---

[7] The *Bread of the Presence* refers to the twelve loaves set out on the golden table in the Tabernacle to represent the twelve tribes of Israel before the Lord (Exodus 25:30; Leviticus 24:5–9).

[8] The word for *cloth* means literally *cloak*, and was probably Goliath's own battle cloak. Because of David's earlier devotion, he is now armed and clothed for life on the run.

[9] David wrote Psalm 52 after his lying led to the slaughter at Nob, and it talks about Doeg's decision to serve money instead of God in verse 7. Since Doeg was Saul's chief shepherd, he also serves as a picture of the *antichrist* and *man of lawlessness*.

test the heart and are pleased with integrity."[10] As a result of this short-term failure, he developed the long-term character which would one day make his reign so pleasing to the Lord. We need only to look at his commitment to the covenant which he makes with Jonathan in chapter 20 many years later in 2 Samuel 9. This trial taught David the importance of integrity and made him more and more into a king that God could use.

Billy Graham was probably the most successful evangelist of the twentieth century. He communicated with more people in that century than anyone else did about anything, and he used the platform he was given to be the kind of person God could use. What most people do not realize, however, is that Billy's successful public ministry began at a private retreat with friends in Modesto, California, where they resolved to be truthful in little things so that lying would not destroy what they held dear. His Modesto Manifesto read:

> *We will be accountable, particularly in handling finances, with integrity according to the highest business standards. We will tell the truth and be thoroughly honest, especially in reporting statistics. We will be exemplary in morals – clear, clean and careful to avoid the very appearance of any impropriety.*[11]

Billy Graham and his friends learned from David's lessons in God's school of purity, and so must we if we are to be the truthful kind of people God can use.

---

[10] 1 Chronicles 29:17.

[11] Harold Myra and Marshall Shelley in *The Leadership Secrets of Billy Graham* (2005).

Madness and Sanity
(21:10–22:23)

So he feigned insanity in their presence; and while he was in their hands he acted like a madman.

(1 Samuel 21:13)

Saul was going increasingly mad, but so too was David. The more time David spent in God's school of purity, the more of Saul's character came floating to the surface from the hidden places of his heart. The Lord allowed him to spend about a decade living as an outlaw in the desert because he knew that water flows downhill, and he was determined to refine him into the kind of leader he could use.

David had been mad to leave God's worship centre at Naioth in order to run to Jonathan. Now he repeats the same madness by leaving the Tabernacle at Nob in order to take refuge among the Philistines. Seeing Goliath's sword had reminded him that Saul would be too scared to pursue him if he went to Goliath's city. Instead of staying at the Tabernacle and receiving guidance from the Lord, he relied on his own wisdom like Saul and took refuge in the Philistine city of Gath.[1]

It didn't take him long to see how insane he must have been. The Gittites didn't take kindly to seeing their champion's executioner strolling around their city wearing his over-sized sword. They went to King Achish and reminded him of the Israelite women's song. This was their golden opportunity to

---

[1] David did consult the Lord at Nob (22:10), but evidently not about where he should go.

execute the man who was now heir to the Lord's promise to deliver Israel from the Philistines.

Achish means *I Will Terrify*, and David was terrified when he saw the mistake he had made.[2] When he heard the Philistines guessing in verse 11 that he was the true *"king of the land"*, he panicked instead of trusting in the Lord. Although the bread and sword he had collected from Nob both served as pictures of the Word of God, verse 12 tells us that he *"took these words to heart"* instead of the words of the Lord. Samuel's prophecy that David would be king effectively made him immortal until it was fulfilled, yet he was so scared for his life that he pretended to be mad to persuade King Achish to dismiss him as a threat and send him back to Israel.

Ironically, it was during this pretence of madness that David finally regained his sanity. He wrote Psalm 56 while in the hands of his Gittite enemies, praying *"In God I trust and am not afraid. What can mere mortals do to me?... In God, whose word I praise, in the Lord, whose word I praise – in God I trust and am not afraid. What can man do to me?"* Returning to faith in God's Word, David remembered that the name Achish can also be translated *Only A Man*. The Lord used Scripture to burn away the last traces of the cowardice which characterized Saul in David's heart, and prepared him to lead his People to victory over all their enemies once he became king. David wrote Psalm 34 as soon as he made it back over the border into Israel: *"I sought the Lord, and he answered me; he delivered me from all my fears."*

Restored to sanity, David moves into a fresh term in God's school of purity. He gathers 400 discontented soldiers in the cave of Adullam and begins to learn how to rule over them as

---

[2] We discover from the title of Psalm 34 that Achish also bore the name of all the firstborn princes of the Philistines, which was *Abimelek* or *My Father Is King* (see Genesis 20:2; 21:32; 26:1).

king.[3] Saul's jealousy is so intense that David's seven brothers join him rather than become a target for Saul themselves. Since Jesse was a quarter Moabite through his grandmother Ruth, David sends his parents to safety in Moab while he drills a mighty new army in his desert stronghold.[4] He has been so humbled by his adventures in Gath that he now waits in 22:3 to *"learn what God will do for me"*, and immediately obeys the prophet Gad when he tells him to leave the stronghold and hide in the forests of Judah instead.[5]

We can read some of what he learned in the cave of Adullam in two psalms which he wrote at this time. He wrote Psalm 142 first, full of fear and loneliness which is soothed by fresh trust in God. He wrote Psalm 57 afterwards, on a day when he was so depressed he did not feel like worshipping the Lord at all, too worried in verse 4 that one of the 400 might prove to be a double agent like Doeg.[6] Yet rather than surrender to the same madness which had taken him to Gath, he reminds himself of God's character, promises and faithfulness, singing literally in verse 2 that he is the *"God who fulfils his purposes for me"*. If you are currently being tried and tested in your own life, you will find great comfort in both of these two psalms. They show how each trial destroyed a little more of Saul in

---

[3] Adullam means *The Lord's Justice for His People*, and it was there that David learned the character he needed to rule Israel justly. Saul could only muster 600 men through his position and resorts to bribery in 22:7. David could gather 400 simply through his anointing with the Spirit.

[4] 2 Samuel 23:13–14 tells us that David's stronghold was the cave of Adullam, but 1 Samuel 23:14 tells us he also had several other desert strongholds. We can read an example of the devotion which David and his men developed for one another at this time in 2 Samuel 23:13–17.

[5] This is the first mention of the prophet Gad, but he would become integral to David's task of leading Israel back to worship (2 Samuel 24:11–19; 2 Chronicles 29:25). He would also become a key historian of David's reign (1 Chronicles 29:29).

[6] Although the debtors and malcontents who flock to David look like an unreliable rabble, they were part of his pointing to Jesus, the true Messiah. We read in Matthew 5:3 that spiritual beggars flock to him too.

David's heart, and how the Lord replaced Saul's madness with godly sanity instead.

Saul, however, still refused to repent of the madness in his soul. Every time he resisted God as teacher, he slipped further down into the drowning mire of his own insanity. When David's worship had failed to drive away his demons, he threw a spear in anger, and now we find him in 22:6 sitting permanently *"spear in hand"*. He ignores the Lord's rebuke when Doeg and Ahimelek inform him that David, unlike him, is a regular visitor to Moses' Tabernacle at Nob. Instead, he accuses David in verses 8 and 13 of plotting to kill him when it is in fact the other way around,[7] and he rushes further down the path of disobedience and rebellion until even the Lord's priests cannot be tolerated to stand in his way. A final rebuke comes when his soldiers refuse to obey his order to kill the priests of God, and the only person who will do so is the uncircumcised Edomite Doeg, but Saul is far too mad to listen. He and Doeg go even further than killing the eighty-five priests by including their women, children and animals too. What Saul was too disobedient to do to the Amalekites, he now does to God's priests instead.

So do not complain when the Lord takes you through trials, and do not harden your heart to what he teaches in his school of purity. If you feel scared, depressed and lonely at the moment, then take a prescription of these chapters and of the psalms which go with them. God will use them to train you and to turn your madness into sanity.

---

[7] Similarly, he accuses the priests of siding with David in 22:17, when in fact they have simply sided with the Lord. It is Saul who has chosen the wrong side.

The Return of the Ephod
(23:1–14)

When David learned that Saul was plotting against him, he said to Abiathar the priest, "Bring the ephod."
(1 Samuel 23:9)

God loves to speak. He likes nothing better than to let people hear his voice. He speaks the world into being on the first page of the Bible, and then carries on speaking to the world on every page. He talks to saints and sinners, rich and poor, male and female, young and old. The God of the Bible is a God who speaks and invites the world to listen.

It therefore comes as no surprise that Israel's history begins with God speaking. He calls Abraham out of Ur of the Chaldees, then continues speaking to him and his descendants as friends. He turns them into a thriving nation of Hebrews and speaks to them at every turn. He speaks to Moses and tells him to command Pharaoh to let his People go, and when Moses leads the Hebrews out of Egypt God speaks to them at Mount Sinai for a whole year. He tells them to build a Tabernacle where he will speak to them constantly in two particular ways. Their leaders will be able to stand before the Ark to hear him speak in general, and their priests will be able to use the Urim and Thummim in the pocket of their ephod to hear him guide them in particular. Israel would be a nation which heard the Lord's voice daily and which acted as his messengers to the world.[1]

---

[1] This is what the Lord meant in Exodus 19:5–6 when he told the Israelites at Sinai that they were to be a *kingdom of priests* and a *nation set apart* for the world.

But Israel had forgotten this during the period of the Judges. They had forgotten to visit Moses' Tabernacle at Shiloh during those days when *"everyone did as they saw fit"*, and they had preferred to worship the mute and lifeless idols of the nations rather than to listen to the words of the Living God. By the time of Eli, *"the word of the Lord was rare; there were not many visions"*, but the Lord had raised up Samuel to bring them back to where their history all began. Under Samuel the Israelites began to hear the word of the Lord again, and to renew their national mission as the messengers of God.[2]

We have already seen that Saul did not understand God's plan. He didn't return Israel to the calling of Mount Sinai but to the waywardness of Judges. He left the Ark of the Covenant unvisited at Abinadab's house in Kiriath Jearim, and never visited the Tabernacle at Nob except as an executioner. We are meant to read with horror in 22:18 that he killed the priests *"who wore the linen ephod"*, because this was the violent culmination of his refusal to lead Israel in listening to God. In case we fail to grasp how seriously the Lord takes our unwillingness to listen to his voice, we read in 1 Chronicles 10:13–14 that *"Saul died because he... did not enquire of the Lord. So the Lord put him to death and turned the kingdom over to David son of Jesse."*

One of the mandatory subjects in God's school of purity is therefore always listening to God. David had learned it as a madman in Gath and in the quietness of his cave. One of the first people he added to his motley entourage was the prophet Gad, and in the aftermath of the slaughter at Nob he also added the new high priest Abiathar.[3] Ahimelek is dead but his son survives as the last hope of Eli's house and, most importantly, brings the ephod with its Urim and Thummim to David's hideout. David honoured the Ark too much to fetch it from Abinadab's house

---

[2] Judges 21:25; 1 Samuel 3:1, 21; 9:6–9.

[3] Unlike Saul's reign, which was characterized by blame-shifting onto others (13:11–12; 15:15, 20–21, 24), David confesses to Abiathar in 22:22 that he is fully responsible for the slaughter of his family.

and subject it to the dirty lifestyle of an outlaw,[4] but at least he now had the ephod through which he could learn to lead Israel as a king who listens to the voice of God.

We are meant to notice a difference in the first verses of chapter 23 – not just between David and Saul, but also between David and the man he used to be. As a teenager, he had learned to hear God's voice personally and had sung the words of Psalm 23: *"The Lord is my shepherd… He leads me… He guides me."* Now, however, he learns to hear God's voice to govern God's People as a viceroy working for the divine King. He does so straightaway when he makes use of Abiathar and the ephod to find out if the Lord wants him to attack the Philistines who are raiding Keilah.[5] When his men protest that they are frightened enough running away from Saul without having to fight his battles for him too, David responds by going back to the ephod.[6] When he hears God speak a promise of victory, he learns to lead reluctant followers through to complete obedience to God's Word. David is learning how to rule very differently from Saul. The more Saul tries to kill him, the more of Saul God kills in David's heart instead.

When news reaches David's ears that Saul is marching out to besiege Keilah,[7] common sense tells him that its citizens will not open their gates and betray their deliverer to Saul. However, David is learning not to rule through common sense alone.[8] He

---

[4] David felt the same when he was forced to flee Jerusalem in 2 Samuel 15:24–26 after becoming king. However, he brought the Ark up to Jerusalem as one of the first actions of his new reign.

[5] Keilah means *Fortress* and was in southern Judah. The nearest Philistine city to it was Gath.

[6] Saul is still king technically, but David has the anointing, the high priest, the ephod, the prophets and the commitment to God's promise to deliver Israel from the Philistines.

[7] Saul is so backslidden that he acts more like the Philistines than the king of Israel. While David rescues Keilah from being sacked, Saul marches out to sack his own city!

[8] As an example of how misleading common sense alone can be, Saul actually concludes from circumstances in verse 7 that the Lord is on his side and is helping him to murder David!

goes back to the ephod to hear God speak and discovers that the men of Keilah are far more treacherous than he might ever have imagined. He remains gracious and does not destroy the city as he flees, for he is learning how to lead as viceroy under God.[9] His 400 men quickly become 600, as the Lord entrusts him with more and more responsibility in order to teach him how to be the kind of king that he can use.[10]

So if you struggle to hear God speaking to you, slow down and take time to listen. Resolve in your heart that he wants to speak to you and will reward you if you give yourself to Bible study and to prayer. Believe the words of Jesus in John 16:14 when he tells you that God wants to glorify himself by revealing things to you today so that you can hear him and obey.

And if you still struggle to hear God speak to you, then cry out in faith until he does. He will even turn his silences into fruitful times for you in his school of purity. He will use them to teach you the command of Jeremiah 33:3: *"Call to me and I will answer you and tell you great and unsearchable things you do not know."*

---

[9] Here lies another lesson for church leaders in God's school of purity. We must serve for God's sake alone because the people we serve will often turn on us with base ingratitude. See Hebrews 6:10.

[10] See Luke 16:10, 12.

Second Fiddle (23:15–29)

You shall be king over Israel, and I will be second to
you. Even my father Saul knows this.

(1 Samuel 23:17)

I was never any good at playing the violin, but I know that
playing second fiddle is even harder. Saul refused to play second
fiddle to God, but both Jonathan and David learned to play it to
perfection.

David has left Keilah behind and is now hiding in the
Desert of Ziph. Since Ziph means *Melting* in Hebrew, we are
meant to understand that the Lord's process of melting and
refining his heart continues. Sure enough, the Ziphites prove
to be as treacherous as the men of Keilah, and we can tell how
David felt when they betrayed his whereabouts to Saul from the
words which he wrote in Psalm 54.[1] How did David write such
a beautiful melody of trust in the Lord and refusal to retaliate
when he was treated so unfairly? Because he was accompanied
in his melody by Jonathan, who had heard the intelligence which
the Ziphites gave his father and had slipped away to meet him in
his desert hideout. David passed his test in Ziph because he had
a best friend who strengthened him in God.[2]

Some readers of 1 Samuel take a dim view of Jonathan.

---

[1] Their betrayal was particularly hurtful since they were the descendants of
Caleb's grandson and therefore from David's tribe of Judah (1 Chronicles 2:42;
Joshua 15:55). Unlike the men of nearby Keilah, they volunteered their betrayal
without receiving any threat, and went on to do so a second time in 26:1.

[2] The word Horesh means *Forest*, and since the Hebrew concept of a desert
meant a wasteland rather than a sandy desert, it appears that David was hiding
in arid woodland.

They point out that he failed to confront Goliath in chapter 17, and that he stayed with his father instead of throwing in his lot with David. They ignore his gutsy faith in chapter 14 and the way he risks his life to comfort David here in chapter 23. Though he had more reason than anyone – even his father – to hate the one who had been anointed to inherit the throne which he had long assumed was his, he submitted to the Lord's sovereign choice and started playing second fiddle. As he does so in this chapter, he teaches many of us to do the same.

Not all of us will be called to lead mighty ministries for the Lord. Jonathan recognized this very soon after David killed Goliath. We are told in 18:1 that he *"became one in spirit with David, and he loved him as himself"*, and that he gave him the royal robe which belonged to Saul's heir.[3] He risked his own life to save David's in chapter 20 and hinted that he knew that David was God's chosen king by wishing him in verse 13, *"May the Lord be with you as he has been with my father."*[4] He asked David to promise to bless his descendants, not the other way around, because he had already submitted himself to the Lord's perfect will. If you suspect similarly that God will never choose you to lead a church, pioneer a ministry or launch a fresh initiative in his Kingdom, then the writer of 1 Samuel records Jonathan's visit to David here for you.

Jonathan strengthens David by focusing him on the Lord. He doesn't seek to strengthen him through sympathy or kind words of human friendship alone. Like all good pastors, he strengthens him by giving reasons to rely on God. He reminds him that the Lord has promised he will be the next king, and confesses that even he and his father Saul know this full well.

---

[3] Although David loved Jonathan deeply in return, it is always Jonathan's love for David which is emphasized in 1 Samuel 18:1, 3, 19:1 and 20:17 and 2 Samuel 1:26.

[4] Jonathan's use of the Hebrew perfect tense here is tragic. Saul still had a decade left to rule, yet he was already a has-been as far as God's presence was concerned.

He spells out for him that this means he is effectively immortal until the Lord's promises to him have all come to pass. Saul can no more lay a hand on him than beat the Lord in mortal combat. Even though David has been shaken by the disloyalty of the men of Keilah after he rescued them, and by the Ziphites after he trusted them as fellow men of Judah, Jonathan reaffirms his covenant of love towards him in the presence of the Lord in order to give him concrete proof that all God's promises are true. Jonathan plays second fiddle so well that David picks up his own instrument and starts to sing Psalm 54.

Saul, on the other hand, will be the lead violinist or nothing at all. When he told Jonathan in 20:30 that he was acting like another man's son, he spoke far more truly than he knew. Jonathan was his flesh-and-blood heir, but he was much more like David than he was his father. Saul is still so self-deluded in his bitter refusal to submit to the Lord's will that he actually tries to bless the Ziphites in the name of the Lord for their act of treachery.[5] He spits out murder in his determination to reign as king instead of God and in his refusal to govern as viceroy under the Lord. That's why God delights to use great irony to thwart Saul's plan to murder David. Because Saul failed to destroy the Philistines as he was commanded, it is one of their raids which forces him to call off his hunt for David when he almost has him in his grasp.

Meanwhile, David is strengthened by Jonathan to pass this next test in God's school of purity. He happily plays second fiddle to the Lord as King and learns to let him take the lead. *"I will sacrifice a freewill offering to you,"* he sings as he plays on his stringed instrument in Psalm 54. He surrenders his own will to the Lord and lets the Lord deliver him in his own time. Sure enough, God leaves his rescue to the very last minute in order to teach David to play second fiddle right down to the final note of

---

[5] Saul admitted to Jonathan in 20:31 that he knew that the Lord had anointed David as his successor.

his concerto, but he rescues him in time. Saul is on one side of the ridge and David is on the other – a reminder that we should also expect our own trials to take us to the wire too – but David is able to name the ridge the *Rock of Departure* or *Rock of Escape* once he has finished playing second fiddle till the very last bar. Jonathan never sees David again but he has strengthened his friend to pass this fresh test through his own example. David learned in the desert to be a *nāgîd*, a second-fiddle viceroy to God the King, and he was made ready to govern Israel as a ruler under God.

Perhaps you are not destined to lead a great work for God. If not, then learn from Jonathan to make another person great by playing second fiddle by their side. Perhaps you are destined to lead great works in due time. If so, then learn from Jonathan while you wait, as David did, so that in due time you will know how to play second fiddle as you govern for your King.[6] As David finds refreshment at the fountain of En Gedi,[7] he hands you the sheet music which he learned to play through his best friend's example. He urges you not to imitate the jarring notes of Saul's ambition but to play the lovely melody of second fiddle for the King.

---

[6] One of the ways leaders can tell if they are doing this is by whether they release people who are more gifted than themselves (2 Samuel 23:8–39) or only gather those who make them look good (1 Samuel 14:52).

[7] En Gedi means *Fountain of the Young Goat* or *Kid Fountain*. It was in the desert of Judah by the Dead Sea.

The Messiah (24:1–7)

*The Lord forbid that I should do such a thing to my
master, the Lord's anointed, or lay my hand on him;
for he is the anointed of the Lord.*

(1 Samuel 24:6)

If you want to access my Internet bank account, it's very easy.
All you need to know is the single password that unlocks it. If
you want to understand why over fifteen chapters pass between
David being anointed king and his finally coming to the throne,
all you need to know is a single password too. It is a Hebrew
word, but a famous one. The password is *Messiah*.

Messiah is one of the most important words in the whole
Bible, but it doesn't occur until 1 Samuel 2:10.[1] It is only when
Israel starts moving towards a monarchy that the Lord starts
littering the pages of the Old Testament with references to his
Messiah. Translated *Christ* in Greek and *Anointed One* in English,
it serves as a password to this entire phase in Israel's history.

The Lord was not pleased when the Israelites demanded a
king *"such as all the other nations have"* in chapter 8. He punished
them by giving them a man-made messiah. Saul wasn't from
the tribe of Judah, which Jacob prophesied in Genesis 49:8–12
would be the messianic tribe, but from the tribe of Benjamin,
which Jacob warned in Genesis 49:27 would be *"a ravenous
wolf"*. When Samuel called down judgment on the Israelites
in chapter 12 for demanding Saul as king, he stated firmly in
verses 3 and 5 that God had made him their *messiah*. They

---

[1] A similar-looking adjective is used to describe God's anointed priest in
Leviticus 4 and 6, but *messiah* never occurs as a noun until a few years before
the establishment of a monarchy in Israel.

had refused to wait for God's true king and had chosen a false messiah, an antichrist, so they would have to suffer forty years of judgment under his rule. Unless we understand this, we will find the second half of 1 Samuel very confusing.

David was probably in his mid-teens when Samuel anointed him as God's true messiah, but he had to wait until he was thirty for the throne of Judah and until he was thirty-seven for the throne of Israel.[2] The Lord decreed a lengthy period in which the antichrist ruled as king over Israel in order to demonstrate how Jesus the Messiah would overcome the man of lawlessness between his First and Second Comings.[3] God gave us these chapters so we will not be too surprised that Satan's crumbling regime often seems strong and Jesus' Kingdom often seems weak. He wants to use chapters like this one to teach us how to assert Jesus the Messiah's rule throughout Church history.

That's why 1 Samuel 24 begins with Saul scoring a victory. He is only able to renew his hunt for David because he has just repelled the Philistines. His army is five times bigger than that of David, and he manages to force David into such a dark dead end that he looks to be on the brink of destroying God's messiah and his kingdom once and for all.[4] We must not be surprised when Satan wins many skirmishes throughout Church history, or forget that it only takes one blunder for the Lord to turn the tables on him in an instant.

Saul's mistake is the direct result of his listening to his own royal propaganda. He is so full of himself as a superhuman King

---

[2] Samuel makes it clear in 16:6 that he has been sent to Jesse's house to find the true *messiah*.

[3] Matthew 24:24; 2 Thessalonians 2:3; 1 John 2:18, 22; 4:3; and 2 John 7 tell us there have been many antichrists or men of lawlessness throughout AD history, which will culminate in a great Antichrist or Man of Lawlessness towards the end. Daniel 11:36 says their key trait is lusting to be King instead of God.

[4] The victory should have caused Saul to repent, but his disobedient pride made him an easy tool for Satan to use in his bitter goal of killing David before he could found the royal dynasty of Jesus the Messiah.

that he does not even allow one of his bodyguards to accompany him into the cave he has chosen as a latrine.[5] He has no idea that David and his men are hiding at the back of the cave, or that David's men are goading him to creep forward and stab him in the back. He doesn't hear them marshalling religious arguments that this is God's provision and the fulfilment of an unrecorded prophecy which they either embellish or make up altogether. He doesn't notice when David cuts off the hem of his robe as a re-enactment of what Samuel did in 15:27–28. He only finds out when David feels guilty, repents of his sinful pragmatism and starts acting as Jesus has done throughout Church history. He refuses to get impatient with the Lord's timing or to use shady tactics in order to usher in God's Kingdom prematurely.

David recognizes that Saul is still the Lord's messiah, at least in a limited sense.[6] Saul still has genuine authority to rule as king because of Israel's continued sin. There will come a moment when God's judgment gives way to mercy and salvation, but that moment is for the Lord alone to decide. Many Christians fail to grasp this and get impatient with the Lord that Satan and his minions continue to assert their defeated rule. They resort to underhand tactics and argue that the end justifies the means, but Jesus rebukes them in John 7:6 as David rebuked his followers, saying, *"My time is not yet here; for you any time will do."* Even though Saul has tried three times to spear David, it does not justify a stab in return, for David's eyes are on the Lord. He lets God carry out his judgment upon Israel for as long as he decides, and grasps that if he seizes the throne on his own initiative then he will not do so as an obedient viceroy, but merely as King Saul II. Jesus asks the Father to save the nations

135

---

[5] The Hebrew says that *he went in to cover his feet* or his *genitals*. He didn't want to spoil his propaganda by showing his humanity to those he led. In contrast, Jesus showed his full humanity in John 13:1–5.

[6] David does *not* spare Saul's life because he is king or Jonathan's father or his own father-in-law. He stresses that he spares him because he is still in a limited sense the Lord's messiah (24:6, 10; 26:9, 11, 16, 23).

through him in Psalm 2:8, but then he proceeds to conquer in the Father's timing in a manner which will fuel our praise forever.

You may live in a nation where the Church appears weak and outnumbered and backed into such a dark place that you fear it may not survive. In that case, this chapter was written particularly for you. It was written to make you like the followers of David who *"understood the times and knew what Israel should do"* in order to turn Saul's kingdom over to David in 1 Chronicles 12:32. It was written to warn you that God judges the world through the men of lawlessness that it has chosen, and that he alone has the right to decide when to revive a nation or open up a new one to the Gospel. It was written to warn you that the end never justifies the means, and that we must not try to advance his Kingdom through sinful means. It was written to prepare you for God's school of purity and to warn you that he uses the frustrations, trials and long delays of Church history to test our willingness to wait in humble obedience for his timing.

David passed this test and refused to exchange his cave for a crown at any cost. Let's learn from him to follow Jesus as he submits to the Father's perfect plan to save the nations.[7] Let's see what God is doing at our own point in Church history, and become the kind of people he can trust to serve as ambassadors of his Kingdom.[8]

---

[7] If you still need convincing, read John 6:15 and 2 Corinthians 4:1–18.

[8] David tells us in 1 Chronicles 16:22 that God has also anointed us as little reflections of his Messiah and called us to preach his Gospel in weakness throughout the nations.

How to Shout at Your Enemies (24:8–22; 26:1–25)

Then David went out of the cave and called out to Saul, "My lord the king!"

(1 Samuel 24:8)

The voice on my answerphone spoke with a thick Pakistani accent: *"I know who you are. I'm going to kill you! I know who you are and who your family are. I'm going to kill you, you little ——!"* The answerphone cut out partway through the caller's final expletive. I had spent the day delivering Gospel tracts in Urdu to the local Pakistani community with my phone number at the bottom for people to find out more about Jesus the Messiah. Somebody hadn't liked it.

It is all very well to note that Satan's fallen reign still feels very strong, but what should we do when the modern-day equivalents of Saul hate us because we love God's true Messiah? Should we assert our rights and retaliate, or should we beat a hasty retreat to await a less offensive time to talk about Jesus? That's the question which the writer of 1 Samuel tries to answer through David's two encounters with an angry Saul in chapters 24 and 26. He wants to teach us how we should shout back at our enemies whenever they attack us for preaching Jesus and his Kingdom.

First, these chapters warn us *not to retreat* in the face of threats from Jesus' enemies. When we admire the way that Patrick's faith converted the nation of Ireland, we must not forget that the druids ambushed and poisoned him, and that he only survived because of the grace of God.[1] When we admire the way that Martin Luther's faith brought revival to sixteenth-century Europe, we must not forget that it required him to walk into the equivalent of Saul's camp in the German city of Worms, declaring: *"Even if there were as many devils in Worms as tiles on the roofs I would still come."*[2] We must not forget that Jesus really meant it when he told his followers that *"Everyone will hate you because of me. But not a hair of your head will perish. Stand firm, and you will win life."*[3]

In both of these chapters, David risks his life to call Saul to repentance. He emerges from the cave and calls after him, and he creeps into his camp by night fully aware that one false move will spell an early grave. He is determined to gain a platform to shout the Gospel to his enemy. Ahimelek the Hittite is a foreigner to the Gospel and finds the risks too high, but David's nephew Abishai risks death at his messiah's side.[4]

Second, these chapters warn us *not to retaliate* towards those who hate us. When David shouts after Saul, he attributes his violence to evil powers at work within his court in 24:9 and 26:19. In the same way, Paul tells us that *"Our struggle is not against flesh and blood, but against the rulers, against the authorities, against the powers of this dark world and against the spiritual forces of evil in the heavenly realms."*[5] Abishai may want to skewer Saul while he sleeps,[6] but David remembers that Saul

---

[1] These stories are recorded by the twelfth-century writer Jocelin his *Life and Acts of St Patrick*.

[2] Hans Hillerbrand in *The Reformation in Its Own Words* (1964).

[3] Luke 21:17–19. Sure enough, the Lord protects David by putting Saul's camp into a deep sleep in 26:12.

[4] 1 Chronicles 2:16. Uriah the Hittite would prove himself a genuine foreign convert in 2 Samuel 11.

[5] Ephesians 6:12. David does not even retaliate towards the Ziphites for their second betrayal in 26:1.

[6] We will look at the general unruliness of Abishai and his brother Joab in the chapter "Joab, Son of Saul".

is still the Lord's messiah in a limited sense and looks for means through which to save him.

Third, these chapters tell us *to shout back the love of God* to our enemies. David humbles himself, addressing Saul as *"my lord the king"*, and describing himself as nothing more than a flea on a dead dog or as a game bird. He addresses Saul affectionately as his father-in-law, and points out that he has been a better friend to him than his closest confidant Abner.[7] He does not stand on his rights and rebuke Saul harshly for marrying off Michal to another in his absence, for he has a greater aim in view. He wants to shout out his submission to the Lord's will and his trust that the Lord will vindicate him, because he hopes to win Saul over to salvation before it is too late. He lives out the command of 1 Peter 2:12 to *"Live such good lives among the pagans that, though they accuse you of doing wrong, they may see your good deeds and glorify God on the day he visits us."*

Fourth, these chapters tell us *to expect to see our enemies saved.* Don't miss the incredible turnaround which David's actions provoke in Saul. In both chapters he addresses David as his son-in-law and confesses that he knows David is God's true messiah. He praises David's righteousness, confesses *"I have sinned"*, and comes the closest in his life to genuine repentance. He blesses David's future reign and begs to have a share in David's covenant with godly Jonathan. Do not underestimate the power which is unleashed when Christians shout back words of love to those who hate them.

Nevertheless, these chapters tell us fifthly *to be shrewd in our dealings* with our enemies. David is not naïve enough to think that Saul's profession of faith means that the danger has necessarily receded. He wisely stays in his stronghold at the end of chapter 24, and tells Saul to send a boy to fetch back his spear at the end of chapter 26. He somehow grasps that Saul

---

[7] David points out in 26:16 that Abner and his men deserve to die for failing in their duty to protect the Lord's anointed king.

is simply remorseful like Judas Iscariot in Matthew 27:4, and not repentant like Peter in Matthew 26:75.[8] This is David and Saul's last encounter, and Saul comes close, but not close enough, to repentance before he hardens his heart again to the Holy Spirit.

In 1956, a twenty-eight-year-old American named Jim Elliot stepped into the equivalent of Saul's camp when he visited the Huaorani Indians of Ecuador, a violent unreached people group who didn't want to hear about God's Messiah. He had written in his diary that *"He is no fool who gives what he cannot keep to gain that which he cannot lose,"*[9] and he proved it when his visit was terminated abruptly by the sharp end of one of their spears. His widow, Elisabeth Elliot, responded by shouting at the Huaorani Indians like David in these two chapters. She came to live among them with her fatherless daughter and told them to take their guilt to the Messiah who continued to shout at them through her. *"Leave it all in the Hands that were wounded for you,"* she told them.[10] As a result, many Huaorani Indians found repentance where Saul had failed and were saved through faith in Jesus, God's true Messiah.

If you want to live for Jesus in a nation of Sauls, therefore, don't be surprised that they hate you and want to harm you. Refuse to retreat or retaliate, and continue to shout back the love of God. Because if even Saul himself can come close to repentance, and if even the Huaorani can be saved, then you can trust God to save your own enemies when you shout at them like David.

---

[8] Perhaps David guessed this from the way Saul was more concerned with preserving his dynasty to make a future bid for the throne in 24:21 than he was with calling David back to court as an act of true repentance.

[9] Diary entry for 28th October 1949. He was probably quoting from the seventeenth-century preacher Philip Henry.

[10] Elisabeth Elliot in *Keep A Quiet Heart* (1995).

How to Save a Nation
(25:1–44)

David accepted from her hand what she had brought to him and said, "Go home in peace. I have heard your words and granted your request."

(1 Samuel 25:35)

In September 1857, a businessman named Jeremiah Lanphier could bear it no longer. He was sick of living in a city of Sauls which refused to submit to Jesus as Messiah. He began a lunchtime prayer meeting in the third-floor room of a church in Fulton Street, New York, and cried out in prayer for the Lord to change his city and nation.

On the first Wednesday lunchtime, he prayed on his own for half an hour before six other people finally came to join him. On the following two Wednesdays, he gathered twenty to forty people and they decided to make their lunchtime prayer meeting a daily event. Within several weeks, many more prayer meetings like it had sprung up across the city, and within several months prayer meetings had sprung up across the nation. Rich northern merchants and poor southern slaves were united in a single cry for the Lord to end his judgment on America, and even the former president Franklin Pierce came to pray. As the nation cried out to God together for revival, tens of thousands started receiving the Lord Jesus as their King. Charles Finney claimed that *"This winter of 1857–58 will be remembered as the time when a great revival prevailed. It swept across the land with such power that at the time it was estimated that not less than 50,000 conversions occurred weekly."*[1]

Perhaps the writer of 1 Samuel had individuals like Jeremiah Lanphier in mind when he wrote chapter 25. He was a prophet and wanted to teach future generations how to pray to avert God's judgment on their nation when it is full of Sauls. He takes the godly example of Abigail and uses her as a picture of what we all must do. He wants her bold act of faith to teach us how to change a nation.

David is still hiding in the Desert of Ziph and extends particular protection towards the flocks of one of the richest men in the land.[2] The name Nabal means *Fool*, however, and he represents a culture which refuses to serve the Lord. When David sends messengers to remind him that he has protected his flocks for free and would like a share in his celebrations, Nabal makes it clear that he has no need for any would-be king but himself. Even though David sends the messengers in the authority of his name, and Jonathan told us in 23:17 that everyone knew that David was God's true messiah, Nabal rejects David's rule with all the contempt he would show towards a runaway slave.[3]

It is significant that Samuel died in verse 1 of this chapter. He must have been aged about 100 when he died, and he had promised in 12:23 to pray for Israel for the rest of his life. Without Samuel's prayers to hold back God's judgment, Nabal's affront provokes David's full fury and he straps on his sword to lead his men out to slaughter Nabal and his household.[4] Unless

---

[1] Charles Finney in *The Memoirs of Charles G. Finney* (1876).

[2] Joshua 15:55 confirms that *Carmel* in verse 2 does not refer to the mountain in the north, but to one of the cities near Maon and Ziph. These towns were related as fellow descendants of Caleb (1 Chronicles 2:42–45).

[3] David presents himself humbly as Nabal's *son* in verse 8, but Nabal mistakes his meekness for weakness.

[4] Some readers assume that David is wrong to march out against Nabal. They see verse 22 as a rash oath uttered in anger, and his use of the Hebrew euphemism *one who urinates against a wall* to mean *men* in verses 22 and 34 as proof that he was full of unrighteous anger. However, Nabal's servants and

God finds another person who can step into Samuel's praying shoes, his judgment is sure to fall. He finds the kind of person he can use in Nabal's wife Abigail, whose name means *Source of Joy* and who is as intelligent and beautiful as her husband is stupid and wicked. The Lord is about to use her to avert his anger. As he does so, he also teaches us how we can also save a nation.

Nabal's servants point out to Abigail in verse 17 that her husband is a *son of Belial*, or literally a *son of lawlessness*.[5] She quickly grasps that radical action is needed to save her household. She musters a small group of intercessors and sets off with gifts to seek the face of God's messiah.[6] When she meets him, she bows down in worship and confesses her husband's sin as if it were her own in verses 24 and 28. *"Let the blame fall on me,"* she prays literally with the same willingness to sacrifice herself to appease God's wrath as Moses displayed in Exodus 32. She appeals to David's character in verse 26, pleading with him not to avenge himself with his own hands – the very thing he promised he would not do in 24:12–13 – and to remember that his true desire is to save and not to judge.[7] She confesses his righteousness and that he is on the Lord's side in verse 28, and that the Lord has appointed him to found an everlasting messianic dynasty. Abigail ends by urging him in verse 30 to act in line with his calling to be a viceroy who governs for the Lord, and not a self-assertive king like Saul. Because Abigail goes to meet David in prayer and pleads with him to hold back his

---

Abigail have no doubt that he is in the right within their culture, and God himself uses the same euphemism in 1 Kings 14:10!

[5] We examined this phrase earlier in the chapter "How to Make God Your Enemy".

[6] There is a play on words in Hebrew in verse 18 since the word for wineskin is *nebel*.

[7] The *wrong* which David might have committed in verses 26 and 39 would have been to judge and destroy a community when a praying woman made room for him to save and revive it instead. This should reassure you that the Lord will never allow your prayers to be uttered in vain.

judgment for the sake of his own name, she manages to save her entire household.

David's forgiveness is so complete in verse 35 that even Nabal himself is given ten days in which to repent. He has a stroke while hung-over but still refuses to give David the honour due his name and finally dies the death of all those who oppose the Lord's messiah. Because he refused to share any of his property with David, he loses it all to him when David marries his widow. In Church history terms, God's Kingdom comes. Abigail is rewarded for her fervent prayer when David chooses her as his queen. Although David's polygamy will cause many problems for him later,[8] the Lord allows this to happen as a prophetic picture for you and me. He wants to encourage us that he delights in Abigails and Jeremiah Lanphiers and will delight in us praying too. He wants to promise us that, when Jesus returns to earth to usher in the fullness of his Kingdom, we will not regret a single moment we have spent in laying hold of him in prayer to have mercy on the nations.

So if you live in a city or nation which is full of Sauls and Nabals, do not simply tut and point the finger. Go to meet the Lord in prayer and plead with him to turn away from his righteous anger. Plead with him until he saves your city or nation through your prayers.

It only took a Jeremiah Lanphier who prayed on his own to start a revival in New York, and it only took a city which prayed to start revival across an entire nation. Through that revival in America, men like D.L. Moody went out to the nations of the world. Through what was achieved in those nations, a missionary movement was birthed which still affects every corner of the world today.

---

[8] We will look at these problems later in the chapter "The Home Front".

Man-Made Plans
(27:1–29:11)

> *In those days the Philistines gathered their forces to fight against Israel. Achish said to David, "You must understand that you and your men will accompany me in the army."*
>
> (1 Samuel 28:1)

The closer you get to graduation, the harder the tests generally become. David's graduation day was just around the corner, so the Lord gave him a final test which showed how much of Saul was still left in his heart.

There is plenty in these three chapters to remind us of the hallmarks of Saul's reign. He quickly returns to his man-made plans after his momentary remorse at the end of chapter 26 and disobeys the Lord by renewing his hunt for David. Because he refused to fulfil the calling God gave him in 9:16 by destroying the Philistines with David as his trusted general, they survive to launch a fresh invasion of his land.[1] Saul is about to discover that pride and disobedience never go unpunished.

As Saul's man-made plans start to unravel, he finally decides to listen to the Lord. He realizes too late that Samuel is dead, that David has the priest with the Urim and Thummim, and that David also has the prophets such as Gad who receive dreams and visions. Isaiah 55:6 warns us to *"Seek the Lord while he may be found; call on him while he is near"*, and Saul reaps the

---

[1] Shunem and Gilboa were only fifteen miles south of Lake Galilee, so the Philistine raid had gone very deep into Israel, virtually unopposed by Saul's man-made kingdom.

bitter fruit of having ignored the Lord for many years. Because he has refused to play second fiddle to the Lord, he finds the Lord unwilling to dance to his tune now that he has decided he finally wants to play.

Saul refuses to repent of his man-made plans because he thinks he has found a way to bypass the Lord and still get what he needs.[2] He knows that consulting mediums is explicitly forbidden in the Law of Moses, since he himself exiled them from Israel during the brief moment at the start of his reign when the Holy Spirit fell upon him, but he finds a medium near to the battlefield who can conjure up the dead spirit of Samuel to guide him. She is petrified when what appears is not a deceptive spirit but Samuel himself,[3] and Saul is petrified when he hears him speak God's verdict on his man-made plans. In words reminiscent of the Lord's curse on Eli, Samuel tells him that his army will be defeated and that he and his sons will die on the battlefield. He tells him for the first time explicitly that God's new messiah is David, and he gives him one last chance to repent before his reign ends in tragic judgment.

All of this is true to form for Saul, but note how similarly David acts in these chapters. When he sees that Saul's remorse is short-lived at the start of chapter 27, he despairs at the thought of many more years of hiding as an outlaw. He does not consult the Lord through the Urim and Thummim or through one of the prophets, since his common sense assures him that *"the best thing I can do is to escape to the land of the Philistines"*. His common sense ignores the Lord's promises and track record, and it robs him of the memory of his disastrous visit to Gath several years earlier. David would need to retake the test

---

[2] He actually tries to blame this on the Lord in 28:15, as if it were God's fault for refusing to answer him.

[3] Her surprised reaction shows that mediums normally conjure up deceptive demons rather than genuine dead souls. This is one reason why the Lord forbade consulting mediums on pain of exile in Leviticus 20:6.

of chapter 21 before he could graduate, and this time the test would be considerably harder.

David soon remembers why he had to plead with the Lord to deliver him from King Achish the first time around. However, rather than repenting of coming to Gath altogether, he simply tweaks his man-made plan. He persuades Achish to let him leave the capital and settle in the country town of Ziklag, telling a lie that he feels unworthy to dwell in the royal city. Once in Ziklag, he faces the fresh problem of providing for 600 men and their families now that he cannot employ his usual tactic of raiding Philistine settlements.[4] Yet again, he tweaks his man-made plan instead of repenting and slipping back across the border to Judah. He raids the Amalekites and the other foreign settlements between Philistia and Egypt, then lies to Achish that he has been raiding the towns of Judah.[5] Since David is careful to slaughter every witness, Achish falls for the lie and assumes that David is now hated in Judah as a collaborator with the Philistines.

The time has come for the Lord to show David how much his man-made plans have made him like Saul. Achish launches an invasion of Israel and tells David that he and his men must play a leading role. David cannot refuse on principle since he has lied to Achish that he has been invading Judah for the past year, so the hero who once fought Goliath is forced to fight for Goliath's city against the People of God! If Saul dies in the battle, there is no way that Israel will receive as their new king a man who has been fighting for the Philistines. His future reign hangs in the balance as a result of his man-made plans.

Even when the Lord stirs the Philistine commanders against him so that Achish sends him back to Ziklag, David does

_____

[4] Governing a city was a fresh stage in God's training school for David in how to rule as king. We can read about some of the new warriors who joined him at Ziklag in 1 Chronicles 12:1–7.

[5] Jerahmeel was the older brother of Caleb and founder of a clan in Judah (1 Chronicles 2:9). The Kenites were the Midianite descendants of Jethro, who dwelt as worshippers of God within Judah (Judges 1:16).

not repent. He should have repeated Psalm 34 and praised God for delivering him from Achish,[6] but instead he addresses the leader of the enemies of God as *"my lord the king"* and tries to persuade him to let him fight.[7] David's stubborn commitment to his man-made plans convinces the Lord that he must do one last thing to force him to face up to his inner Saul. When David and his men arrive back at Ziklag, they find their homes on fire and all their women and children gone. They have been raided by the people they themselves have raided. David's men are so furious that they plan to stone him to death, and the man who gathered an army through his godliness loses it through pursuing man-made plans like Saul. The Lord has brought him to the same point as Saul in the medium's house at Endor, and he urges him to respond differently.

We read in 28:20 and 30:4 that when Saul and David saw the Lord's judgment on their man-made plans, Saul's *"strength was gone"* and David *"had no strength left to weep"*. Saul fails the test by trying to fast as a sign of his repentance and reliance on the Lord's strength, but quickly being won over by his friends to eat a royal feast in order to find *"the strength to go on your way"*.[8] David passes the test when he repents of his man-made plans and 30:6 tells us that he *"found strength in the Lord his God"*.

Saul would die in the Battle of Mount Gilboa, but he died within the heart of David shortly before. David had passed this final test and renounced his reliance on man-made plans. At long last he was ready to reign as the kind of king that God could use.

---

[6] David had promised in the cave in Psalm 57:9 that he would proclaim the Lord's greatness to the nations. By God's grace, 29:6 and 9 suggest that he had some small evangelistic impact on Achish, who refers to the Lord as *Yahweh* and says David has been a pleasing *messenger of God* to the Philistines.

[7] If the Lord had not graciously made this request fall on deaf ears, David and his men would have returned to Ziklag too late to pursue the Amalekites and rescue their families.

[8] Saul had been called to *restrain* God's People in 9:17, but it only takes two men and a woman to break his resolve to fast before the Lord. He knows all the language of religion in 28:10 but nothing of its substance.

Sweet Discipline (30:1–30)

But David found strength in the Lord his God.

(2 Samuel 30:6)

I don't know what it is with toddlers, but all four of my children have been the same. If a toddler gets hold of your car keys while you are strapping them into their car seat, there is no way that you will get the keys back without a fight. It doesn't matter that you want to use the keys to drive them to the park or to swimming or to Legoland. They are so determined that they want to hold the car keys that they will cry over being disciplined by a father who insists that it is time for him to drive.

If you are a parent, you will have observed this for yourself, but even if you are not you can identify with David. For three long chapters he has been holding on to his man-made plans and rejecting the Lord's call to stop and let him drive. Chapter 30 is not therefore just an aside from the main story. It is a glimpse at what might have been for Saul if he had repented under the Lord's sweet discipline.

We noted at the end of the last chapter that David repented of his man-made plans in verse 6 and *"found strength in the Lord his God"*. Almost as soon as he stops snatching the car keys away from God, he begins to see what happens whenever we surrender and let him drive. He calls for Abiathar to bring the Urim and Thummim – the very thing he forgot to do in 27:1 – and he receives a promise from the Lord that if he pursues the Amalekites he will recover all that has been lost.[1] Since by the

---

[1] The name of Ahimelek's son Abiathar means *My Father Is Great* or *Father of Abundance*. As the new high priest, he is about to help David to know the Lord as his generous Father.

grace of God the Amalekites have not slaughtered the women and children as David did when he raided their towns in 27:9, he and his men can still recover their beloved families because the Lord has responded with mercy to their prayer of repentance.

David is left wondering how he can rally his exhausted army and lead them in pursuit of the Amalekites, when suddenly fresh reinforcements arrive to boost their morale. Although the writer of 1 Samuel does not mention it here, we are told in 1 Chronicles 12:19–21 that brave warriors from the tribe of Manasseh defected to him at this very moment when Ziklag was burning and that *"they helped David against raiding bands."* These men had been senior officers in Manasseh, and they help David to lead his exhausted troops twelve miles south-west to the Besor Valley. When 200 of his soldiers tell him they cannot go on any further, David has a chance to demonstrate that he has truly repented of his man-made plans. If he is still relying on human strength then he will force them to go on, because his hope of beating the Amalekites lies in strength of numbers, but if he has truly learned to rely on the Lord's strength instead of his own then he will trust that *"Nothing can hinder the Lord from saving, whether by many or by few."*[2] David passes the test and allows his men to drop out of the battle because his trust is in the Lord. He has stopped trying to snatch at the car keys of his life, and he looks to see what happens when he lets God do the driving.

As soon as he leaves the 200 behind, David finds an abandoned Egyptian slave of the Amalekites who is worth far more in the battle than the 200. By God's grace, the slave is ill enough to have been left behind but not so ill that he died during three days without food and water. He becomes David's guide so that his exhausted army do not need to squander their remaining strength on an aimless search for the Amalekite camp. It is so well hidden, and the Amalekites are so convinced

---

[2] 1 Samuel 14:6.

that David is marching with the Philistines, that they are drunk and have not even posted guards to warn them of his arrival. He and his men are able to finish the slaughter which Saul was too disobedient to complete back in chapter 15.[3] David's men rescue every single one of their wives and children. The Lord has done just as he promised.

Great victories can lead to great dangers. After Saul conquered the Amalekites, he set up a monument to his own glory in 15:12 and started acting as if the plunder was rightly his. David's treatment of the plunder is therefore the proof of whether the Saul which had until so recently lurked in his heart is truly dead. Some of his men refuse to share the plunder with the 200 who stayed behind,[4] but David reminds them that this victory was the Lord's and was more than any of them deserved. David demonstrates that his days of making man-made plans are truly over, and that he is happy now to let God do the driving. As he passes the plunder test where Saul failed, he opens up the door to discover just how sweet the Lord's discipline always is.

David and his men have captured far more plunder than the Amalekites stole from them. Verse 16 tells us that they had also raided Philistia and Judah, and verse 20 tells us that only a small proportion of what they took could be earmarked as *"David's plunder"*.[5] David therefore sends some of the plunder to the elders of Judah and to some of the key cities across Judah. Although they had failed to rally to his side and some of them had even betrayed him to Saul, he treats them as friends and tells them, *"Here is a gift for you from the plunder of the Lord's enemies."* Although he does not realize what he is doing, his

---

[3] We are not told how large the Amalekite army was, but the tiny percentage which manages to escape in verse 17 is the same size as David's entire army!

[4] Like any church, David's army still contains a few *sons of lawlessness*. They do not simply refuse the 200 a share in the plunder, but also tell them they need to *go away*.

[5] The verses which follow show that *"David's plunder"* was not what he demanded after the battle, but what had originally been at Ziklag before the battle. The *Kerethites* in verse 14 were Cretan settlers in Philistia.

actions buy their support at the very time that he is just about to need it. They are about to receive news that Saul has been abandoned by the Lord and killed, and they have just received lavish proof that the Lord is with his new messiah David.

So don't be like a toddler and complain that the Lord wants to take the car keys of your life out of your own hands. Learn through this chapter to trust that, when we let him drive, the Lord takes us to places beyond our wildest dreams. Don't strengthen yourself, like Saul, to reassert your man-made plans, for the Lord's discipline is sweet for those who gladly let him do the driving. Learn to strengthen your soul in the Lord, as David did in Psalm 25:

> *Show me your ways, Lord, teach me your paths. Guide me in your truth and teach me, for you are God my Saviour, and my hope is in you all day long... Do not remember the sins of my youth and my rebellious ways... Who, then, are those who fear the Lord? He will instruct them in the ways he chooses. They will spend their days in prosperity, and their descendants will inherit the land.*

To Reign in Hell (31:1–13)

So Saul took his own sword and fell on it.

(1 Samuel 31:4)

In John Milton's epic poem, *Paradise Lost*, the Devil refuses to repent of his rebellion against the Lord in heaven, even when he is thrown down to the miseries of hell. *"Here we may reign secure,"* he assures his followers, *"and in my choice to reign is worth ambition, though in Hell: Better to reign in Hell than serve in Heaven."*[1] If you are still in any doubt as to who inspired Saul's pride and disobedience, then look at these famous words reflected in his last stand.

We might have hoped that Samuel's words to Saul at the medium's house in Endor would have driven him to repentance. Instead, we find him taking to the battlefield at Mount Gilboa determined to continue to reign as king instead of God, even if in hell. We discover in 2 Samuel 1:10 that he actually put his crown on before battle, even though he must have known it would make him an easy target for the Philistines.[2] Saul would literally rather die than hand over the car keys of his life to the Lord. In the end, that's precisely what he did.

Note the Lord's continued mercy towards Saul as he gives him reason after reason to repent. In verse 1, the Philistines win the Battle of Mount Gilboa and many of Saul's soldiers lie bleeding and dying all across the battlefield. Still Saul refuses to repent. In verse 2, the Philistines kill Saul's three sons,

---

[1] Book 1, lines 261–263. John Milton first published *Paradise Lost* in 1667.

[2] Verse 2 tells us literally that they *clung* or *stuck like glue* to Saul and his sons. Compare this with 1 Kings 22:29–33 to see that Saul's proud decision to wear his crown was a direct cause of his death.

including Jonathan.[3] Still Saul refuses to repent. In verse 3, the Philistines wound Saul so seriously that he knows he is going to die. Incredibly, he still refuses to repent. He is so determined to reign as king instead of God that he is not even willing to govern as his viceroy when he realizes he is dying. He fumes like Satan in *Paradise Lost* and still believes that *"to reign is worth ambition, though in Hell. Better to reign in Hell than serve in Heaven."*[4]

The Lord continues to be gracious towards Saul and gives him time to think over his final decision before the Philistines capture him. Surely now Saul will repent of his proud disobedience and ask the Lord to save his soul, even as his body breathes its last? Don't be so familiar with this story that you fail to be astonished by what Saul decides to do. He worries about how the Philistines will abuse his body,[5] but not about how the Lord will judge his soul. He asks his armour-bearer to kill him instead of asking the Lord to save him. When his armour-bearer is too scared to kill the Lord's anointed king, Saul has no such qualms, and he falls on his own sword rather than fall on the mercy of the Lord. So ends the life of one of the most tragic figures in the Old Testament. He loved his life so much that he lost it, when if he had surrendered it he could have saved it.

Don't be fooled into thinking that this story is about a man in 1010 BC and not about us. Saul isn't the only one who follows Satan's lead and who prefers to die with the car keys in his hand than surrender his man-made plans to the Lord's will.

A few months ago, I spent a morning with a man who has pioneered many successful Anglican Church plants across London. He explained how he has worked with many dying

---

[3] Saul had four sons in total (1 Chronicles 8:33), three of whom were strong enough to fight in battle and be listed in 14:49. Only his weak and ineffective son Ish-Bosheth (also known as Esh-Baal) survived.

[4] When Samuel told Saul in 28:19 that he would soon be *"with me"*, he did not mean *in heaven* but simply *in the place of the dead*.

[5] For an example of what the Philistines did when they captured their enemies alive, see Judges 16:21 and 25.

churches to help them surrender their empty buildings so that he can fill them with hundreds of excited church-planters. Then he told me something which reminded me of the Devil's words in *Paradise Lost*. He said that when he spells out to a church that they must let go of their old ways of working and be prepared to die to be reborn, two-thirds of those churches which express an initial interest refuse. They would literally rather die than surrender to the next stage in God's plan. He pointed to nightclubs and restaurants and mosques which now meet in the defunct buildings of churches which made the same mistake as Saul.

A few years ago, I had lunch with an old lady who had a history of depression. During the course of lunch we were able to talk about the Gospel, and I gave her some of David's psalms to read to help her when the darkness descended on her again.[6] We talked much about her need to surrender to Jesus as King, and we identified that many of the underlying causes of her depression were linked to her desire for control. I discovered shortly afterwards that in her next fit of depression she had committed suicide, and I have to say that her funeral was one of the bleakest services I have ever been to. Faced with the Gospel call to surrender, she had sung the Devil's tune: *"To reign is worth ambition, though in Hell. Better to reign in Hell than serve in Heaven."*

Both for individuals and for churches, therefore, this third section of 1 Samuel ends with a firm challenge. Unless we graduate from God's school of purity with humility and obedience, we cannot be surprised when verse 7 is repeated and Philistines come to occupy the places over which we tried to reign instead of God. We cannot be surprised to find that God treats us as his enemies.

---

[6] David's worship songs help lift Saul's dark moods in 16:23. Many people who suffer from depression have also found that his psalms still help lift their dark moods when they read them today.

David cut off Goliath's head and impaled it on a pole outside Jerusalem to proclaim that the city was next on God's shopping list. The Philistines cut off Saul's head and impaled his body to the city wall of Beth Shan in Manasseh near Mount Gilboa. The writer of 1 Chronicles starts to tell his own parallel story of David's reign from this point onwards, and he reveals in 10:10 that the Philistines put Saul's head in the temple of Dagon to proclaim that their idol also had a shopping list of his own. The Philistines divide the rest of Saul's armour between their other idols and rejoice that the gods of Philistia have triumphed over the God of Israel. What they fail to realize is that the Lord was the true victor at Mount Gilboa. He poured out his judgment on the one who preferred to reign in hell than serve in heaven, and he paved the way for a new king to sit on Israel's throne as a demonstration of his glory.

So, as the men of Jabesh Gilead come at the end of 1 Samuel to express their thanks to Saul for delivering them from Nahash as part of God's advertisement for obedience back in chapter 11, let's remember that what happened on Mount Gilboa was the second half of that advertisement. It was God's clear warning to us against disobedience. The Chronicler sums up the message of this third section of 1 Samuel:

> *Saul died because he was unfaithful to the Lord; he did not keep the word of the Lord and even consulted a medium for guidance, and did not enquire of the Lord. So the Lord put him to death and turned the kingdom over to David son of Jesse.*[7]

A PURE PERSON

156

---

[7] 1 Chronicles 10:13–14.

2 Samuel 1–10:

A Person Who Loves God's Name

David's Greatest Passion
(1:1–2:7)

Tell it not in Gath, proclaim it not in the streets of Ashkelon, lest the daughters of the Philistines be glad, lest the daughters of the uncircumcised rejoice.

(2 Samuel 1:20)

According to Shakespeare, at least, the future King Henry V of England was so desperate to rule that he snatched the crown from his dying father's pillow. In Shakespeare's play, the dying Henry IV responds with anger at his son's *"hunger for my empty chair"* and complains that *"Thou hidest a thousand daggers in your thoughts, which thou hast whetted on thy stony heart."*[1] As the writer of 2 Samuel begins the fourth section of his story, he makes it clear that, unlike Henry V, David's greatest passion was never to rule as king.

For a start, we find David surprisingly unconcerned with what is happening on the battlefield of Mount Gilboa. We might have expected him at the very least to send spies to discover if the moment had come at last for him to be king. Instead, he is too busy being faithful in the little God has given him at Ziklag to waste time lusting impatiently for Saul's crown. The Amalekite who arrives at Ziklag on the third day assumes that David is so eager to snatch Saul's crown that he will give lavish rewards to whoever tells him that the king is dead. He is about to discover to his cost that David's greatest passion was not to become king

---

[1] *Henry IV, Part II* (Act IV, Scene iv). Shakespeare wrote the play in about 1597.

at all. It was to demonstrate the greatness of the Lord's name to the nations of the world.

The Amalekite is unfortunate to be related to those who have just sacked and looted Ziklag, but there is nothing unfortunate about the rest of how he comes to die. He deliberately lies that Saul begged him to kill him so that he would not be captured and tortured by the Philistines.[2] He assumes that David is as desperate for the king to die as Henry V, so he doesn't think about the way his story offends the Lord. To his surprise, David and his men respond to his "good news" by tearing their clothes, weeping, fasting and mourning. He is shocked to find that they are more concerned with God's glory than with Saul's crown. David condemns him to death for daring to lay a hand on the Lord's messiah,[3] and reveals his greatest passion in 1:12. He doesn't simply grieve for his father-in-law Saul and his best friend Jonathan.[4] He grieves *"for the army of the Lord and for the nation of Israel"*, because disaster has fallen on the People who bear God's name.

David's way of expressing his emotions was usually to write a psalm.[5] He does so now in 1:19–27, and it is far more than a simple funeral dirge for fallen leaders. He focuses in 1:19 on what has happened to Israel, and he curses Mount Gilboa in

[2] Since the Amalekite says he *happened* to be on the battlefield, he may well have been one of the predatory scavengers who plundered the corpses of the dead after a battle. Saul had disobeyed the Lord's command to destroy the Amalekites, and he was plundered by one in death. Sin always comes back to bite us.

[3] Not only does David refer to Saul as the Lord's messiah in 1:14 and 16, but 1:21 can also be translated as *"… the shield of Saul, as if he had not been anointed with oil"*.

[4] David now has three wives but he praises his friendship with Jonathan as a source of greater joy than any of them. There is no hint of impurity here, since Spirit-filled churches always foster great same-sex friendships.

[5] David wrote more songs than are recorded in Psalms, and this one was recorded in the *Book of Jashar*, or *Book of the Upright* instead. Joshua 10:13 suggests this was an old collection of histories and worship songs.

1:21 for being unworthy to be part of God's Promised Land.[6] Although he tells no lies about Saul's virtues, he graciously neglects to list his faults, because his true passion is something which goes beyond Saul's place in history.[7] The key sentence is 1:20, as David grieves over what he knows his Philistine friends must be doing in Gath and Ashkelon and their other cities. He grieves over the thought that their celebration of Saul's death is also a celebration that their own idols have won. David thinks back to the day when he placed Goliath's sword in the Tabernacle to proclaim that the Lord was greater than any foreign god, and he weeps to think that Saul's armour and weapons are now in the temples of Baal and Dagon and Ashtoreth and are being used to bolster Philistine faith that their idols are stronger than Israel's God.

David is so consumed by a passion for God's name that he is still not in any hurry to put Saul's crown on his own head. The writer tells us in 2:1 that he only turns to the question of succession *"in the course of time"*, and that even when he does so he first enquires of the Lord what he should do. Common sense demands that he should muster his troops to seize the throne by force, but he uses the Urim and Thummim to ask the Lord if he should go at all, and if he should go then to which city.[8] When the Lord says Hebron in the south instead of one of the more influential northern towns, David does as he says and waits for the elders of Judah to seek him out rather than demanding that they come. He might have acted differently before he enrolled in God's school of purity, but by the time he graduated he had

---

[6] Cursing a place or event was less strange in Hebrew poetry than it is to us. Job curses his birthday in Job 3:3–10, and Jeremiah even curses the man who told his father he had a son in Jeremiah 20:14–16!

[7] One sign that we care for the Lord's glory more than our own is if we also refuse to badmouth our potential rivals and predecessors.

[8] Although the writer does not mention the Urim and Thummim by name in 2:1, the Lord's one-word answers in Hebrew point to the use of the priest's ephod rather than the prophet's gift.

put to death the little Saul inside his heart which lusted to rule at any cost.

The men of Judah come to Hebron and willingly anoint David as their new king. He doesn't need their anointing since he has already been anointed by Samuel as their king in 1 Samuel 16, yet he makes room for them to come and anoint him freely to glorify the Lord. The writer of 1 and 2 Samuel was a prophet and he uses the example of David to prophesy how Jesus the Messiah will extend his reign. He allows people to reject him with cries of *"We have no king but Caesar!"*, because this is a price worth paying for the glory which comes when people freely receive him as *"Son of David"* and *"King of Israel".*[9] Jesus refused to snatch heaven's crown from God the Father, even though he is the Messiah, and he calls us to follow him with the same passion as David for his name.

These opening verses of 2 Samuel end with an account of David blessing Israelites from beyond the borders of Judah for choosing to side willingly with him for the sake of God's glory. He blesses the men of Jabesh Gilead from the other side of the River Jordan and encourages them to continue their faithfulness towards the Lord's messiah by recognizing that Judah has declared David to be the Lord's new king. 1 Chronicles 12:23–40 takes this challenge further by listing over a third of a million Israelites who marched south *"to David at Hebron to turn Saul's kingdom over to him, as the Lord had said... They came to Hebron fully determined to make David king over all Israel."*[10]

David's greatest passion was therefore not to snatch the crown like Henry V, but to do all he could to bring glory to the name of the Lord. This fourth section of the story encourages us to do the same. The Lord is looking for men and women who are consumed with a desire to display his glory. The kind of person God can use is a person who loves his name.

---

[9] Matthew 20:30–31; John 1:49; 12:13; 19:15, 19–22.

[10] The Chronicler is not clear whether they came now in 1010 BC or later in 1003 BC.

Joab, Son of Saul
(2:8–3:39)

May his blood fall on the head of Joab and on his
whole family!

(2 Samuel 3:29)

Joab was the nephew of David, but he acted like the son of Saul. David's nephew through his half-sister Zeruiah plays no part in the story of 1 Samuel, but now the writer brings him onto the stage after the death of Saul.[1] He wants to use Joab as a fresh example of the proud and disobedient person that we are not to be. He will contrast him repeatedly with David in 2 Samuel in order to teach us how to be the kind of people God can use.

Like Saul, Joab has *no passion for God's name*. The eleven northern tribes of Israel have just made the wrong decision. Instead of choosing David as their king, they have chosen Ish-Bosheth, Saul's last surviving son. Saul's old general Abner is the power behind the throne of the weak new king,[2] and he knows full well that Ish-Bosheth is in no way the Lord's messiah and that his actions are inciting Israel to rebel against the Lord and provoke a civil war.[3] David continues to give the Israelites room to decide to end their rebellion and receive him willingly as king, but after two years Abner brings matters to a head

---

[1] David's mother had two daughters by her first husband before she married Jesse (2 Samuel 17:25; 1 Chronicles 2:16–17). This is why her eldest daughter's sons were the same age as her youngest son David.

[2] Ish-Bosheth means *Man Of Shame*, and he was so weak that he is neither mentioned in the list of Saul's sons in 1 Samuel 14:49 nor taken by his father to fight alongside his three brothers at Mount Gilboa.

[3] 1 Samuel 20:31; 24:20; 2 Samuel 3:9, 18.

by leading his army to Gibeon, only five miles from David's border.[4]

Joab means *The Lord Is My Father*, and he ought to have been offended by this rebellion against the Lord. He ought to have been passionate to see God glorified in the eyes of the surrounding nations. Instead, while he is furious and murders Abner for attacking his family, Joab shows no such anger towards Abner's attack on God's glory and happily whiles away the hours in 2:13–16 organizing a tournament with him. When they finally fight and the Lord grants Joab a great victory, he fails to pursue it with a passion to restore the Lord's great name in Israel. He misses the chance to end the civil war in a moment because he falls for smooth-talking Abner's argument that unity matters more than the Lord's name. Don't be mistaken into thinking that Joab pleases God by being merciful in 2:28. He is simply repeating the same sin which his spiritual father Saul committed when he spared the Amalekite king in 1 Samuel 15 because he despised God's glory. The writer tells us in 3:1 that because of Joab's sin, *"the war between the house of Saul and the house of David lasted a long time."*

Like Saul, Joab is also consistently *proud and disobedient*. During the five needless years of civil war he refuses to submit to David as God's messiah. While Abner's sin is obvious – a man of lawlessness who tries to reign over Israel instead of God[5] and who tries to turn David into a king like Saul in 3:12 and 21 by promising to use force *"that you may rule over all that your heart desires"* – it is nevertheless Joab who acts most like a son of Saul. He nurses a grudge against Abner for killing his brother

---

[4] Since 2:11 and 5:4–5 tell us that Ish-Bosheth was assassinated after seven and a half years as king, 2:10 must be telling us that he reigned for two years before the Battle of Gibeon.

[5] Abner claims that Israel is his own land in 3:12, and if he truly slept with Saul's concubine then 16:21 and 1 Kings 2:22 tell us this was a claim to be the true king of Israel. The writer wants us to liken him to Nabal in 1 Samuel 25, since the Hebrew word which David uses for a *fool* or *lawless one* in 3:33 is *nābāl*.

Asahel during the Battle of Gibeon, and he is also jealous of him as a rival. When Abner tires of his man-made king and defects to David, Joab murders him in cold blood and in direct defiance of David's orders.[6] He will go on to defy David's commands again in 18:14 and 20:10, and he will even threaten to name a conquered city after himself unless David dances to his tune in 12:27–28. That's why the writer of 2 Samuel gives him such a prominent place in the story. He doesn't want us to forget what will happen to us if we act like Saul.

As a warning shot across the bows, the writer tells us in 3:13–16 what happened to Saul's daughter Michal. She was David's first wife, who had helped him to escape in 1 Samuel 19 but had then preferred to stay with her father rather than to suffer as an outlaw by her husband's side. She had divorced David in his absence and had married another man, so the Lord now judges her sin by breaking up her adulterous new home.[7] The writer wants us to understand that proud and disobedient people who fail to love his name will always suffer.[8] He wants to turn us into little Davids and stop us being sons of Saul.

David demonstrates his passion for God's name by mourning for Abner as he mourned for Saul and Jonathan. He writes a new psalm to sing at his lavish funeral and majors on the sinfulness of Joab rather than the sinfulness of Abner. He fasts as an expression of his brokenness and humility, and he walks behind Abner's funeral bier as a sign that he had no share

---

[6] 3:30 makes a clear distinction between killing someone in battle and in peacetime: Abner *killed* Asahel but Joab *murdered* Abner. Along with 1 Samuel 25:31 and 1 Kings 2:5, this suggests Christians need not be pacifists.

[7] This is a good object lesson for Christians tempted to divorce and remarry, or even to date an unbeliever. Such relationships may begin sweetly, but they always end in the agony expressed by Paltiel's tears. David's polygamy was also sinful, but we will look at that in more detail in the chapter "The Home Front".

[8] *Bahurim* in 3:16 was the last town in Benjamin before the border with Judah. *Dan* and *Beersheba* in 3:10 were the northernmost and southernmost cities in Israel and Judah.

in Joab's disobedience to the Lord. The writer encourages us in 3:36–37 that David's godly reaction to Abner's death made the Israelites want to choose him as their king, but he also warns us what will happen if we copy Joab and act like sons of Saul.

David curses Joab in 3:29 with words reminiscent of the curse which the Lord placed on the disobedient house of Eli. He asks God to punish Joab and his family for their wickedness, and he repeats this prayer at the end of Abner's funeral service in 3:39. He prays literally in 3:29 that Abner's blood will *go into labour* on Joab's head, and after a thirty-five-year-long gestation period, the delivery date finally comes in 1 Kings 1–2. Joab acts like Saul and Abner by rejecting Solomon as the Lord's messiah and trying to force the accession of David's oldest surviving son Adonijah instead. When he fails, David repeats his prayer for judgment to fall on Joab in 2 Kings 2:5–6, and when Joab launches a second bid to defy the Lord's choice of messiah Solomon executes him. It doesn't matter that Joab runs to the altar in the Tabernacle to beg for mercy. He has not worshipped at the Tabernacle before, and Solomon knows better than to trust the momentary remorse of a son of Saul. Joab had followed his spiritual father by preferring to reign in hell than serve in heaven, and in the end the Lord finally granted him his desire.

David is about to take centre stage in Israel and show us what God can do through a person who loves his name, so don't miss the significance of Joab standing by his side. Even though he was commander of David's army, Joab is not listed among his mighty men in chapter 23.[9] The Lord will not use sons of Saul, like Joab, who have no passion for his name.

---

[9] Although David includes Joab's brother Abishai in the curse of 3:29 and 39, he was not as wicked as his older brother. Abishai and Asahel are both listed among David's mighty men. Joab is conspicuous by his absence.

When a Nation Says Yes
(4:1–5:5)

When all the elders of Israel had come to King David at Hebron, the king made a covenant with them at Hebron before the Lord, and they anointed David king over Israel.

(2 Samuel 5:3)

On Sunday 10th November 1793, at the height of the French Revolution, the cathedral of Notre-Dame in Paris was reopened as the Temple of Reason. Having executed their king earlier that year, the French people gathered to worship the goddess Liberty and to hail her as their nation's new ruler. Statues of church leaders throughout the ages were replaced with busts of human philosophers, as the people sang: *"Descend, O Liberty, daughter of Nature! The people have recaptured their immortal power. Over the pompous remains of age-old imposture their hands raise up your altar... O holy Liberty, come and dwell in this temple. Be the goddess of the French!"*[1]

France was about to experience what happens when a nation says no to Christ and yes to a false messiah. The rule of Liberty would prove to be as disastrous as that of Ish-Bosheth. Many of those who led the worship at the Temple of Reason would be guillotined within the year, and France itself would lurch into twenty years of war which would end in defeat and humiliation. The writer of 2 Samuel wants to teach us in chapter 4 what happens when a nation says no to God's Messiah. He then

---

[1] Emmet Kennedy in *A Cultural History of the French Revolution* (1989).

begins several chapters of encouragement in chapter 5 about what happens whenever a nation repents and says yes.

It is now 1003 BC, seven years after David was accepted by Judah and rejected by the northern tribes. 3:1 tells us that those seven years were a period when *"David grew stronger and stronger, while the house of Saul grew weaker and weaker"*, and chapter 4 updates us on just how weak Saul's dynasty has become. Even though Abner has betrayed him, Ish-Bosheth is still clinging to the hope that he will come back and save his disintegrating reign. When he hears that Joab has murdered Abner, he falls to pieces and the Israelites suddenly realize their stupidity in not having said yes to the Lord's messiah seven years before. Ish-Bosheth has no sons and 4:4 tells us that the last heir to Saul's dynasty is a twelve-year-old lame beggar.[2] The false messiah's rule has proved such a disaster that even his own tribe turns against him and two of his Benjamite officers assassinate him while he takes a siesta.[3] They hope to win David's favour by being among the first Israelites to say yes to him as king.[4]

The two Benjamites have spent so long in Saul's court that they have started to think like him. They assume that David's greatest passion is to see Ish-Bosheth dead. They do not realize that he never saw Saul or his son as an obstacle to his reign, or that he could have conquered Israel by force many years earlier but refused to do so because his greatest passion was for the glory of God's name. He had held back in order to allow the Lord to judge his People for saying no to his messiah, and as a prophetic picture of King Jesus who waits for the world to

---

[2] We discover that Ish-Bosheth had no children in 9:1–3. The ancient Hebrews looked down on disabled people, and we find in 9:4 that Mephibosheth was dependent upon the charity of a friend.

[3] The Hebrew tells us literally in 2:23, 3:27 and 4:6 that Asahel, Abner and Ish-Bosheth were all stabbed *under the fifth rib*. So will Amasa be in 20:10.

[4] Their cowardice and furtiveness is emphasized by the fact that they travel by night down *the Arabah* along the River Jordan and the Dead Sea instead of taking the much shorter but more populated route to Hebron.

hail him freely as Messiah.[5] David therefore executes the two officers who assassinated Ish-Bosheth, as he did the Amalekite in chapter 1, not because Ish-Bosheth was the Lord's messiah but because they have acted wickedly like Saul.

Now, however, the road is clear for the northern tribes to say yes to David as their king. In a scene which is the opposite of what happened at Notre-Dame cathedral, the elders of Israel repent of their sin and pledge themselves to serving God's messiah. They plead with David in 5:1 that he is their brother and must have mercy on them for siding with the son of Saul.[6] Conversion means turning from one master to another, so what the Israelites do here starts a great revival in their nation. They confess that David has a track record of victories under Saul, and that they knew all along that he was God's messiah because of what Samuel prophesied over him when he anointed him as a shepherd-boy over two decades before: *"You shall shepherd my people Israel, and you shall become their nāgīd"* – their *viceroy* under God.[7] Now the Israelites repent of their rebellion and put their faith in the blood of their messiah's covenant with them.[8] They anoint David for a third time as king, but this third anointing is the sweetest. It means that the twelve tribes of Israel have all said yes to God's messiah, and that his blessings can now finally start to flow.

David can now lead Israel into a passion for God's name which has eluded them for centuries.[9] He can lead them to

---

[5] Hebrews 2:8.

[6] This verse points to Hebrews 2:11. It also links to Ephesians 5:30, which in some Greek manuscripts reads that *"we are members of Christ's body, of his flesh and of his bones."*

[7] The writer did not tell us about this prophecy in 1 Samuel 16, nor about the one Abner mentions in 3:18.

[8] 5:3 says literally that David *cut a covenant* with the elders, because Hebrew covenants always involved the slaughter of a blood sacrifice.

[9] 5:2 says literally that David *led out and brought in* Israel. True spiritual leadership means leading people out of their commitment to false messiahs and into the blessing which can be theirs by saying yes to Christ.

accomplish the seven priorities which form the rest of this fourth section of 1 and 2 Samuel. He can lead them to capture *Jerusalem* as the city God has chosen, teach them to treasure *God's presence* and help them to devote their lives to *worshipping* the Living God. He can prepare them to build a magnificent *Temple* and to believe in God's *covenant* to send a better Messiah to save them. He can lead them to *the nations* of the world to preach *the Gospel* through his reign and bring glory to the Lord by saving many. He can cause the nation of Israel to proclaim the Lord's greatness to the Gentiles. He can show us what the Lord does whenever a nation says yes to his Messiah.

The New Testament tells us that the crowds in Jerusalem in 30 AD chose Barabbas as a false messiah and rejected Jesus with shouts of *"We don't want this man to be our king."*[10] It tells us that after Jesus' resurrection, his followers preached *"the good news of the kingdom"* throughout the world, and brought great joy to any city or nation which said yes.[11] David intended his reign to prepare us to carry on their global mission, writing in Psalm 144:15 that *"Blessed is the people of whom this is true; blessed is the people whose God is the Lord."* He wants these chapters which describe his early reign to encourage us to be the kind of people God can use to turn the nations away from their false Ish-Bosheth messiahs, and to the blessing which will be theirs if they repent and say yes to Christ. He wants this whole fourth section to stir our faith to believe the words God spoke to him in Psalm 2 as he pledged his life to proclaiming the glory of the Lord's name:

---

[10] Matthew 27:11–26; Luke 19:14; John 19:14–15. Since *Barabbas* means *Son of The Father*, and some manuscripts of Matthew call him *Jesus Barabbas*, Israel chose a false messiah instead of the true Messiah.

[11] Acts 8:8, 12; 14:22; 19:8; 20:25; 28:23, 31. See also Matthew 3:2; 4:17; 10:7.

I have installed my king on Zion, my holy mountain... Ask me, and I will make the nations your inheritance, the ends of the earth your possession.[12]

---

[12] The Father promised this to David, but Acts 4:24–31 and Revelation 2:26–28 explain that he did so as a picture of what he would promise Jesus the Messiah. This promise is ours as we go to the nations in Jesus' name.

Priority One: Jerusalem (5:6–25)

David knew that the Lord had established him as king over Israel and had exalted his kingdom for the sake of his people Israel.

(2 Samuel 5:12)

"This nation asks for action, and action now," declared President Franklin D. Roosevelt in his inauguration speech on 4th March 1933. It was the height of the Great Depression and he was promising to lead America in bringing recovery to the world. *"There are many ways in which it can be helped, but it can never be helped merely by talking about it. We must act and act quickly... In this dedication of a nation we humbly ask the blessing of God."*[1] The first hundred days of his presidency were so focused that ever since then each new president's agenda has been judged by what he does in his first hundred days.

David revealed his number one priority at the start of his first hundred days as king of Israel. Neither 2 Samuel nor 1 Chronicles takes a breath between David's anointing by the elders of Israel and his leading a united Israelite army to Jerusalem. The first thing he had done after killing Goliath had been to take the severed head and impale it outside the city walls of Jerusalem as a gruesome promise to the Jebusites that their city was next. Now he follows up his promise before the dust settles on his inauguration day.

Jerusalem was a perfect capital city for Israel for

---

[1] This same inaugural speech also contained the famous line: *"The only thing we have to fear is fear itself."*

geographical reasons. It was surrounded on three of its four sides by cliffs and deep ravines which had protected the Jebusites for 600 years since the days of Joshua. It was also a perfect capital city for *political reasons*. It lay between the tribal territories of Benjamin and Judah, and it had been claimed and sacked at least once in its history by both tribes. It was therefore like Washington DC is to America – able to govern every tribe because it was part of none.[2] Yet the main reason David made Jerusalem the first priority of his reign was for *spiritual reasons*.

First, Jerusalem had made Israel's God look like a failure. When Joshua captured it, the Jebusites rebuilt it. When the men of Judah burned it, the Jebusites rebuilt it again. When the Benjamites attacked it, they failed so completely that Saul never tried a fresh assault even though it lay only three miles south of his home. The Jebusites were so convinced that their city proved that Yahweh could not give his People the whole of the Promised Land that they laughed at David from its ramparts that *"even the blind and the lame can ward you off"*. David was determined to conquer Jerusalem because he loved God's name. Once he could tell the world it was the City of David, they would all know that Israel's God was stronger than the strongest foreign idol.

Second, Jerusalem was the site of an unfulfilled prophecy about the Lord's messiah. The city had once been ruled by a man named Melchizedek who was both king and high priest for the Lord. He had served bread and wine to Abraham in Genesis 14:18–20 as a prophecy that God's Messiah would offer his body and blood as a sacrifice for sin outside the walls of his city.[3] David was a prophet and understood this so well that he wrote Psalm 110 about Melchizedek, seeing in him a picture of

---

[2] Joshua 15:8, 63; 18:28; Judges 1:8, 21. This was one of the reasons David had wanted to wait until the northern tribes accepted him as king before launching his attack on the city.

[3] Psalm 76:2 tells us that Salem was the ancient name for Jerusalem. Whereas Melchizedek's city was founded on Mount Zion, Jesus died at Calvary which was part of Mount Moriah opposite.

the coming Messiah. He was therefore determined to capture Jerusalem in his first few days as king of Israel in order to wake up the nations to the urgency of believing that God would send his Messiah to save the world. Zion probably meant *Sunny Place*, since this was where the Lord would reveal his favour to the nations of the earth. It occurs forty times in the Psalms because it was a key part of David's plan to glorify God's name.

Third, Jerusalem was the site of another unfulfilled prophecy about the Messiah. In Genesis 22, the Lord had called Abraham to sacrifice his son Isaac on Mount Moriah on the opposite side of the Tyropoeon Valley from Melchizedek's city on Mount Zion. A hundred feet taller than Mount Zion, Abraham had given it that name because it meant *The Lord Will Provide* and because he recognized that the ram God provided to save Isaac's life pointed to a better substitute sacrifice to come. Abraham had prophesied in verse 14 that *"On the mountain of the Lord it will be provided"*, so David was doubly determined to capture Jerusalem in the early days of his reign in order to proclaim to the nations that this sacrifice for sin was on his way. He built terraces and walls across the valley to join Zion and Moriah together in 2 Samuel 5:9. The name *Jerusalem* is a dual noun in Hebrew, referring to both hills and describing them together as the *Foundation of Peace*. David wanted to teach the nations through his conquest and expansion of the city that the Gospel which would bring them peace with God would be founded in Jerusalem.

The Devil did not ignore David's plan to glorify God's name among the nations. We read in 1 Chronicles 11 that Joab got his dirty hands all over the city from day one. David had been too weak to fire Joab for murdering Abner in 3:39 because he had no other general who was gifted enough to replace him, so he offered command to anyone brave enough to lead his troops to scale the water shaft and break into the impregnable city.[4]

---

[4] David had spotted a weakness in Jerusalem's defences. Since it had no natural river, it drew its water from the Gihon spring outside its walls via a 36-

Joab was too ambitious to leave the assault to a rival, and having retained command of David's army he then played a leading role in the walled expansion of the city. Through proud Joab, the Devil hoped to infect David's godly plan and persuade him to treat Jerusalem as a platform for his own glory.[5] He might have succeeded had David not graduated from God's school of purity, but 5:12 tells us that he *"knew that the Lord had established him as king over Israel and had exalted his kingdom for the sake of his people Israel".*[6]

The Devil therefore tried a second strategy and stirred the Philistines to invade Israel again in 5:17. Instead of hiding in his new stronghold, David consults the Lord and marches out with divine strategies to defeat them twice.[7] He attributes his successes to the Lord who fought on his side,[8] and he routs them so completely that they never dare return during his reign or that of his son Solomon. The Lord has finally fulfilled his promise to Samson, Samuel and Saul, as repeated in 3:18: *"By my servant David I will rescue my people Israel from the hand of the Philistines."* David gathers their abandoned idols and burns them in 1 Chronicles 14:12 to proclaim *"throughout every land"* that his God always keeps his word. Israel's God is stronger than the idols of the nations.

The Devil still has many strongholds today which make the Lord look weak in the eyes of the world. David's commitment

---

foot shaft. Hezekiah remedied this weakness in 2 Chronicles 32:30.

[5] Joab did not *become* commander of David's army in 1 Chronicles 11:6 because he was already its commander in 2 Samuel 2. He retained his position, although David resisted his malign influence.

[6] Even though the writer starts referring to David as a *melek* now instead of a *nāgīd*, he makes it clear that he can do so because David never forgot he ruled under God for the sake of God's People, not for himself.

[7] The Philistines are camped in the same place the second time as the first time, but the Lord's command is different. David warns us not to rely on yesterday's guidance but to seek the Lord afresh each day.

[8] The Philistine idol was called Baal because the word meant *lord*, so when David names the battlefield *Baal Perazim* he is attributing his victory to *the Lord*. This is also why Kiriath Jearim is called *Baalah* in 6:2.

to capture Jerusalem in his first hundred days as king of Israel should encourage us to lay siege to these strongholds in order to proclaim God's splendour. *"David cannot get in here,"* the Jebusites sneered, but *"nevertheless David captured the fortress of Zion."* It doesn't matter what the enemy may say to us if Jesus the Messiah is our leader. Let's ask him to show us the chink in the defences and start climbing up the water shaft.

Your Messiah asks for action, and action now.

Priority Two: God's Presence (6:1–19)

They brought the ark of the Lord and set it in its place inside the tent that David had pitched for it.

(2 Samuel 6:17)

In the legend of Robin Hood, the evil Prince John keeps forgetting that he is merely governing for his brother who is away fighting in the Third Crusade. He sets himself up in King Richard's capital city and starts acting as if he is the true king. Robin Hood and his Merry Men have to remind him he is just a regent until King Richard arrives at the end of the story. Although Saul kept acting like Prince John, David's second priority in his early days as king of Israel shows that he was never in any doubt as to who was King and whose capital city Jerusalem must be.

We saw earlier that David had learned to love God's presence while working as a shepherd-boy in the fields which stretched for eight miles between Bethlehem and Kiriath Jearim. Psalm 132 tells us that he had sworn an oath that *"I will not enter my house or go to my bed, I will allow no sleep to my eyes or slumber to my eyelids, till I find a place for the Lord, a dwelling for the Mighty One of Jacob."* He had nursed this desire to restore the Ark to the Lord's Tabernacle during the years between his anointing by Samuel and his accession to the throne. He took Goliath's sword to Moses' Tabernacle at Nob in 1 Samuel 17:54, and we discover that he was a regular worshipper there in 22:15. His main complaint about the life of an outlaw in 26:20 was that it meant he had to live *"far from the presence of the Lord"*.

Even though the Tabernacle which Saul destroyed at Nob had been re-erected on Mount Gibeon,[1] David pitches a new Tabernacle for the Lord on Mount Zion in 6:17. He rushes excitedly to Kiriath Jearim and leads the Israelites in worship as they bring Israel's true King up on a brand new cart from Abinadab's house to his new palace. Imagine his surprise when, while celebrating his passion for *"the Name, the name of the Lord Almighty, who is enthroned between the cherubim on the ark"*, the Lord suddenly pours out his anger on the happy royal procession. The oxen pulling the cart stumble and Abinadab's son Uzzah puts out a hand to steady the Ark. When he is struck down dead instantly, Israel's celebrations turn into a national disaster.

What had happened? David had forgotten that God's presence is never safe. He had grown over-familiar with the Lord and had lost sight of the majesty and holiness of Israel's King. The author of 1 Chronicles 13:1 implies that David had consulted with his army officers before going down to fetch the Ark but he had not consulted with God. He had put the Ark on a new cart *"because it seemed right to all the people"*, and because it was what the Philistines had done earlier in 1 Samuel 6. However, the Lord had already told the Israelites in the Law of Moses that the Ark must always be wrapped up in the Tabernacle curtains and carried on staffs by the Levites whenever it needed to be moved because his presence was too holy to travel on public transport.[2] It didn't matter that David and Uzzah were very sincere. God's presence is too hot to handle in anything other than what 1 Chronicles 15:13 calls *"the prescribed way"*.[3]

---

[1] 1 Chronicles 21:29; 2 Chronicles 1:3. The Most Holy Place in the Tabernacle was empty, however, since the Ark was still at Kiriath Jearim where it had been brought almost eighty years earlier in 1080 BC.

[2] Exodus 25:12–15; Numbers 4:5–12; 7:9. Instead, David had placed the uncovered Ark next to the backsides of a sweaty team of oxen!

[3] We are meant to contrast *Baal Perazim* in 5:20, where the Lord broke out *for* Israel, with *Perez Uzzah* in 6:8, where the Lord broke out *against* Israel.

At first, David is so angry about his failed plan that he fears to bring the Ark into God's new capital at all. He takes it to the nearby house of a Philistine from Gath by the name of Obed-Edom, perhaps thinking back to where the Ark had been before Kiriath Jearim. However, when he hears three months later that the Ark has brought a mighty blessing rather than a plague on the Philistine, he renews his plan but this time makes sure he honours God's presence as he should.[4] Levites carry the Ark on staffs as Scripture commanded and David offers a blood sacrifice every six steps along the twelve-mile journey. In 1 Chronicles 15:11 we are told that he enlists the help of both the high priest Abiathar and the heir to the other branch of Aaron's family, a man named Zadok or *Righteous*, who will succeed Abiathar when Eli's family is disinherited under Solomon.[5] These joint high priests both assist him in his slow but reverent journey, while singing Psalms 15 and 24 which David appears to have written for the occasion. They sing, *"Lord, who may dwell in your sacred tent? Who may live on your holy mountain?"* as they remember what happened to Uzzah for forgetting the holiness of God's presence. *"Lift up your heads, you gates,"* they sing to Jerusalem, *"lift them up, you ancient doors, that the King of glory may come in!"*

When the Ark finally arrives safely in the city, David shows the Israelites that something has changed in their relationship with Yahweh. He dresses in a priest's ephod and personally offers the blood sacrifices outside his new Tabernacle. This was totally forbidden at Moses' Tabernacle at Mount Gibeon which

---

[4] Obed-Edom could technically have been a *Gittite* by coming from the Israelite city of Gath-Rimmon (Joshua 21:23–24), but the writer never mentions this city and mentions the Philistine city of Gath eighteen times. Obed-Edom appears to have been adopted as an honorary Levite after looking after the Ark, and given a role as a worship leader in David's Tabernacle (1 Chronicles 15:18, 21, 24; 16:4–8, 37–38).

[5] Zadok led the priestly clan of Aaron's son Eleazar. David made him a joint high priest with Abiathar so that he could carry on when the priestly clan of Aaron's other son Ithamar was disgraced under Solomon.

remained the place for Israel to offer their blood sacrifices,[6] but David offers these as the first and last blood sacrifices ever needed at his new worship Tabernacle on Mount Zion. David acts as priest and king because he is re-establishing the order of Melchizedek and pointing forward to the Messiah to whom that order belongs. He prophesies that Jesus will offer a once-for-all sacrifice and invite his followers to worship him with thankful hearts that he has made an offering for them.[7]

That's why David treats this new Tabernacle on Mount Zion as far greater than the one which stands on Mount Gibeon, and makes it home to the Ark and to the oil for anointing kings.[8] It's why he does not create an inner room to hide the Ark away from the worshippers who come, because he wants to point to a day when the Messiah will tear apart the dividing curtain Moses hung between the worshipper and God.[9] It's why he encourages the nation of Israel to come, whether priest or layperson, to enjoy the intimacy of worshipping in the presence of the Lord.[10]

It's also why you should be more scared and more excited than the city of Jerusalem that the true Melchizedek has come. If the Lord did not spare Uzzah for dishonouring his presence by touching an Ark which was only temporary, then we must not dare make light of what God offers us through his Holy Spirit. If the arrival of the Ark caused Jerusalem to rejoice excitedly that

---

[6] Numbers 3:10; 18:7; 1 Chronicles 16:39–42. Moses' Tabernacle remained Israel's *sacrifice centre* while David's Tabernacle became its *worship centre*. Solomon's Temple would combine both.

[7] John 19:30; Hebrews 7:27. The only sacrifices offered thereafter at David's Tabernacle were the sacrifices of praise, obedience and joyful worship (Psalms 27:6; 61:4, 8; 141:2).

[8] 1 Kings 1:39. The Lord now reigned from his throne in the Tabernacle-palace David had erected in his capital city, so the oil which anointed the viceroys who governed for him needed to be stored there.

[9] Matthew 27:51; Hebrews 10:19–22.

[10] Under the New Covenant we are also to bring sacrifices of praise, obedience and joyful worship as we enjoy the Lord's presence (Hebrews 13:15; Revelation 5:8).

they had God's presence in their midst, we must rejoice even more excitedly that the Father promises to send Jesus to dwell in us today:

> *The Lord has sworn [to Jesus] and will not change his mind: "You are a priest for ever, in the order of Melchizedek."*[11]

---

[11] Psalm 110:4. Read this psalm if you have any doubt how much David knew when he built his Tabernacle.

Priority Three: Worship
(6:12–23)

*I will become even more undignified than this, and I
will be humiliated in my own eyes.*

(2 Samuel 6:22)

When Anat's mother arrived back at her house in the suburbs
of Tel Aviv, she immediately saw that her daughter had made
a terrible mistake. She had been busy cleaning her mother's
house all day and expected to be congratulated on her complete
home makeover. She had even dragged her mother's dirty old
mattress outside for the bin men and replaced it with a brand
new mattress as a special surprise. Between sobs, Anat's
mother shouted that her life savings had been in hidden in the
old mattress. Anat had just thrown out over a million US dollars.
Yitzhak Borba, the manager of one of the many landfill sites
which she searched in vain for her money, described the *"totally
desperate"* look on her face. Anat had despised her mother's
mattress and she lost the treasure of a lifetime.[1]

Thirty-seven miles and 3,000 years away, David was coming
home to a similar discovery. He had given a gift of bread, dates
and raisins to the crowds of worshippers before dismissing them
so that they could all return home from God's presence to bless
their families. He returned to the palace and prepared to bless
his newly returned wife Michal, but he was about to discover
the same thing as Anat's mother. She had watched him fulfilling

---

[1] Reported in two British newspapers, *The Times* and *The Daily Telegraph*, on
10th June 2009.

his lifelong goal from an upstairs window and had despised it as fit for nothing but the rubbish heap.

What did you think you were doing today?, she fumed as she went to meet him in the hallway. *You were so... so... unkingly! You might have got away with acting like that as an outlaw in the mountains, but I'm a king's daughter and let me tell you how a king is meant be! My father never even bowed before the Ark at Kiriath Jearim, let alone danced before it like a common slave, as you did!*[2]

Whether through David in the Old Testament or through the woman who anointed Jesus' feet with perfume in the New, we find that not everybody likes to see God worshipped as he deserves. The world can understand our church growth, our social action, our political campaigns and our religious services, but it always hates to see Christians humbling themselves to give glory to God's name. Perhaps the writer splits up David's victories over the Philistines and the other nations in chapters 5 and 8 in order to remind us in the two chapters in between that God is looking for us to be humble worshippers and not just mighty warriors.

You were the daughter of a melek, David corrects Michal in verse 21. *You were the daughter of a man who tried to fool himself that he was king instead of God. I am a nāgīd, a viceroy who governs under God and gives him glory as the true King.* Hadn't she read Psalm 5, where David sang to *"my King and my God"*? Hadn't she listened to the words he had given the Israelites to sing outside from Psalm 24, addressing the Lord five times in just four verses as *"the King of glory"*? He did not want to pretend to be regal like her father, because his greatest passion was for news to spread that Jerusalem's true King was the Lord! *"I will become even more undignified than this, and I will be humiliated in my own eyes,"* he assures her, for this is

---

[2] We can tell that the issue here is a clash between Saul and David's two kingdoms, since the writer refers to her three times in verses 16, 20 and 23, not as David's wife, but as *"Michal daughter of Saul"*.

precisely why the Lord chose him to rule instead of *"your father or anyone from his house"*.

If you have not already experienced this conflict in your own life, then you need to get ready. Becoming a Christian means pledging your life to the glory of a God whom the rest of the world would rather throw on the scrap heap. You can buy off their anger by toning down your worship like a child of Saul, but if you want to follow the Son of David then this conflict is here to stay.

How do you worship the Lord when you are with other Christians? Is your worship characterized by the same things as David's in these verses? Noisy celebration, loud rejoicing, dancing with all your might and leaping before the Lord? David shows enough variety in his psalms to teach us that smiles and noise aren't everything, but he also shows us in these verses that true worship always demonstrates for all to see that God is King and we are his servants. Are you ever like Michal, offering a spectator's critique on other people's worship from the wrong side of the window of your man-made palace, when you should be outside dancing?[3] Do you ever listen to the critics and tone down the honour you bring God's name in worship for fear that it will make you look undignified?[4] This passage should remind us that there is no place which reveals the Saul hiding in our heart quite so clearly as the place of worship.

How about the rest of your life? Do you share the Gospel with unbelievers through your words and your different lifestyle, or are you too worried that speaking up for Jesus will make you appear foolish in their eyes? Do you pray for the sick and reach out to the needy or are you too embarrassed to risk such naked faith in public? Are you willing to forfeit promotion, profit and

---

[3] Michal's criticism sounded clever, but 1 Samuel 19:13 suggests it was a fresh case of dressed-up idolatry.

[4] Like most critics, Michal is just plain wrong. Far from despising him for his devotion to the Lord as she predicted in verse 20, the slave girls saw it as a reason to honour him in verse 22.

popularity in order to improve God's reputation in the world? These daily decisions are the moments when we discover if we are truly followers of the Son of David, or still the children of Saul.

Verse 20 tells us that David was returning home to bless Michal and his household – a hint that she might bear him royal sons. Instead, because she prefers pride and disobedience to David's purity, she receives a curse in verse 23 that she will remain fruitless and infertile.[5] Michal had been given a chance to worship the Lord as a consort to his viceroy, but instead she preferred to reign in her own private hell like her father than serve as the bride of David.[6]

> *True worship always forgets itself,* argues the songwriter Matt Redman. *Isn't it time we saw a bit more holy worship? I'm pretty guilty of this myself, to be honest. I could blame it on my personality, but deep down I know that isn't the whole story... In Luke 6:45, Jesus tells us: "Out of the abundance of the heart [the] mouth speaks." And so, too, out of what's stored up in our hearts we sing and serve and live.*[7]

So let's deal with the Saul in our hearts and worship the Lord like David. Let's be willing to look foolish so that God can look great.

---

[5] These references to *slave girls*, *fruitlessness* and *infertility* are meant to remind us of Hannah's prayer in 1 Samuel 2:1–10. Beware, armchair critics are never fruitful.

[6] The Lord made Michal infertile, but since she now drops out of the story it may also be that David grew estranged from her as an unworthy queen for the new kingdom he was so passionate to pioneer in Israel.

[7] Matt Redman in *The Unquenchable Worshipper* (2001).

Priority Four: The Temple
(7:1–7)

> He said to Nathan the prophet, "Here I am, living
> in a house of cedar, while the ark of God remains
> in a tent."
>
> (2 Samuel 7:2)

One of my children's favourite books is *The Very Hungry Caterpillar*. As the name suggests, the caterpillar has an insatiable appetite for food and no amount is ever enough to satisfy him. After eating his way through an apple, two pears, three plums, four strawberries, five oranges and just about the entire contents of a fridge-freezer, he disappears into a cocoon and something beautiful emerges. Because the caterpillar refused to be satisfied, he becomes a gorgeous butterfly.

If you want to understand David's legacy to Israel, then it may help to stay with *The Very Hungry Caterpillar*. David was hungry for the glory of God's name, and his refusal to be satisfied produced something far more beautiful than a butterfly. That's the background to the fourth priority of David's reign, and in case we miss it in 2 Samuel the writer of 1 Chronicles spells it out in even greater detail.[1]

David's hunger for the glory of God's name made him *bring the Ark of the Covenant* up to his capital city. He led the Israelites

---

[1] Since 1 Chronicles was written during the return from exile in the late fifth century BC, it focuses far more than 2 Samuel on David's Tabernacle and Solomon's Temple, because the Israelites found continuity with their past through their rebuilt Temple in the absence of David's heir being able to sit on his throne.

in a day of such unrestrained worship that he offended his wife Michal, but even a day like that one could not satisfy his hunger. He wanted more than a day's memory. He wanted Israel to live under God's presence every day so that all the other nations of the world could see.

David's hunger for the glory of God's name therefore made him *set up a new Tabernacle on Mount Zion*. Although he sent priests to continue the blood sacrifices at Moses' Tabernacle on Mount Gibeon, he made the new focal point of Israel's life with God the Tabernacle on Mount Zion. Forty times the Psalms speak of what is happening in Zion, yet not once do they mention Mount Gibeon. David set up worship teams to lead Israel in non-stop praise before the Ark, perhaps inspired by some of what he had seen in Samuel's academy of prophets at Naioth in 1 Samuel 19.[2] Through those teams he trained the Israelites in how to worship God, giving them ten instructions in 1 Chronicles 16:8–11 to teach them what the Lord desired: giving thanks, calling on his name, proclaiming his deeds, singing, praising, meditating on his acts, boasting in his name, rejoicing, looking to his strength and seeking his face. The hunger he had felt as a shepherd-boy in the fields near Kiriath Jearim to teach his nation to worship, he was now able to realize as king.

Even so, David's hunger for the glory of God's name was still not satisfied. How could it be when he lived in a palace made with cedar wood and gold while the Lord dwelt in a Tabernacle which was just an elaborate tent? Suddenly his mind went back to the great Philistine temples which he had seen in Gath, and he summoned the prophet Nathan to get permission to upgrade his Tabernacle into a glorious Temple.[3]

Nathan hastily gave his permission but he was forced

---

[2] 1 Chronicles 6:31–32 and 16:4–6. This worship may well have been 24/7, since the Hebrew of 16:6 suggests that it took place *continually* rather than just *regularly*.

[3] This is the first mention of the prophet Nathan in the Old Testament. He and Gad were the two main prophets of David's reign (1 Chronicles 29:29).

to backtrack the following morning after hearing God speak during the night.[4] The Lord was very pleased with *"my servant David"*, but he didn't want a plan which was based more on pagan practices than on his own purpose for the world. Unlike Moses' Tabernacle, we are not given the design or dimensions of David's Tabernacle because the Lord was far more interested in the spirit of what took place inside. God was so pleased with the worship there that he uses the Hebrew word *mishkān*, or *dwelling place*, for the first time in 400 years since Joshua 22:29. He therefore tells David that while pagan gods might want large buildings, he wanted to dwell in human hearts. One day he would unite the blood sacrifices at Moses' Tabernacle and the worship sacrifices at David's Tabernacle through one single Temple, but he did not want to do so before achieving a lasting work in the hearts of Israel.[5]

David's suggestion was ahead of its time, but the rest of chapter 7 makes clear that even the idea brought yet more glory to God's name. Nevertheless, David's hunger for the glory of God's name was still not satisfied. He pressed the Lord for a reason why he could not do this work in the hearts of Israel as easily through a magnificent Temple as through a Tabernacle, and when the Lord told him that he could not build because he had shed too much blood as a warrior on the battlefield, he didn't complain that he had shed that blood in fighting the Lord's wars.[6] Instead, he saw a new way to direct his hunger for the glory of God's name. We discover in 1 Chronicles 21–29

---

[4] Despite his need to revise what he says in verse 3, Nathan teaches that what God puts in a Spirit-filled heart is normally a good gauge of his guidance. He tends to guide us as we put those desires into action.

[5] Solomon's Temple would be structurally like Moses' Tabernacle, but would be marked by the same vibrant worship as David's Tabernacle (1 Chronicles 23:3–5; 25:1–31; 2 Chronicles 29:25–26). Once completed, Solomon would move the Ark into it and dismantle both of the Tabernacles (2 Chronicles 5:5).

[6] 1 Chronicles 22:6–10; 28:2–7. David's son would be called Solomon, meaning *Peaceful*, and the fact that David subdued all of Israel's enemies would mean that Solomon's unbloodstained hands could build.

that he pleaded with the Lord to let him do everything save actually to build the Temple. He bought its future site on Mount Moriah so that the blood sacrifices there would point to the better sacrifice which Abraham had prophesied. He received detailed building plans through the Holy Spirit and gathered all the materials that Solomon would need.[7] He organized the Levites, priests, musicians, gatekeepers and administrators so that Solomon's work would be easy. He devoted the rest of his reign to the building of a Temple which he knew that he would never see. He was simply too hungry for the glory of God's name to take no for an answer.

All of this begs the question: *How like the very hungry caterpillar are we?* Are we easily satisfied with a few minutes of singing on a Sunday, or with a Gospel conversation with an unbeliever once a month? Or are we like David, so ravenously hungry for the glory of God's name that we pour out our lives to build a place where he can dwell in our towns and cities? If there are already vibrant churches doing that, will we go and build in the other cities of the world where there are no such churches? At the very least, if we feel too weak to be a David or Solomon and lead the work of building, will we be as hungry as the hundreds of people mentioned in 1 Chronicles 23–26, who faithfully played a smaller role?

Don't be satisfied with the grubby life of a caterpillar, like so many of the Christians around you. Hunger like David for the glory of God's name and let him use you to produce his beautiful Church throughout the world.

---

[7] Compare *"the hand of the Lord"* in 1 Chronicles 28:19 with Ezekiel 1:3, 3:14 and 8:1. 1 Chronicles 22:14 tells us that he gathered gold and silver alone weighing about 3,500 and 34,000 tons.

Priority Five: The Covenant (7:8–29)

He is the one who will build a house for my Name,
and I will establish the throne of his kingdom for ever.

(2 Samuel 7:13)

In about 260 BC, the ancient mathematician Archimedes had a bath. He needed one from sweating over the task the king had given him of determining, without melting it down, whether or not his crown was made of pure gold. Everybody knew that it was impossible to measure the volume and density of an irregular object, so Archimedes needed inspiration and needed it fast. As he lowered himself into the bath, he displaced some water with his body and suddenly saw a way he could measure the crown's volume and density. *"Eureka! Eureka!"* he shouted in Greek as he ran down the street naked, too excited to stop to put back on his clothes. *"I've found it! I've found it!"*[1] When David asked permission to build a temple for the Lord, all heaven started shouting Eureka too.

It didn't matter that David's timing was all wrong. It was still music to the Lord's ears. He had been searching for centuries for the kind of person he could use, and David had finally proved himself to be the man.

David's request proved he was free enough from Saul's *pride* to be entrusted with true greatness. Saul felt that Israel's king deserved to live in a royal palace, but David was too aware of God's great glory to find peace living in a fine palace while the

[1] The first-century BC Roman architect Vitruvius relates this famous story in *De Architectura* (Book IX).

true King of Israel was dwelling above the Ark of the Covenant in a tent across the road. God had finally found somebody who cared much more for his honour than they did for their own. It was a Eureka moment which could launch the next chapter of God's plan.

When the Lord refused David's request, his response proved he was free enough from Saul's *disobedience* to be entrusted with true kingship.[2] Saul would not have asked a prophet's permission in the first place, and if a prophet had dared to thwart his plans he would have probably ended up like one of the priests at Nob. David had been excited when Nathan told him initially to *"Go ahead and do it, for the Lord is with you"*, but he submitted meekly to his change of heart the following morning after hearing from the Lord. 1 Chronicles fills in some of the gaps in this chapter by telling us that David could not build the Temple because he had shed too much blood on the battlefield to use those same hands to build a holy dwelling for the Lord,[3] but rather than trying to argue that he had shed that blood fighting battles for God's glory, David simply submitted to the Lord's plan instead of his own. Samuel had been right when he called David a man after God's own heart in 1 Samuel 13:14. Heaven shouted Eureka even louder. The Lord had finally found the kind of person he could use.

Like Archimedes and his bath, the Lord holds nothing back in his excitement over David. He makes a personal covenant with him in verses 5–16 which promises he will be the ancestor of the great Messiah who will upgrade the covenant God made with Israel at Sinai with a new and better covenant.[4] David had been passionate to make the Lord's name great, so *"I will make*

---

[2] The Lord reiterates in verse 8 that he made David a *nāgīd*, a *viceroy* who ruled under God as the true King.

[3] 1 Chronicles 22:6–10; 28:2–7.

[4] The word *forever* occurs eight times in this chapter because much of this covenant would be fulfilled through Jesus instead of Solomon.

your name great, like the names of the greatest men on earth."[5] David had been eager to replace God's tent with a great house, so *"The Lord himself will establish a house for you."*[6] David was anxious to ensure that Israel continued to worship the Lord's name long after he himself was dead and buried, so *"I will raise up your offspring to succeed you, your own flesh and blood, and I will establish his kingdom."*[7] David is astonished by God's naked kindness, and his reaction proves that heaven was shouting *"Eureka!"* for a reason.

David does not reply to Nathan, but simply stumbles across to the Tabernacle and sits before the Ark in the presence of the Lord.[8] He sits rather than standing because he recognizes that this covenant is a gift of grace which was not earned through works,[9] and he whispers incredulously: *"Who am I, Sovereign Lord, and what is my family, that you have brought me this far?"* It was enough for him to have been promoted from the sheep pen to the palace, from the shepherd's crook to the ruler's crown, but now the Lord has also made him unprecedented promises about his future. David's prayer is entirely focused on the Lord's plan to gain glory for himself through David and through Israel, so that *"your name will be great for ever. Then people will say, 'The Lord Almighty is God over Israel!'"* He refers to himself ten times as God's servant and to God nine times as either *the Sovereign Lord* or *the Lord Almighty*. Despite the fact that God

---

[5] We see a similar dynamic in Genesis 11:4 and 12:2. The builders of Babel want their names to be famous yet become anonymous, while Abraham wants the Lord's name to be famous yet becomes famous himself.

[6] As in English, the word *house* in Hebrew can refer to both a building and a dynasty.

[7] The Lord also uses a play on words when he promises Israel *a home of their own* in verse 10, since the word he uses is the root of the normal Hebrew word for *tabernacle*.

[8] This is what is meant in verse 18 by his "going in" and sitting "before the Lord".

[9] The Lord hints in verse 14 that Solomon and the future kings of Judah will not be as obedient as David. Nevertheless, the Lord promises to bless David's house and make him ancestor to the Messiah anyway.

has promised him far greater fame than Saul tried to steal, his years in God's school of purity have made him so hungry for the glory of God's name that he maintains a proper focus.

David was a prophet, and there are clues here that he understood the depth of what God truly promised him through this covenant.[10] He uses a strange Hebrew phrase in verse 19 which means literally *"is this the law of man?"* and which is probably best translated *"Is this your normal manner of dealing with a human being?"* The writer of 1 Chronicles, expanding on this passage centuries later, deliberately changes these words to bring out what was on David's heart when he said this, and tells us in 17:17 that he added literally, *"You have seen me as a type of the Man who is on high."* David did not simply praise God for treating him better than most other people. He praised him as a prophet who saw that the son God promised was not just Solomon but Jesus the Messiah.[11] In case we miss this, 1 Chronicles 17:14 also changes the reference to *David's* house and kingdom here so that it is *the Lord's* house and kingdom instead.

As David sits back and enjoys the reward God gives to the kind of people he can use, he also wants us to be stirred to receive the same reward ourselves. He wants us to display this same humility, obedience and commitment to see God's name glorified throughout the nations. David's son Solomon inherited his throne and started building the Temple in Jerusalem in 966 BC, but David's greater Son Jesus has inherited his throne forever and has started building his New Covenant Temple – the Church – in every nation of the world.[12] Jesus is still looking for

---

[10] This is one reason why he didn't receive this covenant passively, but prayed so fervently for its fulfilment.

[11] The Hebrew word for *offspring* in verse 12 is *zera'*, which literally means *seed* and is the same word which the Lord used repeatedly in Genesis to describe both Isaac and Jesus. See Galatians 3:16, 19, 29.

[12] 1 Kings 6:1, 38. 1 Chronicles 22:6–10 and 28:5–7 adds us that the Lord told David at this time that his temple-building son had not yet been born and must be named Solomon, which means *Peaceful*.

people who will become heirs alongside him to the covenant which God made with David in this chapter.[13]

Is this God's normal way of dealing with a human being? Jesus tells us that it is when he sees the kind of person he can use. He invites us to join his building team and to make heaven resound again with excited cries of *"Eureka!"*

---

[13] See Matthew 16:18; 1 Corinthians 3:16; 2 Corinthians 6:16; 1 Peter 2:5. This is why Hebrews 1:5 quotes 2 Samuel 7:14 and applies the promise directly to Jesus the Messiah.

Priority Six: The Nations
(8:1–18; 10:1–19)

King David dedicated these articles to the Lord, as he had done with the silver and gold from all the nations he had subdued.

(2 Samuel 8:11)

For a former shepherd-boy from small-town Bethlehem, David certainly had an expansive view of the world. If you assume from 2 Samuel 8 and 10 that he saw the nations around Israel as nothing more than people groups to be conquered, then you need to think again. David was hungry to share God's glory with the world.

David conquered the nations around Israel in order to demonstrate *God's greatness* compared to their idols. Even as a teenager, David had grasped from the Law of Moses that Israel's battles with the nations were primarily battles between their God and pagan idols.[1] This made him view his struggle with Goliath as a continuation of that unfinished battle,[2] and made it a priority for his early days as king to finish what the Judges and Saul had failed to do – to defeat every nation which dared to boast that its idols were a match for Israel and its God. *"The earth is the Lord's, and everything in it,"* he wrote as the basis for his foreign policy in Psalm 24, refusing to accept that parts of

---

[1] He says this in 2 Samuel 7:23 based on verses such as Exodus 12:12 and 18:11 and Numbers 33:4. Even the Philistines and Joab understood this in 1 Samuel 5:7 and 2 Samuel 10:12.

[2] 1 Samuel 17:26, 36, 45–47, 54. 1 Chronicles 18:1 tells us that *Metheg Ammah* in verse 1 was another name for Gath, so David eventually annexed the city of Goliath and Achish.

the world belonged to Baal or Dagon any more than we should accept terms such as "the Muslim world" or "post-Christian Europe". After each successful campaign, 1 Chronicles 14:12 tells us, he burned the idols of the defeated nation and preached to his new subjects that there was only one true Living God, and that his name was Yahweh.[3]

David also conquered the nations around Israel in order to demonstrate *God's righteousness* in the face of their wickedness. These verses make uncomfortable reading for our twenty-first-century eyes because we have forgotten what these nations had done to Israel for several centuries. The Philistines had repeatedly occupied and plundered Israel, the Moabites had tried to curse them and to seduce them into sexual sin,[4] and the Ammonites brought shame on Israel's God in chapter 10 while sacrificing babies in the fire to their own national god Molech.[5] If we are uncomfortable with these verses, we simply show that we have not grasped God's righteous anger against sin as well as David did. We need to grasp it because these verses also serve as a prophecy of Jesus the Messiah's final judgment.[6]

David also conquered the nations around Israel in order to demonstrate *God's faithfulness* to his promises. The Lord had defined the borders of the Promised Land for Joshua and the Israelites, but they had never fully conquered it. Despite

---

[3] 8:11–12 and 1 Chronicles 18:8 underline this by telling us that David dedicated his plunder to the Lord to build his Temple in Jerusalem. He also made this the theme of Psalm 60 which he wrote at this time.

[4] Numbers 22–25. An eighth Moabite himself through his great-grandmother Ruth, David killed two-thirds of their soldiers but was careful not to annihilate them because of God's command in Deuteronomy 2:9.

[5] King Nahash of Ammon had tried to shame God's People in 1 Samuel 11, and his successor tries to do the same in 2 Samuel 10. David tells his messengers to wait in the ruins of Jericho while he avenges their honour.

[6] The *Moabites* and *Ammonites* to the east were the descendants of Lot. The Aramean cities of *Zobah*, *Damascus* and *Harnath* were in the north. The *Amalekites* and *Edomites* in the south were descendants of Abraham, and the *Philistines* were in the west. The Messiah's judgment will therefore reach in all directions.

God's fresh promises to Samson, Samuel and Saul, nor had they. David therefore took to heart the promise which is recorded in 3:18, that *"By my servant David I will rescue my people Israel from the hand of the Philistines and from the hand of all their enemies,"* and devoted his early reign to proving that God's promises were true. Don't miss the significance of the statement in verse 15 that *"David reigned over all Israel, doing what was just and right for all his people."* The writer is telling us that David finally conquered the entire Promised Land, and that he did so as prophetic assurance that God would be faithful to his covenant with David to install his Messiah as the righteous King of all the earth.

David therefore conquered these foreign nations in order to proclaim God's great name to the nations,[7] but he was less concerned with slaughter than he was about salvation. David wanted the nations to see God's glory because he was hungry to see the fulfilment of the Lord's promise to Abraham in Genesis 12:2–3 that he would save the nations through Israel. When the writer tells us literally in verses 6 and 14 that *"the Lord saved David wherever he went"*, he wants us to understand that these chapters do more than simply prove that one day God will judge unbelievers. He wants us to see them as a promise that even now God wants to come and save them.

1 Chronicles 16:7–36 holds the key which helps us to understand these chapters,[8] since it records the psalm which David wrote for the opening of his Tabernacle, and which invites the Gentile nations to come and find salvation through

---

[7] We discover in 8:13 that, as in chapter 7, the Lord responded to David's hunger to make him famous by making David famous too.

[8] 1 Chronicles 18:4 and 19:18 also suggest that our surviving manuscripts of 2 Samuel may contain a few copying errors. 8:4 should read that David captured *1,000 chariots and 7,000 charioteers*, and 10:18 should read that he killed *7,000 charioteers and 40,000 foot soldiers*. 1 Chronicles 18:12 and Psalm 60 also clarify that Joab and Abishai helped David defeat the Edomites, killing 12,000 on the battlefield and 6,000 in the pursuit.

Israel's God.[9] He tells the Israelites in verse 24 that their calling is to share the Gospel with foreigners – something which David evidently modelled personally since the list of his mighty men in 2 Samuel 23 includes a Zobahite, an Ammonite and a Hittite. He preaches to the Gentiles in verses 25–30 that their gods are mere idols (literally *worthless things*) and that they need to join Israel in recognizing Yahweh as the true King of all the earth.[10] He ends by appealing to them to cry out to the Lord in verse 35: *"Save us, God our Saviour, gather us and deliver us from the nations, that we may give thanks to your holy name, and glory in your praise."*[11] This was David's global vision for his Tabernacle on Mount Zion, so it is not surprising that the apostle James quotes from Amos 9:11 in Acts 15:16–18 to teach Jewish Christians that God wants to rebuild the Tabernacle of David (not of Moses) through the Church and to save an international community of believers from every nation of the world.

So don't be confused by these two chapters and their gory description of David's military victories over the nations. He fought these battles in order to demonstrate that the Lord is greater, more righteous and more faithful than any foreign idol, and he did so in order to save people from every nation, tribe and tongue. He did so to encourage us to play our own part in God's plan to conquer every nation through the Gospel. He did so in order that we will take the Messiah seriously when he commands us in Matthew 28:

---

[9] 1 Chronicles 16:8, 14, 23–24, 28, 30–31, 33, 35. This psalm was adapted later by the Levites into Psalms 96, 105 and 106 and became a key reminder of Israel's calling to preach the Gospel to the nations.

[10] The word for the Lord *reigning* in verse 31 is the root of the word *melek*. The nations needed to confess that their own kings were mere viceroys, and that the Lord was as much King of their nations as of Israel.

[11] This appeal goes out to every *clan* or *family* within each nation in verse 28, because the Lord wants to save people from every tiny people group, and not just from every nation.

All authority in heaven and on earth has been given to me. Therefore go and make disciples of all nations, baptizing them in the name of the Father and of the Son and of the Holy Spirit, and teaching them to obey everything I have commanded you. And surely I am with you always, to the very end of the age.

Priority Seven: The Gospel (9:1–13)

So Mephibosheth ate at David's table like one of the king's sons.

(2 Samuel 9:11)

Anthony Garcia tried to plead the fifth amendment when he was arrested for murder in April 2011, but he had already waived his right to remain silent at a tattoo parlour. Detectives found guilt literally written all over him when they examined the tattoos on his chest and found a detailed picture of the murder scene outside a liquor store at Pico Rivera, eleven miles from Los Angeles, underneath the tell-tale words *"Rivera Kills"*.[1] Sometimes David ran out of opportunities to preach the Gospel verbally to the Israelites and Gentiles, so he looked for fresh ways to tattoo the Gospel in bold letters across his life. He did so in large things such as offering blood sacrifices outside his new Tabernacle, but chapter 9 gives us a smaller, more everyday example in order to provoke us to share the same priority as David and to scrawl the Gospel across our daily lives.

Mephibosheth was the *lowest of the low*. Verse 3 tells us that his life was dominated by the fact that his nurse panicked when he was a five-year-old and dropped him at the news that the Philistines had won the Battle of Gilboa. His legs had been irreparably shattered, and we can tell how disabled people were treated in his culture by the insults which the Jebusites traded with David and by the fact that Hebrew law barred disabled

---

[1] This story was reported in the *Los Angeles Times* on 22nd April 2011.

people from entering the royal palace or the Tabernacle.[2] As the only son of Saul's eldest son Jonathan, Mephibosheth ought to have been hailed as heir to his grandfather's dynasty, but the wily Abner had known that Israel would never follow a crippled king and had sidelined him in favour of his Uncle Ish-Bosheth instead.

Mephibosheth was also *David's greatest enemy*. There was a reason why David had to calm his fears in verse 7, since the first thing any founder of a royal dynasty did was to destroy the final remnants of the one which went before. That was why both Jonathan and Saul pleaded with David to spare their descendants' lives when he came to the throne,[3] and why Mephibosheth was hiding in a home across the River Jordan in faraway Lo Debar where Abner had taken him along with Ish-Bosheth for safety in the early days of Israel's civil war in 2:8. His exile from the true Promised Land, from the People of God and from the Lord's Tabernacle are a picture of the unsaved as Paul describes them in Ephesians 2: *"You were separate from Christ, excluded from citizenship in Israel and foreigners to the covenants of the promise, without hope and without God in the world."*

Mephibosheth was *not looking for David*. He knew his crippled body was not strong enough to curry favour through loyal service or lavish gifts. He knew that the worst he could expect was execution and that the best he could hope for was to be ignored. His greatest wish was for David, like the rest of Israel, to forget all about him, but David was about to tattoo the Gospel across his chest for all to see.

Verse 3 tells us that David came looking for Mephibosheth when he least expected it because of *"God's kindness"*. Verse 1 explains that he did so for the sake of his beloved friend who had died as the innocent victim of another person's sin on

[2] Leviticus 21:18–19; 2 Samuel 4:4; 5:6–8.

[3] 1 Samuel 20:14–17; 24:20–21. Contrast this with 1 Kings 15:29 and 16:11 and 2 Kings 10:11 and 11:1.

Mount Gilboa. With hindsight we can see that Jonathan's death serves as a picture of Jesus' crucifixion in the story, but the prophet who wrote 2 Samuel also grasped something of this too. Mephibosheth means *Dispeller of Shame*, and his other name Merib-Baal means *The Lord Pleads My Cause*.[4] The writer wants us to see that David removed the man's shame because the Lord had convicted him of his desire to proclaim the Gospel through his followers playing by very different rules from the rest of the world.

Mephibosheth needed to *admit* that he was in desperate need of being saved. If he had tried to insist that he was a royal heir and deserved recognition, his audience with David would have ended with an executioner's sword. Instead, he bows low as David's servant and refers to himself in verse 8 as *"a dead dog"*. This humble confession paves the way for him to receive salvation beyond his wildest dreams.

Second, Mephibosheth needed to *believe* that David's offer of salvation was genuine and permanent.[5] He needed to believe that David would truly grant him the inheritance which his grandfather had sinfully squandered in verse 11,[6] and that God's grace could truly transform a dead dog into a king's son through the innocent death of the beloved. He needed to accept this grace as a gift which involved no effort of his own (that's why verse 10 emphasizes that another must work instead of him), and to trust that this offer involved no probation period

---

[4] The word *Baal* was used in David's day to mean *the Lord* (5:20), but by the time that 1 and 2 Samuel were written it was only used to refer to the Canaanite idol. Therefore the writer uses the name Mephibosheth instead of Merib-Baal (1 Chronicles 8:34; 9:40). He does the same in 11:21 compared with Judges 9:1.

[5] Since Mephibosheth named his son *Mika*, which means *Who Is Like [God]?*, these verses suggest that he was a man of bold faith like his father, not a man of weak disobedience like his grandfather.

[6] Verse 7 and Luke 19:10 tell us that Jesus won back for us all that Adam lost in the Garden of Eden.

because it was a permanent gift of grace.[7] Paul explains again in Ephesians 2:

> *God raised us up with Christ and seated us with him in the heavenly realms in Christ Jesus, in order that in the coming ages he might show the incomparable riches of his grace, expressed in his kindness to us in Christ Jesus. For it is by grace you have been saved, through faith – and this is not from yourselves, it is the gift of God – not by works, so that no one can boast.*

Third, Mephibosheth needed to *commit* his life to David, leaving his old life in Lo Debar behind in order to begin a new life at the royal court in Jerusalem.[8] The mighty men listed in chapter 23 would know David through their deeds, but Mephibosheth could know him better than them all through grace if he was willing to die to his old life and commit his future into David's hands.

So if you have read this far into 1 and 2 Samuel but have not yet surrendered your life to Jesus, don't read any further until you have responded to him like Mephibosheth. Admit, believe and commit your life to him. It's as easy as A-B-C.

If you are already a saved follower of Jesus, don't read any further until you have lifted your eyes up to see the millions around you who are not. God wants you to talk to them about Jesus, but he also wants you to tattoo his message across your life like Anthony Garcia in Los Angeles or like David in Jerusalem. He wants you to look out for ways to express his kindness towards those who are far from him through sin, yet are also loved through the death of Jesus Christ and the undeserved kindness of God.

---

[7] Verses 7, 10 and 13 stress that this offer of salvation was for *always*. It would even include his son Mika.

[8] Lo Debar means *Place of No Pasture*. What we give up to receive Christ is not worth clinging onto.

2 Samuel 11–24:

A Repentant Person

The Comeback King
(11:1–27)

After the time of mourning was over, David had her brought to his house, and she became his wife and bore him a son. But the thing David had done displeased the Lord.

(2 Samuel 11:27)

Anyone who watches horror movies can tell you that the villain rarely stays dead the first time they are killed. I forgot that once and was caught by such surprise that I spilled an entire bowl of cornflakes down myself. It was stupid and embarrassing, but it was nothing compared to the tragedy which hit David when he assumed that the Saul in his heart had died once and for all during his time in God's school of purity. He was about to be caught completely unawares by the comeback King Saul.

David's trouble was partly caused by Joab's failure to follow up diligently on his victory over the Ammonites the previous summer in chapter 10. David had been forced to march against the Ammonites again that autumn, but he had done so too late in the fighting season to conquer the capital city of Rabbah before winter.[1] When spring arrived, David therefore sent Joab out to complete what he had failed to finish the previous year.[2]

---

[1] Rabbah stood on the site of the modern-day city of Amman, the capital of Jordan.

[2] Since Solomon was aged about eighteen when he became king in 970 BC, the events of this chapter must have taken place in around 990 BC, halfway through David's forty-year reign.

David was left alone in Jerusalem and was ambushed as he walked on his palace roof by the undead Saul in his heart. He saw Bathsheba bathing naked on her roof, stopped to ogle her, invited her to the palace and ended up sleeping with her. When he discovered that she was pregnant, he brought her husband back from fighting the Ammonites and got him drunk so that he would sleep with her and conclude that the baby was his own. When Uriah proved more passionate for the Lord's glory than David and refused to enjoy the comforts of his wife while the Lord's Ark was out on campaign, David ordered Joab to murder him and then married Bathsheba while her husband's grave was still freshly laid. How could the man after God's own heart behave so much like King Saul? What is the meaning behind this shocking story, and behind the fifth and final section of 1 and 2 Samuel?

The writer uses David's failure to show us the kind of person God can use.[3] If he had stopped after the fourth section, we might have assumed that God only uses perfect people who are not like us. In section five we discover that David was a picture of the perfect Messiah, but that this didn't mean that he was always picture-perfect himself. God wants to encourage us that alongside humility, obedience, purity and passion for his name, he also prizes heartfelt *repentance*. David sinned like Saul at times, but unlike Saul he quickly repented of his sin. God wants to encourage us that he can still use us in our sin and weakness, so long as we keep a short account with him and learn how to repent each time we fail.

The writer also uses David's failure in order to warn us against the power of temptation. If you go shark-fishing in a dinghy, you will become the bait yourself, and if you think fighting off the comeback King Saul in your heart is easy, you will have a shock like David. Let's examine the stages through

---

[3] The writer of 1 Chronicles has a different purpose in mind, so he barely records the events of 2 Samuel 11:1–21:14 at all. They do not fit within his wider goal of renewing the Jewish national vision after the exile.

which temptation overcame the man after God's own heart in this chapter, to learn some lessons for our own lives.

David's mistake began over twenty years before he ever set foot on his palace roof. He had ignored the Lord's command in Deuteronomy 17:17 that a king *"must not take many wives, or his heart will be led astray"*, and he had acted like the polygamous kings of the pagan nations. By the time he was crowned king of Judah, he had three wives, and before he was crowned king of Israel he had four more. Once he captured Jerusalem, he married several more women in addition to taking more than ten concubines.[4] He grew complacent to the danger because his sin appeared to go unpunished for many years, but he discovered all too late that he had never properly learned to restrain his desire for women. By the time he saw his friend's beautiful wife naked and remembered that her husband was away at war, he had already built a path to disobedience like Saul.[5]

If first base in David's temptation was his polygamy, then second base was neglect of duty. He sent others to serve the Lord when he should himself have led his troops to war, and the Devil soon found work for his idle hands and eyes to do back home.[6] It didn't take long from the moment that David neglected the seven priorities of his reign until he started to rule in disobedience like Saul.

David moved to third base when he didn't look away from Bathsheba's naked body and sent messengers to find out more about her and invite her to his palace.[7] It was only a short step

---

[4] 1 Samuel 25:42–43; 2 Samuel 3:2–5; 5:13; 15:16.

[5] Uriah the Hittite is listed as one of David's trusted mighty men in 23:39. He trusted David so implicitly that he delivered his own death warrant unsuspectingly in verses 14–15.

[6] Although the Hebrew text says that spring was the time when *messengers* went off to war, 1 Chronicles 20:1 confirms the Septuagint reading that it was the time when *kings* went off to war.

[7] Bathsheba may also have been sinning through her immodesty, but David's palace was so much taller than the other buildings in Jerusalem that she may

from the dining hall into his royal chamber, and only a small step once inside into the warmth of his royal bed. David toyed with this temptation as if it were cute and controllable like a little lion cub, but he forgot that lion cubs grow into terrible man-eating lions.[8]

David moved to the home plate when he discovered that Bathsheba was pregnant. He had forgotten his once-bright passion for God's glory, but Uriah was too pure to sleep in his wife's arms while the Ark of the Covenant was in a military tent.[9] Caught between a pregnant wife and a husband who was too godly to co-operate with his cover-up plan, David feared scandal and planned murder.[10] He enlisted Joab to kill a squad of his own soldiers by sending them on a suicide mission in order to fool people that Bathsheba's baby was her husband's and free her to become his umpteenth queen.[11] David's plan seemed successful at first, but the murder of Uriah had raised from the dead the little Saul in his heart. We are told in words reminiscent of Saul's reign in verse 27 that *"the thing David had done displeased the Lord."*[12]

God wants us to be encouraged that sinful but repentant people are still the kind of people he can use. However, he will also convince us through this fifth section that toying with the

---

have thought that no one could see her in her courtyard.

[8] Genesis 4:7 and James 1:14–15 both treat temptation as a lion cub which grows up into a mighty lion.

[9] Although Uriah was a foreigner, his name means *The Lord Is My Light* and his passion for Yahweh stands in stark contrast with that of the man who called Israel to preach the Gospel to the Gentiles.

[10] Since verse 4 tells us that Bathsheba had purified herself publicly from her period since Uriah went to war (Leviticus 15:19–30), there was no way that anyone would believe the baby was her husband's.

[11] The reference to Abimelek being killed by a woman dropping a millstone on his head while he was besieging her city of Thebez comes from Judges 9.

[12] David says literally to Joab in verse 25, *"Do not let this thing be evil in your eyes."* The writer responds by telling us literally in verse 27 that *"The thing which David did **was** evil in the Lord's eyes."*

pride, disobedience and wilfulness of Saul will turn our lives into a living nightmare.

So let's not be like David who looked, lusted, lapsed and lamented. Let's be like Joseph when he faced a similar temptation in Genesis 39 and refused to go even to first base with temptation. We read in verse 10 that *"though she spoke to Joseph day after day, he refused to go to bed with her **or even to be with her**."*

Let's not forget that horror-movie villains don't die easily, and that the Saul in our hearts is a comeback king.

A Pure Heart (12:1–25)

Then David said to Nathan, "I have sinned against the Lord."

(2 Samuel 12:13)

One of my friends is a top barrister who specializes in defending London gang members who are accused of rape or murder. She is the first to admit that her job is seldom easy. Even when her clients are innocent, they usually have such a terrible track record of previous convictions that it is very hard to convince the jury. Their behaviour in the run-up to a crime is often the pivotal factor in whether or not she can convince a court to show them mercy.

David, on the other hand, had a track record second to none. As a boy, he had written worship psalms and worked so diligently as a shepherd that the Lord chose him to be the ruler of his People. As a teenager, he had risked his life fighting Goliath in order to defend the Lord's honour. In his twenties, he had graduated as a star student from God's school of purity. In his thirties, he had conquered Jerusalem, built a Tabernacle, brought back the Ark of the Covenant and led his nation back to God. If any person's track record could atone for a short period of sin, it was David's. But he showed he was still the kind of person God could use when he repented at a rebuke from the prophet Nathan that the Lord had put his life on trial.

It is one thing to hear God speak, but quite another to have the wisdom to communicate what he says.[1] Nathan uses a

---

[1] Jesus does this perfectly in John 4:16–18, and even Joab knew how to do so in 2 Samuel 14. Compare this with the brashness of the young Joseph in Genesis 37:5–11.

parable to trick David into passing the death penalty on himself. David was used to playing judge and preaching the Gospel. Nathan turns the tables and tells him that he is the accused and the one who needs forgiveness through the Gospel.

We might have expected David to appeal to his *devotion to God's Word*. He didn't simply love Scripture, he wrote large sections of it! He taught Israel to sing that *"The decrees of the Lord are firm, and all of them are righteous. They are more precious than gold, than much pure gold; they are sweeter than honey, than honey from the honeycomb... In keeping them there is great reward."*[2] He loves God's Law so much that he instantly knows in verse 6 that Exodus 22:1 demanded fourfold repayment for a stolen sheep. But David doesn't appeal to his love of Scripture for forgiveness because he knows it hasn't stopped him breaking the sixth, seventh, eighth, ninth and tenth commandments over Bathsheba. He remembers that Deuteronomy 22:22 commands that an adulterous man and woman must be executed.

We might have expected David to appeal to his *virtuous track record*. After all, he had achieved more for God's glory during his thirteen years reigning in Jerusalem than the fourteen judges and Saul had achieved together in 350 years. If anyone had ever earned the right to forgiveness then it was him, but he doesn't try to appeal to his virtuous track record for forgiveness either. He knew the Law of Moses well enough to spot that Adam and Eve had a better track record than his, yet they had been banished from the Garden of Eden for committing just one sin.[3] He also remembered that God was unimpressed when they tried to cover over their sin and shame with man-made clothes of fig leaves, killing an innocent animal to cover them with its sacrificial skin instead.

---

[2] Psalm 19:9–11. He may also have written the anonymous Psalm 119 which extols the Word of God.

[3] Genesis 3:1–24. We do not know how long Adam and Eve lived in the Garden before they sinned, but it may well have been longer than David's entire lifetime.

Like my friend's guilty clients, David knew he had no option but to throw himself on the mercy of the court. When Nathan tells him in verses 9–10 that he has despised both the Lord and his Word, he quickly confesses that *"I have sinned against the Lord."*[4] When Nathan adds in verse 14 that his actions have provided fuel for God's enemies to ignore his hard work in section four and despise the Lord's name, he doesn't try to argue.[5] Instead, he cries out in Psalm 51, which he wrote at this time:

> *Have mercy on me, O God... Wash away all my iniquity and cleanse me from my sin... You are right in your verdict and justified when you judge... Cleanse me with hyssop, and I will be clean; wash me, and I will be whiter than snow... Create in me a pure heart, O God.*[6]

Paul comments on David's repentance in Romans 4:6–8. He tells us that David knew better than to try to rely on works to remain the kind of person God could use. David could see that attempting to earn forgiveness would be as proud and disobedient as his adultery and murder. Instead, he responded to the Gospel he had preached so often through his lifestyle and his words. Although he was the star student in God's school of purity, he pleaded with the Lord to make him truly pure through the blood of a far better Messiah.

Having been forgiven instantly in verse 13, David quickly

---

[4] In contrast, Exodus 20:20 tells us that when we refuse to sin we demonstrate our high regard for the Lord.

[5] The Hebrew of verse 14 reads that David's sin caused the Lord's enemies to despise him, but some English translations change this since his sin was not yet widely known. Either way, sin is the opposite of worship.

[6] The title of Psalm 51 tells the director of music to use it in corporate worship in the Temple. This psalm therefore aims to teach God's People how they must repent too.

returns to his godly character of before.[7] He shows his *humility* by dressing in sackcloth to pray and fast for a week on the floor. He shows his *obedience* by trusting in God's wisdom and worshipping him even when Bathsheba's newborn baby dies. He shows his *passion for God's glory* by naming their second son together Solomon, the name commanded by the Lord for his future temple-builder, which was a sign of recommitment to the Lord's plans for the future.[8] He shows his *purity* by also naming him Jedidiah, which means *Loved By The Lord*, as instructed by the prophet Nathan, as a promise that he will devote the rest of his life to teaching his successor to be the pure-hearted kind of person God can use.

This chapter therefore warns us not to try to seek forgiveness by appealing to our character or track record. If even David's long list of good works could not save him, then nor can ours.

It also warns us not to be discouraged when we sin, because God can still use us if we repent as wholeheartedly as David. By grace, he can renew in us the pure heart which makes us the kind of people he can use.

Psalm 51 ends by telling us what to say to God each time we sin: *"You do not delight in sacrifice, or I would bring it; you do not take pleasure in burnt offerings. My sacrifice, O God, is a broken spirit; a broken and contrite heart you, God, will not despise."*

---

[7] Although there would be terrible consequences to David's sin, he was forgiven immediately and without the need to serve any penance or probation period.

[8] 1 Chronicles 22:6–10; 28:2–7. We can see God's grace towards David since he stops viewing Bathsheba as *Uriah's wife* in verses 10 and 15 and starts viewing her as *David's wife* in verse 24. This grace goes even further in Matthew 1:6, where we read that David and Bathsheba's son became the ancestor of Jesus.

Do Babies Go to Heaven? (12:18–23)

Can I bring him back again? I will go to him, but he will not return to me.

(2 Samuel 12:23)

One of my hardest tasks as a church leader has been to counsel parents after a miscarriage or the death of a child. Since one in five pregnancies ends in miscarriage and one in twenty babies born in the world dies before its fifth birthday, it's a very real issue. The parents often ask for assurance that their baby is in heaven, and it's to these verses that I turn. As David grieves for his newborn baby son, he gives parents vital hope if they ever have to ask that tragic question.

I begin by explaining that God does not fully answer their question for a reason. The Roman poet Lucretius was right when he said that *"Religion can prompt such evil deeds in people,"* because Church history is full of people who have used proof texts from Scripture to justify horrific crimes.[1] Imagine what parents might have done in the Middle Ages if they had believed they had a cast-iron guarantee that their children would go to heaven if they died before their fifth birthday, but not thereafter. Even last year when I googled this question, I found a blog which suggested that *"If babies go to heaven when they die, abortion can't be wrong."* God knew what he was doing when he decided not to give us a complete answer to our question.

---

[1] Lucretius writing in the first century BC in his poem *On the Nature of Things* (1.101).

Next, I have to share the bad news that the Bible doesn't share our culture's sentimental view of children. While David was praying for his dying baby, he wrote in Psalm 51:5 that *"I was sinful at birth, sinful from the time my mother conceived me."* Scripture talks about babies responding positively or negatively towards the Lord while still in their mother's womb.[2] If it assures us that babies go to heaven then it certainly doesn't do so by teaching that they are conceived as innocent little people who are free from sin.

This leads into the good news which David discovered in the midst of his own family tragedy. Although he sometimes talked in general terms in the Psalms about the abode of all the dead, there are clues that he is talking specifically about heaven when he says of his baby in verse 23 that *"Now that he is dead... I will go to him, but he will not return to me."*[3] He said no such thing in 18:33 when his sinful adult child Absalom died, wailing without hope, *"My son, my son Absalom! If only I had died instead of you – O Absalom, my son, my son!"* David worshipped the Lord with faith in chapter 12, but he lamented very differently in chapter 18 because he understood that God judges babies differently from adults. He loved the Law of Moses enough to know that God promised in Deuteronomy 1:35–39 that *"No one from this evil generation shall see the good land I swore to give your ancestors, except... your children **who do not yet know good from bad** – they will enter the land."* Isaiah 7:15 picks up on this verse and suggests a child reaches an "age of discretion" *"when he knows enough to reject the wrong and choose the right".*

Is David therefore promising us that all babies and young children who die go to heaven? No. He is hinting at something which Jesus unpacks further when a paralysed man is brought to him for healing in Mark 2:1–12. The gospel writers do not tell

---

[2] Genesis 25:22–23; Psalm 22:10; 58:3; Job 15:14; Luke 1:41–44.

[3] David echoes 1 Samuel 28:19 when he refers in general to the place of all the dead in Psalms 6:5 and 30:9. However, he makes a distinction between *heaven* and *hell* in Psalms 16:10–11, 17:14–15 and 139:8.

us if the man was mentally as well as physically disabled, but they all agree that his friends were the ones who brought him to Jesus and that he himself had a non-speaking role. Mark tells us that *"when Jesus saw **their** faith"* he turned to the weak and vulnerable man and told him, *"Son, your sins are forgiven."* This suggests that the very young and the mentally disabled tend to believe whatever their parents or their closest friends tell them is true. The paralysed man trusted in his friends' faith that Jesus heals and saves, which suggests that children also do the same to whatever level is reasonable for their age.

I have four children under seven, so this question is not merely academic for my family. When I look at each one of them, I think of what David learned through the death of his baby son in 2 Samuel 12.

When I look at my *six-month-old*, I am reminded that I need to trust God with the full answer to this question. Should anything happen to him – perish the thought – I have enough grounds in this chapter to trust that his eternal destiny is secure. If David could write literally in Psalm 8:2 that the Lord gains glory *"through the praise of suckling babies and breastfeeding infants"*, then I can trust him to build a relationship with my son in a manner that a six-month-old can handle. I can also comfort Christian parents who have miscarried or buried a little baby with the same faith which David found as he buried his own baby.

When I look at my *two-year-old*, I am reminded not to neglect spiritual disciplines while she is still young. Jesus rebuked his disciples in Luke 18:15–17 for thinking he was not interested in building a relationship with toddlers, and I must not make the same mistake as they did. Since my daughter is still at the age where she will believe me if I tell her black is white and white is black, I need to make sure I make the most of this time to instruct her in the basics of the Gospel. I need to tattoo the Gospel across the daily life of our family and to take every opportunity to tell her about Jesus' sacrifice for sin. Were something to happen to her, like the paralysed man in Mark 2, her salvation would depend largely on what she had learned through her parents' faith.

When I look at my *five-* and *six-year-olds*, I am reminded that I need to lead my children to a personal decision. The Bible does not specify when a child reaches the "age of discretion", but since it happens when a child *"knows enough to reject the wrong and choose the right"*, I have to assume that it happens pretty young nowadays. I cannot wait until their teenage years and leave it to chance that they will respond to the Gospel on a youth camp far from home. I need to teach them the Gospel and urge them to respond to it as a five-year-old, as a six-year-old and repeatedly as their understanding grows with age.

In *The Lord of the Rings*, King Théoden kneels at his son's graveside and grieves that *"No parent should have to bury their child."* The wizard Gandalf reassures him that *"He was strong in life. His spirit will find its way to the halls of your fathers."*[4] David gives us far better reassurance in this chapter in case tragedy strikes our own families, or in case we need to bring hope to those around us. The Father who watched his own Son die at Calvary stands next to his People at the graveside and reassures them that they can *"Let the little children come to me."*[5]

---

[4] *The Lord of the Rings: The Two Towers* (New Line Cinema, 2002).
[5] Luke 18:16.

Domino Rally (12:26–13:39)

The king's sons came in, wailing loudly. The king, too, and all his attendants wept very bitterly.

(2 Samuel 13:36)

The Dutch get very excited about domino rallies. Almost a quarter of the entire Dutch population tuned in to watch their nation break the world record for the largest domino rally in human history on 13th November 2009. A single domino was knocked over to unleash a massive chain reaction which toppled almost four and a half million dominoes in ninety minutes of mesmerizing television.

David unintentionally launched the greatest domino rally of the Old Testament when he sinned with Bathsheba. He only realized what he had done when Nathan prophesied in 12:10–12 that his secret sin had unleashed a series of public disasters. His newborn baby would die, his wives would be raped and civil war would tear apart both his family and kingdom. God reassured us in 12:13 that he will forgive us when we repent of our sin, but he warns us for the rest of 2 Samuel that forgiveness does not mean that our sin has no terrible consequences. He promised Moses in Exodus 20:20 that *"the fear of God will be with you to keep you from sinning"*, and he wants to use the chain reaction unleashed by David's sin to teach us how to fear him and avoid a domino rally worthy of a Dutchman.

Domino number one was the effect which David's sin had on ungodly Joab in 12:26–31. Relations between David and his nephew had been poor since the murder of Abner in chapter 2 and David's attempt to replace him as commander of his army in 1 Chronicles 11. While Joab begrudgingly respected his uncle as a man of God, his resentment was held in check, but when his uncle commanded him to murder one of his best officers their fragile relationship broke down. Joab succeeded in his fresh campaign against the Ammonite capital city of Rabbah, and sent a threatening message back to David that he must leave the comforts of the palace and rejoin his army: *"Otherwise I shall take the city and it will be named after me."*[1] David didn't like the thought of Joabsville, so he was forced to dance to his nephew's tune and march out hastily to Rabbah.

Domino two was the effect which David's sin had on his eldest son Amnon. The prince had developed an infatuation with his teenaged half-sister,[2] but the Hebrew word for *virgin* means literally *separated one* and tells us that he had no way to get close enough to tell her about his feelings and to ask if they were mutual. Another of David's nephews, this time Jonadab, was sufficiently disenchanted with his uncle to foment trouble in his home.[3] He advised Amnon to take a leaf out of his father's book and invite his sister Tamar to his house on a pretext in order to lure her into bed, and Tamar's refusal of his advances revealed just how confused Amnon was in the wake of his father's sexual sin.[4] Knowing that his father had used violence to seduce the woman he desired, he didn't fear to rape Tamar before throwing her out of his house once he had used her. 13:20 appears to make a conscious link back to David's crime,

---

[1] His message was not sent out of humility but brash rebellion. He knew he had fresh power over David through his murder, and resented the king's hypocrisy for having lectured him earlier over Abner's murder.

[2] 3:3 tells us that David married the mother of Absalom and Tamar after he became king of Judah in 1010 BC. Tamar was therefore probably in her late teens when her half-brother raped her.

[3] Jonadab cynically uses the trouble he causes as a means to ingratiate himself with David later in 13:32–35.

[4] She was probably stalling for time by suggesting David would ignore Leviticus 18:11 and allow them to marry. Nonetheless, her hope that Amnon might believe her shows how much he had lost his moral bearings.

since it echoes David's attempt to convince Joab in 11:25 that his sin should not be taken too seriously.[5]

Domino three toppled over as a result of David's failure to discipline Amnon's sin. He knew that the penalty for rape in Deuteronomy 22:24 was execution, but he probably felt too ashamed of his own sexual sin to enforce the law. Therefore, like Simeon and Levi when their father Jacob failed to avenge their sister's rape in Genesis 34, Absalom decided to take vengeance into his own hands. He had the added motive that Amnon was David's eldest son and David's second-born had died young,[6] so murdering Amnon would make the third-born Absalom the new heir to the throne. 13:23 tells us that he waited patiently for two years to find an opportunity to lure Amnon to his death as Amnon had lured Tamar to his bedroom. David had started a domino rally through his sexual sin and murder, and now the chain reaction resulted in sexual sin and murder within his family.

Domino four came hot on the heels of this murder, as Absalom sought refuge from Israelite justice with his maternal grandfather in the Aramean kingdom of Geshur.[7] He lived there for three years imbibing his grandfather's pagan thinking, and learned to regard Israel's monarchy like Saul. David may have married the daughter of King Talmai in order to bolster his alliances with the Arameans, but his conquest and plunder of several Aramean cities in chapter 8 meant that the locals had poisoned Absalom's heart towards his father by the time he returned to Jerusalem. God wants us to grasp that Absalom's

[5] There is also a link back to Joseph, since this Hebrew word is only used to describe his ornate robe and hers. Joseph's brothers tore his coat to conceal their sin, but she tore her coat to expose her brother's sin.

[6] Amnon, Kileab and Absalom are mentioned in that order in 3:2–3, but Kileab (1 Chronicles 3:1 calls him by his other name, Daniel) must have died young since he is not mentioned in these chapters and David's fourth-born Adonijah believed he was the rightful heir to the throne in 1 Kings 1.

[7] 3:3 tells us that King Talmai of Geshur was the father of Absalom's mother Maakah.

subsequent rebellion was the direct result of the domino rally which David started when he sinned by failing to look away from the naked body of Bathsheba.

Domino five came later, when David's wisest counsellor Ahithophel joined Absalom's rebellion and almost caused it to succeed. At first glance his betrayal seems unfair and unexpected, but not when we compare 11:3 and 23:34. They reveal that Ahithophel was the grandfather of Bathsheba and had been appalled by the way in which David had abused his granddaughter and her husband. He was so disgusted by the hypocrisy of the king who claimed to have a passion for God's name that he nursed this grudge against him for eleven years. Sometimes sin's domino rally takes a long time to fall, but God wants us to understand that it topples all the same.

Domino six falls at the end of 2 Samuel when Absalom's rebellion fails. When David's enemies see how easily his friends and family have managed to defy him, they seize the opportunity to launch fresh attacks of their own. Saul's tribe of Benjamin rebels against his rule in chapter 20, and the Philistines attempt to renew their fortunes through launching fresh raids on the wealthy towns of Israel. Like a Dutchman on Red Bull, the writer of 2 Samuel keeps the domino rally falling. He wants us to view sin's deadly consequences as intensely as the English Puritan, Ralph Venning, when he urged his readers:

> *Oh, look to yourself, for sin, notwithstanding all its flattering pretences, is against you, and seeks nothing less than your ruin and damnation... Sin disappoints men; they have false joys but true miseries... There is not, nor can there be any profit to man by sin... Sin costs dear, but profits nothing. They make a bad purchase who buy their own damnation.*[8]

---

[8] Ralph Venning in *The Plague of Plagues* (1669), since republished as *The Sinfulness of Sin*.

God invites you to consider the fate of David, Joab, Amnon, Absalom, Ahithophel, the Benjamites and the Philistines through their sin. He wants you to be afraid because a fear of God will keep you from sinning and from starting sin's devastating domino rally in your own life too.

What God Desires
(14:1–22)

We must die. But that is not what God desires; rather, he devises ways so that a banished person does not remain banished from him.

(2 Samuel 14:14)

Last month I went for a walk with my family to the local duck pond. My wife and I parked our baby son's buggy and started playing a game of chase with our three older children. Imagine how I felt when I looked up and saw a freak gust of wind catch the buggy and cause it to roll towards the duck pond with our baby inside.

Usain Bolt would have struggled to keep up with me as I ran towards my son, but I couldn't reach the pond in time and his buggy fell into the water and started sinking. I was wearing my best clothes and had my iPhone and camera in my pocket, but moments like this reveal what we really treasure. I leapt into the pond and stopped my son from going under the water just in time. If you can picture me, dripping wet but gratefully cuddling my baby son next to the duck pond, it may help you to understand the message of chapter 14 and what God very eagerly desires.

The chapter begins with Absalom effectively exiled to the Aramean kingdom of Geshur. Joab knows that David misses him and, true to form, decides to take the matter into his own hands. He persuades a wise woman from Tekoa[1] to adopt

---

[1] Tekoa was a town in Judah which lay twelve miles south of Jerusalem. It was a wasteland frequented only by shepherds and therefore the perfect home

Nathan's successful strategy from chapter 12 and convince David to recall Absalom by telling him a made-up story. David isn't fooled by her flattering repetition of King Achish's words in 1 Samuel 29:9 and soon spots the hand of Joab behind her story, yet the woman is wise enough to tell him an important truth in verse 14: *"Like water spilled on the ground, which cannot be recovered, so we must die. But that is not what God desires; rather, he devises ways so that a banished person does not remain banished from him."*

Jesus confirms the wise woman's words in the three parables which he tells in Luke 15. He says that God is like a shepherd who leaves ninety-nine sheep in the field to go after one which is lost, like a woman who cleans her house from top to bottom to find a missing coin, or like a father who waits longingly for his prodigal son to return. He might even have said that God is like a dad who gladly sacrifices his iPhone and camera to dive into a duck pond and save his son. He wants us to understand that God is permanently creating ways to bring lost people to repentance so he can save them.[2]

Sadly, it would appear that the people in God's Church largely are not. We are more like the Levite in the Parable of the Good Samaritan in Luke 10 – so busy with our jobs and our Christian activities that we would rather cross the road to avoid those who are far from God than devise ways to bring them back to him. We are more like the priest – so full of fine ideas that we treat seeking and saving banished sinners as somebody else's job instead. One recent survey revealed that in the previous year almost half of Christians did not share their faith with anyone, that two-thirds did not give anyone an evangelistic pamphlet or a gospel, that four-fifths did not send a single letter or email to an unbeliever in the hope of converting them, and that nine-

---

for a wise old hermit (2 Chronicles 11:6; 20:20; Amos 1:1).

[2] Ungodly Joab fails to grasp that real repentance must always precede forgiveness. As a result, his ruse does David a great disservice because Absalom's heart was nothing like his father's repentant heart.

tenths did not take part in preaching the Gospel in a public place.[3] When it comes to devising different ways to reconnect banished people with the Lord, it appears that the majority of us are not doing very well at all.

Perhaps that's why the writer of 2 Samuel devotes three times as much space to the wise woman of Tekoa's audience with David as he does to an event like the capture of Jerusalem. He knows that God's People tend to struggle to feel the same passion as the Lord towards the lost people all around them. We are like the fishermen around the duck pond who looked up in concern when they saw my son's buggy rolling towards the water but did not think to drop their fishing rods and run to save him. So what can we do to increase the amount that we share the Lord's passion for lost souls as described by the wise woman in this passage?

One thing we can do is *go and discover how far away from God most unbelievers are.* As a church leader and author, I am constantly challenged by a throwaway comment by Bill Wilson: *"If I take that approach, I will become what so many other pastors, unfortunately, are – pencil-sharpening, paper-pushing administrators, so alienated from the people that they really think they are ministering by sitting in an office, living in the suburbs and writing books on evangelism."*[4] Therefore I block out days to take people from my church to engage strangers in the street about their spiritual beliefs and their knowledge about Jesus. Every time, I feel I am too busy to do it, but every time I come back feeling freshly dosed up with God's compassion. Matthew tells us it was this way even for Jesus, since two busy chapters of ministry precede his comment that *"When he saw the crowds, he had compassion on them, because they were harassed and helpless, like sheep without a shepherd."*[5]

---

[3] 2005 data from the *How Christians Share Their Faith* survey by the US-based Barna Group.

[4] Bill Wilson in his bestselling autobiography *Whose Child Is This?* (1992).

[5] Matthew 9:36. If Jesus grew in his love for the lost by going out among them, then we are unlikely to grow in our own love for the lost by waiting for it to come as we sit at home.

Another thing we can do is *devise a few experimental ways to bring unbelievers to God*. We tend to worry far too much that our evangelistic plans may fail, and we need to rediscover Jonathan's bias towards faith-filled action in 1 Samuel 14:6, when he attacked the Philistines on the basis that *"Perhaps the Lord will act on our behalf. Nothing can hinder the Lord from saving."* If the wise woman is right and God is constantly thinking up new ways to save the lost, then let's enjoy using our God-given creativity to join him as he does so. Let's think up ways to introduce unbelievers to a network of Christian friendships so they can see the Gospel through our lives. Let's plan events to which we can invite them to hear the Gospel message and a challenge to surrender to the Lord. Let's devise ways to share the Gospel message through mercy ministries, through the media, through politics, through education and through business. There is nothing that will stir our hearts with more passion for lost souls so much as seeing a person saved through an experiment that we have devised.

Our world is full of Absaloms – people who are angry, empty, banished and woefully complacent about their own souls. God wants us to see their lives as pushchairs rolling into the duck pond of hell, and to think up many different ways that we can dive into the water and reconcile them back to him. He wants us to go and lay hold of banished people and to tell them that the Father isn't first and foremost angry. He is waiting for the moment when one of his prodigals accepts a way back home.

The Home Front (14:23–24)

But the king said, "He must go to his own house; he must not see my face."

(2 Samuel 14:24)

Tiger Woods was at the height of his golfing career in November 2009. He had just played some of his best golf ever to lead the United States to victory in the Presidents Cup and had just been paid a record $3,300,000 for playing in a single tournament. *"There isn't a flaw in his golf or his makeup,"* marvelled fellow golfer Jack Nicklaus.

Then came some revelations which hit his career into the bunker. Although famous for his focus and diligence on the golf course, Tiger Woods had not shown the same virtues at home. He was forced to confess to having slept with over 120 women during his five-year marriage, and he lost far more than his wife and children as a result. Gillette, Accenture and TAG Heuer all dropped their big-money sponsorship deals with him, and his problems off the golf course made him go through 2010 without winning a single major tournament. *"I knew my actions were wrong, but I convinced myself that normal rules didn't apply,"* he later reflected. *"I had worked all my life. I felt I was entitled. I was wrong. I was foolish. I don't get to play by different rules."*[1]

Like Tiger Woods, David had assumed that he could play by different rules from the ones God set out for kings in Deuteronomy 17. To his credit, he had obeyed the command of verse 16 when he hamstrung the horses he captured on the

---

[1] This quote and the one at the end of the chapter come from a press conference on 19th February 2010.

battlefield in 2 Samuel 8:4. He knew that he would not succeed away from home if he based his strength on anything other than the Lord.[2] But he forgot to guard himself against more subtle dangers on the home front. He failed to obey the command of verse 17 that Israel's king *"must not take many wives, or his heart will be led astray"*. As the domino rally of judgment starts falling on his life, it emphasizes the importance of how we serve the Lord at home.

David knew the Law of Moses well enough to grasp that polygamy was wrong. Although Abraham and Jacob had married more than once, Genesis 2:24 taught that marriage was meant for one woman and one man, and Genesis 4:19 explained that polygamy was the sinful innovation of the line of Cain. David indulged his passions by taking at least twenty-five wives and concubines, amassing a harem like a pagan king and using marriage to build alliances with important grandees in Israel and in foreign lands.[3] His disobedience on the home front was judged through Amnon's sexual sin, and his sexual sin in private with Bathsheba would be judged through Absalom's sexual sin in public with ten of his concubines in 16:22.

David's polygamy was also the root of his problems with his sons in these chapters. He understood the importance of godly parenting, writing in Psalm 145:4 that *"One generation commends your works to another"*, and he gave his children names which spoke of his desire to shape them into the kind of people God could use. He fully intended to train sons such as Amnon (*Faithful*), Daniel (*God Is My Judge*), Absalom (*Father of Peace*), Adonijah (*My Lord Is Yahweh*), Shepatiah (*The Lord Is My Judge*) and Ithream (*For the Benefit of the People*) to serve the

---

[2] In Psalm 20:7 David says this was why he obeyed Deuteronomy 17:16 in 2 Samuel 8:4.

[3] 1 Samuel 25:40–44; 2 Samuel 3:2–5; 3:13–16; 5:13–16; 11:27; 15:16; 16:20–22. Despite his own sin, David forced Michal to honour her marriage vows when she tried to divorce him and marry someone else.

Lord.[4] However, with over twenty sons from his many wives, he quickly saw that he could not devote himself both to his kingdom and his kids. 1 Chronicles 27:32 tells us that he therefore hired a man named Jehiel to be their tutor and delegated the task of parenting to him. David preached the Gospel to the faraway nations, but he neglected to do the same to his sons back home.

David's neglect spelt disaster for *Amnon*. His firstborn son and heir apparent knew that his father was too weak to discipline him if he sinned. This emboldened him to rape his half-sister Tamar, and he was proven right when David got angry but did nothing in 13:21. Ironically, the king's failure to punish Amnon actually caused his death since it convinced Absalom that murder was his only hope for justice.[5] Perhaps Solomon was thinking about his older brother when he wrote in Proverbs 19:18 that parents who fail to discipline their children become *"a willing party to their death"*.

David's neglect also spelt disaster for *Absalom*. He knew so little about his children's lives that he didn't guess what Absalom had in mind when he invited Amnon to a party in the country. After he killed Amnon, his father let him hide among the Arameans rather than riding out with his army and forcing him to face up to his sin. Even when Joab convinced David to recall his banished son, he still gave him the silent treatment for two years in 14:28 instead of confronting him, and when he finally recalled him to the palace it was merely to sweep his sin under the carpet in 14:33. David had been able to resist large foreign armies on the battlefield, but 13:27 tells us literally that *"Absalom broke past him"* at home.

We will read in chapters 15–16 that David's failure on the home front allowed Absalom to mount an armed insurrection

---

[4] 2 Samuel 3:2–5; 5:14–15; 1 Chronicles 3:1–9; 14:4–7. We read in 2 Samuel 8:18 that he hoped they would serve as priests in his Tabernacle.

[5] David not only refused to carry out the command of Deuteronomy 22:24, but he also shielded Absalom from the Israelites carrying out the command of Numbers 35:31.

against his rule. Even then, David blamed his son's sins on his wicked advisers and refused to face up to the truth about him. The Lord had warned David in 7:14 that the true mark of a father's love is his willingness to discipline, but instead of learning the lesson he killed Absalom with superficial acts of kindness.

If we read on into 1 Kings, we also discover that David's failure on the home front spelt disaster for *Adonijah* and for *Solomon*. He had not taught his eldest surviving son to submit to the Lord any more than he had his brothers, so Adonijah lost his life for opposing David's choice of Solomon to be his successor as king. Solomon then went on to take what he had seen in his father to an even more destructive level. Taking a thousand wives and concubines, he discovered that Deuteronomy 17:17 had been right to warn that it would result in his being led astray to worship foreign gods. His idolatry with his wives plus his own failure to teach his many sons how to serve the Lord led to his kingdom being torn apart within months of his death.[6]

Tiger Woods looks back now and suggests that *"I made my share of mistakes. People can look at that as what not to do."* David suggests we do the same with his mistakes too. He warns us not to succeed at church, at work and far away at the expense of losing the battle where it matters most, at home. He invites us to treat his failure with his wives and children as our reason to be diligent on the home front for the Lord.

---

[6] 1 Kings 3:1–3; 11:1–13.

*Absalom sent secret messengers throughout the
tribes of Israel to say, "As soon as you hear the sound
of trumpets, then say, 'Absalom is king in Hebron.'"*

(2 Samuel 15:10)

David's son Absalom went into exile in Geshur, but by the time
he returned three years later he was very much the son of Saul.
The writer deliberately mirrors David's struggle with a false
messiah in 1 Samuel and his struggle with another false messiah
in 2 Samuel. He wants us to recognize that Absalom was King
Saul II, and he uses his rebellion against his father to remind us
about the kind of person God can use.

Absalom was just as *proud* as Saul. The writer wants us
to see the parallel between 1 Samuel 9:2 which tells us that
Saul was *"as handsome a young man as could be found anywhere
in Israel... a head taller than anyone else"* and 2 Samuel 14:25
which tells us that *"In all Israel there was not a man so highly
praised for his handsome appearance as Absalom. From the top
of his head to the sole of his foot there was no blemish in him."*
Absalom had inherited impressive outward appearance from his
uncles. It didn't bother him that the Lord had told his father that
his much younger half-brother Solomon was the next messiah.
One look at his face in the mirror and at his manly locks on the
hairdresser's floor was enough to convince him that he knew
better than the Lord.[1]

---

[1] Although 14:27 tells us that Absalom had three sons and a daughter, they
must have all died in childhood since 18:18 tells us that their father died without
an heir.

Absalom was just as *disobedient* as Saul. He had grown up as a neglected but pampered prince in his father's palace, and he was not accustomed to having his will crossed by anyone, not even by the Lord. We can see from 14:28–32 that he had learned from his Aramean grandfather in Geshur to reign as an independent king instead of co-operating with God's search for a viceroy. He summons the commander of Israel's army to his house like a common servant, and when Joab rightly refuses to dance to his tune he responds by torching his barley field in order to get his attention. He despises God's Tabernacle by saying that if he cannot get into the royal palace then he is no better off in Jerusalem than he was in Geshur. Like Saul, he is not interested in serving in heaven while he thinks he has a chance to reign in hell.

Absalom was just as *unrepentant* as Saul. He had lied to his father, murdered his half-brother and thrown in his lot with the Arameans, yet he still has the audacity to demand an audience with God's messiah and dare him in 14:32 to prove *"if I am guilty of anything"*! Unlike David, who murdered Uriah yet remained the kind of person God could use because of his soft-hearted repentance, Absalom hardens his heart so much like Saul that his conscience is too calloused to sense God's cry that he needs to be forgiven.[2] He bows before David in a false show of penitence in 14:33, but his words betray that in his heart he refuses to bow down to the Lord.

Absalom was just as *impure* as Saul. The Lord had graciously taken him into exile like his father for a three-year intensive stint in his school of purity, but he had dropped out of the course early on. While David had learned to surrender his ambitions to the Lord to such an extent that he refused to snatch at the crown even when his rival died, Absalom returned from Geshur with his ambition still strong and growing ever stronger.

[2] David hoped that two years of waiting in Jerusalem would convince Absalom to seek forgiveness at one of the Lord's two Tabernacles. Instead, it simply gave him courage to demand an audience with the king.

We read in 15:1–6 that he provided himself with a king's chariot and a royal entourage in the belief that if he looked the part then he would get the job. He went out early to meet those who came to plead their case at his father's court at the city gate, and he stole their hearts through false humility and flattering promises of what he would do for them if they made him king.[3]

Absalom had the same *lack of passion for God's name* as Saul. 15:7–12 tells us that he was as skilled as David's predecessor at using spiritual language and play-acting as a worshipper of the Lord. After four years of groundwork, he tells his father that he wants to fulfil a vow he made to the Lord in Geshur that he would worship him at Hebron if he brought his exile to an end.[4] He offers blood sacrifices on the Lord's altar, but he is rebelling against the very God he claims to serve. He does not care that the Lord has told his father that the young Solomon is the new messiah who will build a Temple to glorify God's name.[5] Now that Amnon is dead, Absalom is the natural heir apparent, so he hijacks Israel's religion as a vehicle towards achieving his ambition to glorify his own name. Therefore the Lord decides to deal with King Saul II as decisively as he had King Saul I.

This week I have been fitting a new kitchen in my home. I needed to adjust two old pipes – one made of lead and the other of cast iron. The lead pipe was soft and bendable like David, and I was easily able to twist and turn it into the kind of pipe

---

[3] When 15:6 tells us that Absalom *stole* the hearts of the Israelites, it is reminding us that at least God appointed Saul as his messiah, whereas Absalom was never anything more than a self-appointed messiah.

[4] Although a copyist's error in the Hebrew manuscript of 15:7 reads *forty* years, some manuscripts of the Septuagint still contain the correct reading of *four*. Absalom killed Amnon in *c.*988 BC, returned to Jerusalem in *c.*985 BC, was restored to David in *c.*983 BC and launched his rebellion in *c.*979 BC.

[5] 12:24–25 only hints that the prophet Nathan told David that his newborn baby son Solomon was God's beloved messiah rather than his older half-brothers, but 1 Chronicles 28:5–7 tells us plainly. Absalom's rebellion was therefore not just against his father, but against the Lord's sovereign choice of heir.

that I could use. The cast-iron pipe, however, was far too hard and unyielding so I had to take out an angle grinder, chop it up, throw it away and replace it with the kind of piping I could use. The writer of 2 Samuel wants to use the example of Absalom to remind us that if we refuse to repent and submit to God's plans like lead pipes then we must expect to feel his angle-grinder attacking the cast-iron rebellion of our hearts.

Solomon observed in Proverbs 16:18 that *"Pride goes before destruction, a haughty spirit before a fall,"* and God judges Absalom by using the Saul in his heart as the very means by which he thwarts his plans. Absalom's refusal to repent and submit to the Lord's will takes him into a battle with his father's army which he cannot win. His lack of passion for God's name means that he falls for Hushai's trickery instead of consulting the Urim and Thummim. Absalom's pride leads to his capture in 18:9 when his perfectly coiffeured head gets caught in a tree during the battle. His disobedience leads to his death in 18:14–15 when Joab finds him hanging from the tree and defies David's express instructions in order to avenge the destruction of his barley field.

So if you did not learn from the first King Saul how to be the kind of person God can use, then listen to the sound of God's angle grinder in these chapters. If we refuse to let God shape us like a lead pipe in his hands, then God offers us a cast-iron guarantee of judgment like King Saul I and King Saul II.

If he says, "I am not pleased with you," then I am
ready; let him do to me whatever seems good to him.
(2 Samuel 15:26)

When Absalom rebelled against him, David refused to assert his rights. He saw it as an opportunity to take a postgrad course in God's school of purity. He responded to Absalom's threat in the same way as he had done Saul's: he surrendered to the Lord's will as an old man as completely as he had when he was young. In doing so, he gives a masterclass in how we should respond to opposition.

David was about the same age that Saul had been when he realized David was a threat to his throne, and Absalom was about the same age as David at that time. This was therefore a moment of truth which would reveal if he would fight like Saul to remain king, even if it meant damaging God's Kingdom in the process. David passes the test with flying colours by deciding that hanging on to his throne by force as an old man would be just as sinful as seizing it by force as a young man. He decides to abandon Jerusalem in 15:14, even though it could have served as a perfect stronghold from which to fight, because he refuses to put God's People in danger in order to save himself or to risk defiling the city which is home to the Tabernacle which bears God's name.

In 15:13–37, David trusts that the Lord who put him on the throne will also restore him to it, even if he flees, because God still considers him the kind of person he can use. Since he loved the Law of Moses, it is likely that he remembered Numbers 16 and the way that Moses had refused to resist Korah's rebellion by force and had simply cried out to the Lord to vindicate his chosen ruler. Sure enough, as David leaves the city he finds that Joab declares that he is still on his uncle's side. He resents Absalom even more than he resents David, and his vote of confidence brings over to David large numbers of Israelite soldiers and foreign mercenaries. Among them is a Philistine from Gath named Ittai, who declares for David despite his many campaigns against his home city. He pledges that he would rather die as a fugitive alongside David than live in comfort under Absalom.[1] When the two high priests bring him the Ark of the Covenant and declare for him as well, David begins to see that when we trust God with the future, he never fails to help us in the present.

Although David refuses to subject the Ark to the dirty conditions of a fugitive, he is greatly encouraged by what their offer signifies. 1 Samuel 4:4 reminds us that the Ark was the Lord's earthly throne, so the prophet David seems to have grasped that the priests were telling him that by refusing to act like Saul he had acted like the true Messiah. Jesus would walk that same route 1,000 years later, from Jerusalem across the Kidron Valley to the Garden of Gethsemane on the Mount of Olives. He would take the words which David wrote at this time in Psalm 49 and apply them to his own rejection as Israel's King and to his own betrayal by Judas Iscariot, just like Ahithophel.[2] When the crowds sneered as he died that God had obviously rejected him, he remembered Shimei's curses upon David in chapter 16 and forgave them. David's reign as king might have been shattered, but he had never been more like God's Messiah.

---

[1] Since these chapters prophesy Jesus' rejection in Jerusalem a thousand years later, Ittai represents the Gentiles receiving Jesus as Messiah while the Jews run after Absalom. Hebrews 13:11–13 urges us to follow his lead.

[2] John 13:18; 18:1; Matthew 26:30. This is the first mention of the Mount of Olives in Scripture.

He trusted in the Lord and showed that he was still the kind of person God delights to use.

In 16:1–4, David takes his surrender to the Lord's will even further. He has covered his head and is walking barefoot as a sign of his humble repentance, worshipping as he goes,[3] when he receives another blow. Ziba is lying when he tells him that Mephibosheth has betrayed him and used his place at David's table to reassert his claim to be king, but David is so punch-drunk that he believes him enough to give Ziba all the land which he had restored to his master. Nevertheless, he does not command Ziba to go home and execute his master for his ingratitude. Mephibosheth can fight Absalom but not David for the throne. David would rather yield his own glory freely than risk seeing God's Kingdom torn apart by human ambition.

In 16:5–14, David refuses to react like Saul even when one of his predecessor's Benjamite supporters throws stones at him and shouts his verdict that *"The Lord has given the kingdom into the hands of your son Absalom. You have come to ruin because you are a murderer!"*[4] Joab and his brother Abishai want to kill Shimei there and then for his insolence, but David rebukes them for responding like Saul.[5] He left room in 15:26 for the Lord to be finished with him as a leader because of his sin, and he leaves room again in 16:11 for the possibility that his accuser is right and the Lord has indeed instructed Shimei to curse him. David knows that the only way for him to save his kingdom is to be willing to give it away, so he prefers life as a hunted has-been within the Lord's plan to life in a royal palace in defiance of

---

[3] A literal reading of 15:32 is actually that *"David came to the summit where he worshipped God."*

[4] To understand Shimei's astonishing courage, we need to note that Psalm 41:3 and 7–8 tells us that David was so ill at this point that many people assumed he would die. This illness may have been what provoked Absalom's rebellion, since he feared that Solomon was about to inherit the throne.

[5] David says literally, *"What do you and I have in common, sons of Zeruiah?"*, and repeats the question in 19:22. He is telling Joab and Abishai that they are working to Saul's agenda while he works to the Lord's.

his will. The God who chose to put him on the throne must also choose to keep him there.

In 16:15–17:29, David finds that the Lord is delighted with the way he has responded to this opposition. For a start, his friend Hushai manages to trick Absalom into giving David enough time to recover from his flight and to rally his troops. During this vital time of regrouping, three rich friends appear with enough provisions to feed his entire army. Shobi the Ammonite had not forgotten that David made him a puppet ruler instead of his older brother when he captured Rabbah. Makir had not forgotten the kindness which David showed towards his one-time houseguest Mephibosheth. Barzillai had not forgotten that David delivered his estates from the Moabite and Ammonite raiders who had long been the scourge of Gilead. Their grateful gifts turn the tide of the civil war in David's favour, but he is less excited about the food than he is about what it says about God's vindication. He finishes Psalm 41 and his lament over Ahithophel with a celebration to the Lord that *"I know that you are pleased with me, for my enemy does not triumph over me."*[6]

If God has entrusted you with any level of Christian leadership, you can expect opposition. What matters is how you respond to the Absaloms who challenge your position and resist your God-given authority. Will you resist them and cling on to power like Saul, or will you follow the example of David and Jesus instead? Will you trust the Lord to vindicate you as you walk through the valley of tears? Will you cast your crown at Jesus' feet and let him lead you out the other side?

---

[6] David also wrote Psalm 3 and possibly Psalm 63 at this time.

*Do you understand? Go back to the city with
my blessing.*

(2 Samuel 15:27)

Sometimes retreating with Jesus is easy. It's going back into the
world for him that's hard. David let Ittai the Gittite go with him
into exile, but he told Zadok, Abiathar and Hushai to go back into
the city. As they walked back down the Mount of Olives, crossed
the Kidron Valley and re-entered Jerusalem, they discovered
that the only thing harder than following God's Messiah is to be
sent by him into the world.

We know very little about Hushai the Arkite except that
he was from the tribe of Ephraim and held a special place in
David's court.[1] 1 Chronicles 27:33 tells us literally that he *"was
the king's friend"*. Life is lonely at the top, and David had found
in Hushai a companion with whom he could share his life and
mission. When David told him that he didn't want to take him
into exile because he had a plan for him in Jerusalem, he must
have felt like one of the disciples when Jesus reassured them:

> *I am going away and I am coming back to you... I no
> longer call you servants, because a servant does not
> know his master's business. Instead, I have called you
> friends... You are filled with grief because I have said
> these things. But very truly I tell you, it is for your good
> that I am going away.*[2]

[1] Joshua 16:2. His home town was either called *Arki* or *Erek*.

[2] John 14:28; 15:15; 16:6–7. 2 Samuel 15:33 suggests that Hushai was very
old, which would fit well with Absalom's other adviser Ahithophel being old

Hushai needed to go back into a city which was in enemy hands in order *to speak up for his messiah*. Ahithophel, David's wisest adviser,[3] had defected to Absalom and was determined to make him king. He had the brains of a chess grandmaster and fulfilled the curse of 12:11–12 by persuading Absalom to burn his bridges with his father by sleeping with his father's concubines on the same rooftop where he had lusted over Bathsheba. We see why David sent Hushai behind enemy lines when Ahithophel advises Absalom to finish off his father while his camp is in disarray, because disaster is looming unless he speaks. Hushai takes advantage of Absalom's pride since he knows that the upstart will think he means himself and not his father if he greets him with *"Long live the king!"* and promises to serve *"the one chosen by the Lord, by these people and by all the men of Israel"*. Don't judge Hushai for his willingness to speak the grubby language of the enemy's court in order to get a hearing for his master. These chapters teach us that we must not to retreat like the idealist Jean-Paul Sartre criticizes in his play *Dirty Hands*:

> *How you cling to your purity, young man! How afraid you are of dirtying your hands!... Purity is an idea for a yogi or a monk. You... use it as a pretext for doing nothing. To do nothing, to remain motionless, arms at your sides, wearing kid gloves. Well, I have dirty hands. Right in to the elbows. I have plunged them in filth and blood.*[4]

Hushai plunges his hands into the filth and blood of Absalom's court in order to thwart the enemy's plans. He reads the young man perfectly by making a counter-proposal which plays on his fear that his father is tougher and more experienced than

---

enough to be grandfather to David's wife Bathsheba.

[3] Ironically, his name meant *Brother Of Foolishness*, and the Lord answered David's prayer in 15:31 by turning his wisdom into folly.

[4] Jean-Paul Sartre in *Les Mains Sales* (1948). John 17:19 tells us that true purity involves engagement.

he is, and which is full of bravado about his leading the army into battle and destroying cities *"until not so much as a pebble is left"*. Absalom is won over, and Ahithophel sees so clearly that it means checkmate for his plans that he goes out and hangs himself.[5]

The prophet who wrote 2 Samuel wants us to see this as a picture of how we are to serve Jesus as Messiah. The one who suffered outside the city of Jerusalem also told his followers to *"Stay in the city... Do not leave Jerusalem... You will be my witnesses in Jerusalem, and in all Judea and Samaria, and to the ends of the earth."*[6] He prayed to the Father as he crossed the Kidron Valley and climbed the Mount of Olives that his followers would imitate the example of Hushai the Arkite: *"My prayer is not that you take them out of the world but that you protect them from the evil one... As you sent me into the world, I have sent them into the world."*[7] He prayed for an army of friends who would follow him like Bertrand Moncrif, the ally of the Scarlet Pimpernel who fights against the French Revolution at the very heart of Paris, and who said:

> *It is the still small voice that is heard by its persistence even above the fury of thousands in full cry... Our aim is to take every opportunity by quick, short speeches, by mixing with the crowd and putting in a word here and there, to make propaganda against the fiend Robespierre... One of us will find the word and speak it at the right time, and the people will follow us and turn against that execrable monster and hurl him from his throne.*[8]

---

[5] Because he tried to install King Saul II, Ahithophel commits suicide just like King Saul I. In doing so, he prophesies that Judas Iscariot will kill himself in Matthew 27:3–5 after betraying Jesus the Messiah.

[6] Luke 24:49 and Acts 1:4 and 8.

[7] John 17:15 and 18.

[8] Baroness Orczy in *The Triumph of the Scarlet Pimpernel* (1922).

That's why David provides Hushai with some friends who will *watch and pray for him*. Zadok and Abiathar were the king's two high priests who had been at the heart of his project to build a Tabernacle on Mount Zion and bring the Ark back to Jerusalem. They find it as difficult as Hushai to be told that they cannot go with him into exile and to receive a commission to go back into the enemy-held city. People see them carrying the Ark into Jerusalem, but it is actually a Trojan horse, for they are like Odysseus and his Greek friends when they smuggled themselves inside Troy in order to open its doors from the inside. They pay a high price to cry out to the messiah on Hushai's behalf, since they have to risk their sons' lives to get word to him at the fords in the desert, but their words open the gates of Jerusalem from the inside in the same way that Odysseus opened the gates of Troy.[9] Because of his praying priests on the inside of the city, David makes a swift change to his plans and is able to regroup and win the battle against Absalom.

So don't complain about the wickedness of the world without rolling up your sleeves and getting your hands dirty to fight it.[10] Don't talk about your desire to follow Jesus unless you are also willing to be sent by him into the world. Learn to live like C. T. Studd who went deep into pagan China, India and Africa, saying: *"Some wish to live within a yard of church and chapel bells; I want to run a rescue shop within a yard of hell."*[11]

Because if you speak up for your Messiah like Hushai the Arkite in Absalom's Jerusalem and like Bertrand Moncrif in revolutionary Paris, and if you open the gates of your city and nation like Zadok and Abiathar in Jerusalem and like Odysseus

---

[9] Zadok's son was rewarded for his faithfulness as a messenger in 17:17–22 by being allowed to run as the messenger who told David he had won in 18:19–28.

[10] Don't be offended by the lie the woman tells to protect Ahimaaz and Jonathan in 17:20. The writer tells you this detail in order to shock you that God prefers even such grubby engagement to pious retreatism.

[11] Norman Grubb in *C. T. Studd: Cricketer and Pioneer* (1933).

in Troy, then you have done something harder than simply following Jesus. You have obeyed the commission which he gave you when he sent you into the world. Your reward will come in the form of rejoicing when at last you see his Kingdom come.

Time to Repent
(18:1–19:43)

> *"Should anyone be put to death in Israel today?*
> *Don't I know that today I am king over Israel?" So the*
> *king said to Shimei, "You shall not die."*
>
> (2 Samuel 19:22–23)

David's return from exile as king was dramatic, but it wasn't the messiah's second coming. His journey out of Jerusalem had foreshadowed Jesus' rejection and crucifixion, so his return to Jerusalem foreshadowed Jesus' resurrection.[1] That's why he comes back to the city, not with judgment, but with grace, as a picture of how Jesus will rule as King throughout AD history. Jesus gives people time to repent but warns them that a final judgment day is coming for anyone who despises his patience and mercy.

David returns as king in weakness, not in triumph. It is about 979 BC, so David is aged sixty-one, and his generals convince him that he is too old to fight. He sends his army out to battle under the command of a converted Philistine and the two unruly sons of Zeruiah. This is not a picture of Jesus returning at the head of his angel army to judge the earth but of his setting out to conquer the world after his resurrection and ascension through a ragtag collection of 120 unlikely followers. Have you

---

[1] David was as good as dead by the end of chapter 17, but God's power through Hushai and his three rich friends resurrects him from the grave to restore his kingdom. Psalm 69:22–28 shows that David was not embarrassed about judgment day, and that he stayed his hand simply because this was the day of salvation.

ever wondered why the Lord appears to let the wicked get away with their sin while the Church looks so weak? If you have, you will find some answers in these chapters.

You will find them in the way that David weeps over *Absalom*. David was weak in dealing with his sons, but there is far more than parental failure in his bitter grief as a father. He knows that God wants to give rebels time to repent, and he weeps that Absalom has been robbed of such an opportunity. *"Be gentle with the young man Absalom **for my sake**,"* he pleads with his generals in 18:5, just as Jesus pleads with the Father on our behalf for his own name's sake in heaven right now.[2] *"Is the young man Absalom safe?"* he asks in 18:29 with the same concern as Jesus when he prayed for his crucifiers, *"Father, forgive them, for they do not know what they are doing."*[3] He weeps inconsolably for his unrepentant son in 18:33, willing to lay down his own life to save him, just like Jesus when he wept for unrepentant Jerusalem and cried over what could have been *"if you, even you, had only known on this day what would bring you peace"*.[4]

David even gives *Joab* time to repent. Murdering Abner had been criminal, but it was nothing compared to murdering Absalom in defiance of a direct order from the king in the hearing of the whole army. Joab had defied his lord's will in order to get vengeance for his barley field,[5] and now that David

---

[2] David's plea foreshadows Romans 8:34–39, Hebrews 7:25 and 1 John 2:1–2.

[3] Luke 23:34. Stephen also shows in Acts 7:60 that God wants to give people time to repent during AD history.

[4] Luke 19:41–44. Joab is too much like Saul to understand God's heart towards sinners in 19:1–8, but David expresses God's heart as revealed in Ezekiel 18:23 and 32, 1 Timothy 2:4 and 2 Peter 3:9. Sadly, Absalom was more interested in building monuments to his own name in 18:19 than he was in learning from his father.

[5] If you are in any doubt that Joab's action was the sinful fruit of his being a son of Saul, then compare his heart in 18:14 with Saul's in 1 Samuel 13:8–14 and 14:18–19.

finally has a gifted replacement in Amasa he can afford to carry out the death penalty on Joab.[6] Yet even though Joab grasps nothing of the Gospel in 19:1–8, David merely relieves him of his command and gives him time to repent instead. This isn't the final judgment day. It is still the day of salvation.

David gives *Israel* time to repent. They admit in 19:10 that they have been following a false messiah, but David does not force himself on them now any more than he did back in the days of Ish-Bosheth. He is secure in the knowledge that he is their anointed king by right and therefore waits for them to surrender willingly to his rule in 19:9–15. He is delighted when some of them share one heart and mind to call him home as king. The Church often looks weak because Jesus prefers a small group of willing followers to a whole world of browbeaten slaves.

David even gives wicked *Shimei* and *Ziba* time to repent. Joab's brother Abishai had begged David to let him kill Shimei for cursing David, pelting him with stones and calling him a murderer when he fled Jerusalem. Now he quotes David's words back to him from 1 Samuel 26:9 in order to try a second time to get permission kill him. David rebukes Abishai for thinking it is judgment day and not the day of salvation,[7] then accepts Shimei's confession of sin and his grovelling for forgiveness in 19:16–23. He grants a similar pardon to Ziba in 19:24–30, despite the fact that Ziba had lied to him in order to steal his master Mephibosheth's lands. Even these two rebels are given plenty of time to repent.[8]

---

[6] Amasa was Joab's cousin, another nephew of David. 1 Chronicles 2:17 shows that the correct reading of the variant manuscripts of 2 Samuel 17:25 is that Amasa's father was an Ishmaelite.

[7] David tells Abishai literally in 19:22 either that *"You are like an adversary to me today"* or *"You are like Satan to me today."*

[8] David's friend Barzillai warns us not to write ourselves off as too old to change in 19:31–39. Moses began leading Israel at eighty, Joshua led Israel across the Jordan at eighty-four and Caleb conquered new land at eighty-five,

Therefore 18:19–32 serves as the Old Testament equivalent of Luke 15:20. David looks into the distance like the prodigal son's father and longs for signs that rebels are making use of the time which he gives them to repent. He is delighted when Mephibosheth arrives with such devotion that he gladly shares his lands with Ziba if that means he can see his messiah's face again.[9] He smiles when the tribes of Israel try to outdo one another in their love for him.[10] But he grieves when Joab and Shimei's actions betray their lack of repentance, and that they would rather try to rule in hell with Saul and Absalom than submit on earth to the Lord's messiah.

Joab murders his new rival Amasa in the same way that he murdered his old rival Abner in chapter 2. He continues to rebel against his uncle by conspiring to put Adonijah on the throne instead of Solomon while David is on his deathbed in 1 Kings 1–2. Since Joab has squandered the day of salvation, David is forced to tell Solomon to declare that it is judgment day. Joab is executed alongside Shimei, who continued to rebel against God's messiah by ignoring a direct order to stay in Jerusalem where Solomon could watch him. Jesus has declared that AD history is the day of salvation, but don't let that fool you that judgment day isn't just around the corner.

So if you have ever wondered why King Jesus often lets the wicked prosper and the Church look weak, these chapters give an answer. They also challenge each one of us to make the most of the time he has given us to repent before his final judgment day. Will we be the repentant kind of people he can use, like Mephibosheth? Or will we mistake his meekness for weakness,

---

yet Barzillai feels so old at eighty that he lets his son Kimham receive land near Bethlehem instead (Jeremiah 41:17).

[9] In this sense Mephibosheth is the exact opposite of the prodigal son's older brother in Luke 15.

[10] Even though Shimei was from the tribe of Benjamin, he refers to the ten northern tribes as *"the tribes of Joseph"* since the largest were Ephraim and Manasseh. The two southern tribes were Judah and Simeon.

like Joab and Shimei? Paul asks us that question with a challenge in Romans 2:4:

> *Do you show contempt for the riches of his kindness, forbearance and patience, not realizing that God's kindness is intended to lead you to repentance?*

How to Repent (20:1–26)

Then the woman went to all the people with her wise advice, and they cut off the head of Sheba son of Bikri and threw it to Joab.

(2 Samuel 20:22)

When the Lord prophesied to David in 12:10 that *"the sword will never depart from your house, because you despised me"*, he really meant it. No sooner has David's army quashed Absalom's rebellion than Saul's relative Sheba starts a second one. David deals swiftly and decisively with this rebellion, and the writer of 2 Samuel uses it to teach us some practical lessons on how to repent.

Sheba takes advantage of the disagreement between the northern and southern tribes at the end of chapter 19 over which of them loves David the most.[1] He uses it to turn the ten northern tribes against David on the basis that he comes from the tribe of Judah in the south, whereas Saul came from Benjamin which was one of the ten northern tribes.[2] This gives Amasa a chance to prove himself as the new commander of David's army, but he takes so long to muster his troops that Sheba manages to escape to the far-northern city of Abel Beth

---

[1] He persuades Israel to renege on the covenant they made with David in 5:1–3, and he lays the ideological grounds for Israel's rebellion against Rehoboam about fifty years later in 1 Kings 12:16.

[2] Saul's home town of Gibeah was actually less than ten miles further north than Bethlehem. However, it was part of the ten northern tribes which had initially sided with Ish-Bosheth instead of David.

Maakah, part of the tribal territory of Naphtali to the north of Lake Galilee and one of the border fortresses of Israel.[3]

When Joab and his army arrive at the city, a wise woman cries out to him with *humility*. She has plenty of reasons not to be humble, since Joab is even more sinful than Sheba. He has shamefully and deceitfully murdered Amasa en route to Abel Beth Maakah,[4] and he has no real authority to act as commander of David's army. The king appointed Joab's younger brother Abishai as his new commander, and Joab is only back in his former position because of an agreement with his brother. The woman has plenty of reasons to point the finger at Joab and demand his withdrawal, but instead she comes with the humility which always accompanies true repentance. She does not even tell Joab her name as she introduces herself as *"your servant"*. Her humility shows that her repentance is real and it makes her the kind of person God can use to save a city.

The woman comes to Joab with a *frank confession of sin*. She could have tried to flatter Joab into withdrawing, since Abner was successful in using smooth words to hoodwink him into calling off his assault in chapter 2 and since he failed to press home his advantage when he had a chance to besiege the Ammonite capital in chapter 10. Joab has a track record of weakness when flattered by his enemies, but the woman shows her repentance is real by the way she confesses that her city is not what it used to be. They are still *"the Lord's inheritance"* and ought to be living for the Lord, but they are not as they were *"long ago"* when people used to treat the city as a place to hear the Word of God. *"We are the peaceful and faithful in Israel,"* she remembers, which stands in contrast to their current status as the headquarters of a civil war against God's anointed king. The

---

[3] The wise woman refers to the city in verse 19 as a metropolis, or mother-city, in Israel.

[4] The fact that Joab kissed Amasa and made his intestines spill onto the ground in 20:9–10 may even point to the fate of Judas Iscariot in Matthew 26:48–49 and Acts 1:18.

woman proves that her repentance is real by not trying to flatter Joab or sweep her sin under the carpet.

The woman comes to Joab with *faith in his Gospel message*. Joab speaks far more truly than he knows, just like the high priest Caiaphas did in John 11:50 when he prophesied that *"it is better for you that one man die for the people than that the whole nation perish."* When Joab tells her that the violent death of one man can save her sinful city, she isn't offended by his message. She responds with faith to the Gospel message which Paul warns in 1 Corinthians 1:18 is so repulsive that only those who are truly repentant can receive it: *"For the message of the cross is foolishness to those who are perishing, but to us who are being saved it is the power of God."*

The woman comes to Joab with *a willingness to pay the price* of repentance. Salvation is free but repentance is never cheap. She convinces her fellow citizens to make a radical turnaround and change their city from being the rebel headquarters into one of David's most loyal towns. She persuades them to decapitate Sheba as a clear-cut moment of conversion, and throws his severed head over the ramparts to Joab and his men below. Repentance means far more than saying sorry, it means turning from sin, and seeing Sheba's head convinces Joab that the city's repentance is real. He lifts the siege and returns to Jerusalem with the city forgiven and free from the threat of judgment. It's a picture of what happens to any person who comes to the Lord in genuine repentance like the wise woman of Abel Beth Maakah.[5]

This fifth and final section of 1 and 2 Samuel teaches us that God is looking for repentant people he can use. We therefore need to grasp the terrible warning at the end of this chapter that it is possible to nod at this lesson yet remain as unsaved as before. Joab witnessed the wise woman's repentance firsthand,

---

[5] Although the details are different, Solomon may have had this story in mind when he commends such wisdom in Ecclesiastes 9:14–15.

but he failed to apply it to his own life and paid the price. When David restored him formally to the position of commander in verse 23, he forgot to make the most of the day of salvation which he had been given. He rebelled against Solomon in 1 Kings 1–2 and then tried to lay hold of the Lord's altar for forgiveness, but he had lived in such unrepentance for the nine years since his return from Abel Beth Maakah that Solomon saw at once that his words of sorrow were a sham.[6]

Let's therefore learn the wise woman's lesson far better than Joab. Let's come to the Lord with humility and frank confession of sin, without trying to argue our case or charm our way out of his judgment. Let's believe his Gospel message about the one who died on a cross to save the sinful people of the world, and be willing to pay whatever it costs us to stop being rebels and become devoted followers of Jesus the Messiah.

In the past, people went to Abel Beth Maakah to hear direction from the Lord. Because of this one wise woman who knew how repent, God tells us that the same is true today.

---

[6] Joab was executed by the same Benaiah that verses 7 and 23 tell us marched with him as commander of David's foreign bodyguard. Benaiah would then replace Joab as the commander of Solomon's army.

What Stops Repentance
(20:9–13)

*The man saw that all the troops came to a halt there.
When he realised that everyone who came up to
Amasa stopped, he dragged him from the road.*

(2 Samuel 20:12)

For supposedly rational creatures, we can get very irrational when God calls us to repentance. We can find a hundred and one excuses why we should either leave it to another day or not repent at all. These reasons can become such barriers to faith that no amount of Gospel preaching can get through unless those beliefs are dealt with first. That's why the French philosopher Pascal taught that *"Men despise religion. They hate it and are afraid it may be true. The cure for this is to show that religion is not contrary to reason, but worthy of reverence and respect."*[1] It's also why the writer of 2 Samuel warns us that we need to deal with such beliefs if we are to succeed in calling people to repentance.

The belief which forms an obstacle in 20:12 is *I Can't Believe in God because Religious People Are Hypocrites*. The soldiers are running towards a lesson in repentance at Abel Beth Maakah when they are stopped in their tracks by finding Amasa's bleeding body in the road. They like David, but they have second thoughts about his call when they see the hypocrisy of Joab who claims to follow him. This is the issue which causes Christopher Hitchens to reject Christianity in his book *God Is Not Great*, arguing that Jesus cannot be taken seriously because

---

[1] Blaise Pascal's 187th thought in his *Pensées* (1670).

"Religion has been an enormous multiplier of tribal suspicion and hatred."[2] A soldier needs to drag Amasa's body from the road so that his comrades can get past this obstacle and continue on their road towards repentance. We need to do the same in conversation with unbelievers.

We can drag this question out of the way by querying whether religious hypocrites might in fact be unbelievers in disguise. God gives people time to repent before his judgment falls, so it shouldn't surprise us that the Church is as full of sinners as a hospital is of sick people, but more often than not such hypocrites are just like Joab – unbelievers who dress their wickedness up in religious clothes. Their sins are not an example of what people who are devoted to Jesus do but a provocation to unbelievers to repent and show what true devotion to Jesus really means. This belief shouldn't be an obstacle to repentance but a challenge to be like the countless Christian heroes throughout history who have truly repented then worked to eliminate injustice and suffering in the world.

This links back to another obstacle to repentance in 2:23: *I Can't Believe in God because Bad Things Happen to Good People.* There are deliberate parallels between the killing of Amasa in chapter 20 and the killing of Joab's more virtuous younger brother in chapter 2. We are told that soldiers who encountered Asahel's corpse on the road also stopped and gave up their pursuit, because the question of suffering is one of the biggest obstacles to faith of them all. Note the way it distorts the soldiers' perspective – they have killed eighteen times more people than Abner's army, yet they lose courage to follow David any further.

We can drag this question out of the road by agreeing that the existence of suffering is a real problem. In fact, it's as big a problem for unbelievers as believers. If God created us then why doesn't he stop the suffering in his world, but if life came

---

[2] Christopher Hitchens in *God Is Not Great: How Religion Poisons Everything* (2007).

about by chance and by survival of the fittest then why do we care so much about suffering at all? The fact we do care lifts our eyes to see God, and when we look we find that he has suffered more than us all. He is no mere spectator on this question, having suffered more than any of us at the crucifixion. What's more, if God was even able to turn around the death of his Son for good, then we can trust him to bring good out of our own suffering too. We mustn't shake our fists at God like Joab. If he is big enough to blame for our suffering, he is also big enough to know what he is doing and to comfort us in the meantime.

Later in the same chapter, we find another obstacle to repentance in 2:26: *It Doesn't Matter What We Believe so long as We Are Sincere.* Abner is defeated and his army is about to be slaughtered, so he convinces Joab to let him go by arguing the equivalent of *you say tomahto and I say tomayto.* He stresses that Israel and Judah are people of faith from the same family, and brushes over the fact that they are divided by following true and false messiahs.

We can drag this question out of the road by pointing out that all major world religions do agree on two things: First, that people have sinned and are liable to judgment, and second, that people need to find forgiveness for those sins. They may disagree over the nature of the god who has been sinned against and over what needs to be done to find forgiveness, but they all agree that modern Western secularism is wrong. When people use the plethora of world religions to avoid travelling along God's road to repentance, they are not claiming all religions are valid at all. They are claiming that all of them are equally *in*valid: twenty-first-century Westerners are clever enough to know that sin isn't real and forgiveness is unnecessary, while people in every other culture, time and place are wrong. It's preposterously arrogant.

A final obstacle to repentance appears in 10:14: *I'll Think about it Another Time.* Once again, the problem involves Joab, who has routed the Ammonites and forced them back into the city of Rabbah, but who decides that it is too late in the year for him to finish off what he has started. He is like Governor Felix when Paul told him to repent and he replied in Acts 24:25, *"That's enough for now! You may leave. When I find it convenient, I will send for you."* He is like King Agrippa when Paul told him to repent and he replied in Acts 26:28, *"Do you think that in such a short time you can persuade me to be a Christian?"* Joab delays his pursuit, and his fatal complacency leads to David's sin with Bathsheba in 11:1. That's why the writer warns us that putting off a decision to repent can be as dangerous as any of these other obstacles. Now is the day of salvation. The Day of Judgment is just around the corner.[3]

The eighteenth-century novelist Jonathan Swift observed that *"It is useless to attempt to reason a man out of a thing he was never reasoned into."*[4] The writer of 2 Samuel agrees. But he also warns us that unless we use reason to drag these obstacles from people's paths then they will never reach the place of repentance. If we are as diligent to drag away these obstacles as the nameless soldier in Joab's army, the writer promises that we will lead many to repentance and teach them how to become the kind of people God can use.

---

[3] 2 Corinthians 6:1–3; Hebrews 4:7–11.

[4] Quoted by Maturin Murray Ballou in his *Treasury of Thought* (1872).

Kingdom Army
(21:1–22; 23:8–39)

These are the names of David's mighty warriors.

(2 Samuel 23:8)

The writer is conscious that we have almost finished 1 and 2 Samuel. He has been honest with us in this fifth and final section about David's failings so that we will not fall into the trap of thinking God can use a man like David but can't use people like us. Now he starts to draw this fifth section to a close by telling us that God wants to raise a Kingdom army of men and women like David who will fight for his Messiah.

The writer begins with a warning in 21:1–14 that simply *being zealous for the Lord is not enough.*[1] Even Saul dreamed up big dreams for the Lord, but they were dreams of his own making. Little over two miles from his home town of Gibeah lay Gibeon, a town which was still inhabited by some of the last Canaanite survivors of Joshua's conquest of the Promised Land.[2] Saul was passionate about this issue as a Benjamite and decided to finish off what Joshua had failed to do. Sadly, he wanted to fight for the Lord but he didn't want to listen to what he said. He didn't bother to read in Joshua 9 that the Israelites

---

[1] Chapters 21–24 have an ABCCBA structure, since 21:1–14 and 24:1–25 deal with sin and judgment, 21:15–22 and 23:8–39 deal with David's mighty men, and 22:1–51 and 23:1–7 record David's worship. However, 21:1–14 also belongs with the passages on David's mighty men in order to show that zeal for the Lord is not enough.

[2] They were technically *Hivites*, but the writer uses the term *Amorite* as a generic term for all seven Canaanite nations, just as the Lord does in Genesis 15:16.

had made a covenant with the Gibeonites and promised never to harm them. As a result, the Lord judged Israel with three years of famine until David let the Gibeonite survivors avenge themselves on Saul's family.[3] Being zealous for the Lord is not enough for him to use us. We need to apply what these two books have taught us about how to be the kind of people he can use.[4]

The writer reminds us in 21:15–22 that *the Lord uses the humble*. Even though David was a former giant-slayer and Abishai flatters him he is *"the lamp of Israel"*, he got so tired in battle on one occasion that he was nearly killed by a Philistine.[5] There were many giants besides Goliath and there were many other people God used to kill them.[6] He invites us to join his team of giant-slayers, as part of his Messiah's army.

The writer reminds us in 23:8–12 that *the Lord uses the obedient*. How could one man kill 800 men with just a spear?[7] How could another take his stand in a field and single-handedly repulse the Philistines? We discover the answer in 1 Chronicles 12:18, which tells us that *"the Spirit came on Amasai, chief of the Thirty, and he said: 'We are yours, David! We are with you, son of Jesse!'"* These men were only mighty because the same Holy Spirit came on them as came on Samson in Judges 14:6

---

[3] Although some Hebrew manuscripts of 21:8 tell us that these were children of *Michal*, 6:23 and 1 Samuel 18:19 suggest that this is a copying error and that the correct manuscripts are the ones which read *Merab*.

[4] We are so far removed from David's culture that passages like 21:1–14 strike us as horrific. We need to see David's action in the context of Numbers 35:33, and grasp that failure to listen to God always ends in tragedy.

[5] David was only *"the lamp of Israel"* in the same way that Rehoboam was in 1 Kings 11:36 – as a prophetic picture of Jesus the Messiah who would be the true *"Light of the World"* (John 8:12).

[6] Although the Hebrew of 21:19 appears to have been corrupted in the copying, the parallel 1 Chronicles 20:5 clarifies that Elhanan killed *Lahmi the brother of Goliath the Gittite*.

[7] The Hebrew of 23:8 also appears to have been corrupted in the copying. 1 Chronicles 11:11 suggests that it should read that Josheb-Basshebeth killed *300* men and that Adino the Ezite killed *800*.

and 15:14 when he killed a lion with his bare hands and 1,000 Philistines with a jawbone. The Holy Spirit loves to fill people who are devoted to God's Messiah and to grant them power to fulfil his mission. The Lord promises to use us as mightily as these warriors to extend his Kingdom if we commit our lives to Jesus the Messiah as entirely as Amasai.

The writer reminds us in 23:13–17 that *the Lord uses the pure*. He tells us a beautiful story about what happened when David longed to drink from the well at his home town of Bethlehem while he was stuck in his hot and arid desert stronghold. Even though Bethlehem was in the hands of the Philistines and the Valley of Rephaim means literally *the Valley of the Giants*, three of David's mighty men felt such pure devotion towards their leader that they took enormous risks for no military gain simply in order to put a smile on the face of their messiah. David responds with no less purity by pouring out the water on the ground rather than drink water which was bought at the risk of his people's lives. We are meant to grasp from this event that Jesus is not simply interested in our deeds but in the purity of our love towards him. He will never forget any of our courageous acts of love, and he delights more in the purity of our hearts than David did in the purity of Bethlehem's drinking water.

The writer reminds us in 23:18–23 that *the Lord uses those who are passionate for his name*. Suddenly, the talk turns to fame and reputation as the writer tells us Abishai and Benaiah both became more famous than the Three.[8] He tells us that the Three were held in high honour but that the names of Abishai and Benaiah were held in even greater honour still. Because Joab was passionate for his own name, he is conspicuous by his absence from these verses, but because these other mighty

---

[8] Since Abishai means *My Father Gives Gifts* and Benaiah means *Built Up by the Lord*, these men show us that the Lord likes to make himself famous by making his followers famous on his behalf.

men were passionate for David's name they became famous members of *"the army of God"*.[9]

The writer reminds us in 23:24–39 that *the Lord uses the repentant.* Don't miss the motley nature of this list of thirty-seven mighty men. There are Gentiles such as Zelek the Ammonite and Uriah the Hittite, men who were excluded from God's covenant with Israel but who proved their repentance through actions such as those described in 11:6–13.[10] There is also a man from Saul's home town of Gibeah, who had rejected Saul's ways in order to fight for the Lord by David's rules. As if to emphasize the importance of repentance, the writer mentions Joab's two brothers and his armour-bearer, but not Joab himself. A royal nephew who refuses to repent will not be used by God, but a common armour-bearer who repents will.

Above all, the writer turns to us and tells us that *the Lord uses people like us.* He talks about the Thirty, then lists thirty-seven names. He talks about the Three, then lists two commanders of the Three who were not part of the Three.[11] Confused yet? You are meant to be, because the writer wants to show you that his list is incomplete. When he tells you literally in 23:18 that Abishai *woke up his spear* to fight for David, he is also telling you that it is time for you to wake up and join the Messiah's army too.[12]

Jesus told his followers that *"I will build my church, and the gates of Hades will not overcome it. I will give you the keys of the kingdom of heaven; whatever you bind on earth will be bound in heaven, and whatever you loose on earth will be loosed in*

---

[9] 1 Chronicles 12:22 tells us to see this list as a picture of God's true army which marches behind Jesus, his true Messiah. Abishai and Asahel make it into the list because they were less unruly than their older brother.

[10] 1 Chronicles 12:4 also mentions that one of his mighty men was one of the foreign Gibeonites whom Saul had tried to kill in 2 Samuel 21:1–14.

[11] The parallel list in 1 Chronicles 11 gives us a further sixteen names, and 1 Chronicles 11–12 names three separate chiefs of the Thirty!

[12] Note also the warning in 23:20 not to wait for the perfect weather conditions before we begin.

heaven." He is still looking for soldiers to take their place in his Kingdom army and devote their lives like these mighty men to establishing his rule in every nation of the world.[13]

---

[13] 1 Chronicles 11:10; Matthew 16:18–19. Although Jesus gave this charge to Peter specifically in 16:18–19, he made it clear in 18:18 that it applies to us all.

Weak People Wanted
(22:1–23:7)

He rescued me from my powerful enemy, from my foes, who were too strong for me... It is God who arms me with strength.

(2 Samuel 22:18, 33)

You've probably heard the well-known story about the ventriloquist whose act contained a lot of Irish jokes. On one occasion, an Irishman in the crowd was so incensed that he leapt up and demanded that he stop implying Irish people are stupid. *"I'm so sorry I've offended you. I was only trying to have a little fun,"* apologized the ventriloquist. *"You keep out of this,"* shot back the Irishman. *"I'm not talking to you. I'm talking to that little fellow on your lap."*

The writer of 2 Samuel didn't know that story, but as he draws to a close he is concerned that we might make the same mistake as the Irishman. Despite all he has said about the kind of person God can use, he still suspects that we might slip into hero worship and think that the God who used David can't use the likes of you and me. That's why he records one of David's psalms and one of his prayers which both describe the secret of his ministry. Since this song is already recorded for us in Psalm 18, he doesn't include it because we can't read it elsewhere. He does it to convince us as he finishes 1 and 2 Samuel that God wants to use weak people just like us.[1]

---

[1] In fact, when David re-edited this song for congregational singing in Psalm 18 he included a new first line which read simply, *"I love you, Lord, my strength."*

In 22:1–6 the writer tells us *David's strength was entirely the Lord's*. He reminds us that it was the Lord who delivered David from all his enemies in verse 1, and goes on to tell us in the verses which follow that the Lord was David's *rock*, *fortress*,[2] *deliverer*, *shield*, *horn*,[3] *stronghold*, *refuge* and *saviour*. David freely confesses in verse 6 that unless the Lord had strengthened him he would have ended up dead long ago.[4]

In 22:7–16 the writer reminds us that *the Lord is strong enough to use even the weakest person*. He uses mighty angels as his chariots and the wind as his taxi service. He uses lightning bolts as arrows to shoot at his enemies.[5] He even parted the Red Sea – one of the greatest miracles in the Old Testament – by sniffing with his nostrils rather than by blowing with his mouth, because his challenge was not to summon enough strength to part it but to limit his strength enough to part it without destroying the Israelites at the same time.[6] If you think that you are too weak for God to use you, then you are not so much confessing what you believe about yourself as what you believe about God.

In 22:17–30 the writer tells us *what attracted the Lord's strength to David*. Even though he was weaker than his enemies, David's character drew on God's strength *"because he delighted in me"*. He became the kind of person God could use because he was humble in verse 28, obedient in verses 22–23, and pure

---

[2] The Hebrew word translated *fortress* in 22:2 is the same word which was used for David's desert *stronghold* in 5:17 and 23:14 and in 1 Samuel 22:4–5 and 24:22. The word translated *rock* is the same word which was used in 1 Samuel 23:25 and 28.

[3] In Hebrew thought a *horn* represented an animal's strength. Luke 1:69 picks up on this verse to refer to Jesus as *"a horn of salvation for us in the house of his servant David"*.

[4] The Hebrew word *she'ol* in 22:6 may even mean that unless God had saved David he would now be in *hell*.

[5] See also Psalm 77:17 and 144:6 and Habakkuk 3:11.

[6] See also Exodus 15:8. Since the Tabernacle was referred to as God's *Temple* in 1 Samuel 1:9 and 3:3, the temple mentioned in verse 7 was probably David's Tabernacle on Mount Zion.

in verses 21 and 24–25.[7] Even though Abishai flattered him in 21:17 that he was *"the lamp of Israel"*, David is so passionate for the God's name that he confesses in verse 29 that the Lord is the true lamp, not him.[8] If we embrace the first four sections of 1 and 2 Samuel by being humble, obedient, pure and passionate for God's name, then David promises that God will also strengthen us to overcome any obstacle.

In 22:31–43 the writer tells us that *the Lord trained David to use his strength*. God armed him with divine power in verse 33, then he taught his hands and feet to use it in verses 34–37. God armed him with strength for the fight in verse 40, and he will do the same for anyone else who follows him as David did. How can we strike down spiritual giants and rout Satan's forces single-handedly, like the mighty men in chapters 21 and 23? By laying hold of Jesus' promise in Mark 1:17 that he will do the same for us as he did for David: *"Come, follow me, and **I will make you** fishers of men."*

In 22:44–51 the writer tells us that *the Lord strengthened David for the sake of his Messiah's name*. This psalm of praise ends on a crescendo which speaks of God's true King and Messiah who will be the *"seed of David"*,[9] and says that the Lord's plan is to strengthen his Messiah in order to save the nations.

This leads into David's final prayer in 23:1–7, in which he tells us in verse 1 that God made him Israel's hero and messiah in order to inspire him to prophesy that a far greater Messiah

---

[7] Although we can find David's absolute confidence that the Lord delights in him inappropriate, the writer warns that it is far more inappropriate for us to doubt that we are also the kind of people God can use.

[8] The parallel verse in Psalm 18:28 simply says that *"you keep my lamp burning."* David changes the words here in order to stress that the Lord is the true King of Israel.

[9] Although many English translations refer simply to *"David and his descendants"*, the Hebrew literally speaks about *"David and his seed"*. Galatians 3:16 suggests this is a prophecy about Jesus the Messiah.

was coming.[10] The prayer celebrates the messianic covenant which the Lord made with him in 7:12–16 and anticipates the prophecies about Jesus in Isaiah 9:7 and 11:1–5, as well as those in Jeremiah 23:5–6 and 33:15–16. Our salvation is meant to lead to fruitfulness, David promises us at the end of his prayer, because we are like ventriloquist's dummies in the hands of a powerful Master. He promises us that if we follow his lead then we will also be the kind of people God can use.

So if your response at the end of 1 and 2 Samuel is nothing more than admiration for David, you have missed the point like the Irishman who shouted at a dummy. God's strength has not changed and nor has his desire to employ it on behalf of people like you and me in order to glorify his Messiah's name. If we are humble, obedient, pure, passionate for his name and repentant like David, then he promises to strengthen us to advance Jesus' Kingdom. He promises that we are the kind of people he can use.

---

[10] Since the Greek for *"I have put my trust in him"* in Hebrews 2:13 may well be taken from the Septuagint translation of 2 Samuel 22:3, the New Testament suggests that this psalm is a prophecy about Jesus, and that 22:6 and 17 is a prophecy about his death and resurrection.

God Has a Better Messiah
(24:1–25)

These are but sheep. What have they done? Let your hand fall on me and my family.

(2 Samuel 24:17)

Everybody knows that a great story needs a happy ending. The goody beats the baddy, the hero gets the girl and the kind of person God can use finally wins the day. Everybody knows that, it would appear, except for the writer of 2 Samuel.

The writer doesn't end with David's handover to Solomon or with his death aged seventy in 970 BC (that comes at the start of 1 Kings and at the end of 1 Chronicles). Instead, he ends with David forgetting the lesson he sang about in chapter 22 and counting the number of warriors in his army like a miser counting money.[1] Even Joab can tell that such reliance on human strength is likely to bring a curse on Israel so, true to form, he secretly disobeys David's order.[2] But the damage is done. Jeremiah 17:5 warns that *"Cursed is the one who trusts in man, who draws strength from mere flesh and whose heart turns away from the Lord."* God therefore presents David with a menu of punishments to choose from, and he selects three days of deadly plague. What made the writer of 2 Samuel choose

---

[1] Taking a census was not sinful in itself (Numbers 1:1–3; 26:1–4), but 1 Chronicles 27:23–24 tells us that this census was prompted by self-reliance rather than by God's command.

[2] 1 Chronicles 21:6 tells us that *"Joab did not include Levi and Benjamin in the numbering, because the king's command was repulsive to him."* Comparing 24:9 with 1 Chronicles 21:5 shows that Joab counted 1,100,000 and 470,000 men but reported back 800,000 and 500,000 to David.

such an unhappy ending to his story? When we understand the reason, it's incredibly exciting.

First, the writer is seizing a final chance to convince us that God can use people like you and me. David was humble, but not always. He was obedient, but not always. He was pure, but not always. He was passionate for God's name, but not always. Yet he was always repentant, and that's what distinguishes him first and foremost from Saul and Absalom and Joab. The writer wants to tell us that no matter how often we fail, we can still be a man or woman after God's own heart if we are quick to repent. He doesn't want us to put David on a pedestal and worship him as a hero. He pulls him back down to our level so that we will see him simply as a man that we can follow.

Second, the writer wants to end the story with the spotlight firmly on the true and better Messiah about whom he has prophesied again and again. David was the kind of person God could use, but he was only a faint shadow of another who would one day come from his dynasty and become the ultimate Person God could use. Let's walk slowly through this final chapter together and examine the clues which the writer gives us as he draws his prophetic history book to a close.

The chapter begins with *the utter sinfulness of humankind*. Joab effectively admits that he is not a follower of the Lord when he says *"the Lord **your** God"* to David in verse 3, yet even he can tell that reliance on human strength is sinful. David refuses to be won over and fails to change his mind even when the task takes the best part of a year to complete (verse 8). It is only at the end of the year that he is conscience-stricken with his sin. David was godly, but the writer wants to emphasize that even the best of men are still men at best.

The chapter then emphasizes *the grace of God towards human sin*. Whereas 1 Chronicles 21:1 tells us that *"Satan rose up against Israel and incited David to take a census of Israel,"* the writer tells us in verse 1 that the Lord only let him do so because he wanted to bring Israel's sin to a head so that he could save them.[3] David's subjects had been so disappointed by his sin with Bathsheba that they had waned in their devotion to worshipping the Lord at his Tabernacle, and this judgment would renew their commitment to build a Temple where they could be saved through blood sacrifices which pointed to a better Messiah. Verse 14 tells us that judgment at the hands of the Lord can be beneficial, *"for his mercy is great"* towards us even when we sin.[4]

The chapter then paints a picture of *Jesus the Messiah dying to save a sinful world.* Judgment falls throughout the length and breadth of Israel,[5] and in only three days 70,000 Israelites die because of sin.[6] The Hebrews viewed seven as the perfect number, so the number 70,000 emphasizes that the Lord's judgment is great but not arbitrary. He measures his judgment perfectly and is eager to forgive as soon as anyone expresses their faith in Jesus Christ as the sacrifice for sin. David does not fully know what he is saying when he cries out in verse 17 *"These are but sheep. What have they done? Let your hand fall on me and my family"*, but the Lord knows and he stops his avenging angel in a moment. Someone from David's family would indeed soak up God's judgment on the sinful world one day.[7]

---

[3] Don't be confused by this apparent contradiction. Job 1:12 and 2:6 make it clear that Satan can only operate within the sovereign limits God sets for him.

[4] Moses listed all three of these options in his curse on sin in Deuteronomy 28:15–25. He also warned Israel in Exodus 30:12 that a plague would destroy them if they ever took a census without collecting the silver redemption money which pointed to the death of Jesus the Messiah.

[5] *Dan* was the northernmost major city in Israel and *Beersheba* was the southernmost. The writer wants us to understand that none of us will escape God's judgment for sin except through his Messiah.

[6] The Lord was not judging the Israelites unfairly for David's sin. Verse 1 tells us David sinned because the Lord decided to judge the Israelites for neglecting his Tabernacle and returning to the ways of Saul.

[7] We looked at the Hebrew verb *nāham* and the idea of God *changing his mind* in the chapter "Act like a Little Girl". The writer uses the same verb again in verse 16 as soon as David prays.

The chapter therefore ends with a prophecy about *the day when a better Messiah will die.* The original readers of 2 Samuel knew exactly where the threshing floor of Araunah the Jebusite was because it was the site where Solomon built his Temple.[8] It was on Mount Moriah, the place where Abraham had sacrificed a sheep to save the life of Isaac and where he had prophesied in Genesis 22:14 that *"On the mountain of the Lord it will be provided."* It included a rocky crag which would later be known as Calvary.[9] That's why David refuses to receive the land from Araunah for free or to *"sacrifice to the Lord my God burnt offerings that cost me nothing".*[10] As a prophet, he grasps that his sacrifice points to a better Messiah than himself who will one day die on that spot to save the world.[11]

That makes the final verse of 2 Samuel the happiest of endings, even though it is a happy ending in disguise. The writer prophesies that God has a far better Messiah than David. Jesus would never sin like David, and he would lay down his perfect life as God's blood sacrifice for the rest of us who do.

The curtain falls on the drama of 1 and 2 Samuel with every eye fixed, not on David, but on the true and better Person God can use.

---

[8] 1 Chronicles 21:28–22:1; 2 Chronicles 3:1. The writer of 2 Samuel ends his story with this event, but 1 Chronicles continues with eight final chapters which celebrate the Temple which would be built there.

[9] 24:24 tells us the price which David paid for Araunah's threshing floor, but 1 Chronicles 21:25 tells us the price which he paid for Araunah's bigger tract of land which included much more of Mount Moriah.

[10] In saying this, David encourages us that our worship is actually most precious to the Lord on the days when we feel least like worshipping.

[11] This is why David offers the sacrifice as a priest in the order of Melchizedek instead of getting Zadok or Abiathar to do so as priests in the order of Aaron. Psalm 40:6–8 and 110:4 are fulfilled in Hebrews 7:11–17 and 10:1–10. 1 Chronicles 21:26 adds that fire fell from heaven on the altar, because it pointed to heaven's gift.

Conclusion: The Kind of Person God Can Use

Now, Lord God, keep for ever the promise you have
made concerning your servant and his house. Do as
you promised, so that your name will be great for ever.
(2 Samuel 7:25–26)

Nobody really knows who wrote 1 and 2 Samuel. Some people use 2 Samuel 23:1 to argue that the whole thing was written by David. Others use 1 Chronicles 29:29 to argue it was written by the prophets Nathan and Gad. What seems more likely from the repeated references to Israel and Judah as two separate entities is that somebody wrote it shortly after 930 BC and the break-up of David's kingdom under his grandson Rehoboam.[1] Whoever the writer was, it is clear he was a prophet and that he wrote to train his readers to be the kind of people God could use.[2]

Solomon had started well but had failed. He had built the Temple, and the nations of the world had flocked to worship Israel's God. One of his most distinguished visitors had exclaimed, *"Praise be to the Lord your God who has delighted in you and placed you on the throne of Israel. Because of the Lord's eternal love for Israel, he has made you king."*[3] Then he stopped

---

[1] 1 Samuel 11:8; 17:52; 18:16; 27:6; 2 Samuel 5:5; 24:1–9 suggest it was written after 930 BC. 1 Samuel 27:6 suggests it was written before 925 BC when the Egyptians annexed Ziklag.

[2] The Hebrew Old Testament categorizes 1 and 2 Samuel among "the Former Prophets". It was never just a history book. It is a prophetic sermon about the kind of person God can use and about the coming Messiah.

[3] 1 Kings 10:9. 1 Chronicles 28:5 and 29:23 emphasize that Solomon was as much a picture of Jesus the Messiah during the first half of his reign as David was during his.

being humble and obedient because of his foreign wives and lost the purity and passion for God's name which had made him strong. Because he failed to repent as thoroughly as David, the Lord had told him that the ten northern tribes would be torn out of his successors' hands. Since the writer of 1 and 2 Samuel was probably still reeling from this happening, we can see why he made such a heartfelt plea that God is still looking for the kind of men and women he can use.

Sadly, things would not improve during the centuries which followed the writing of 1 and 2 Samuel. But for a few godly exceptions such as Jehoshaphat, Hezekiah and Josiah, the kings who were born to David's house largely ignored the messianic covenant which the Lord had made with the founder of their dynasty. Jeremiah 21–23 laments that they were not the kind of people God can use and promises that the true Messiah would come and succeed where they had failed:

> *"The days are coming" declares the Lord, "when I will raise up for David a righteous Branch, a King who will reign wisely and do what is just and right in the land. In his days Judah will be saved and Israel will live in safety. This is the name by which he will be called: the Lord Our Righteous Saviour."*[4]

We can therefore sense the excitement when the gospel writers trace Jesus' ancestry back to David and tell us he is God's Messiah. The angels announce that *"The Lord God will give him the throne of his father David... His kingdom will never end,"* and that *"Today in the town of David a Saviour has been born to you; he is the Messiah."*[5] People recognize him as *"the son of David"* and as God's true King.[6] He was perfectly humble, perfectly

---

[4] Jeremiah 23:5–6.

[5] Matthew 1:1–17; Luke 1:32–33, 2:4, 11.

[6] Matthew 1:1; 9:27; 12:23; 15:22; 20:30–31; 21:9, 15; 22:42; John 1:49; 6:15; 12:13; 18:39; 19:19.

obedient, perfectly pure and perfectly zealous for his Father's name. He died on a cross as God's perfect sacrifice for sin on the land which Araunah the Jebusite had sold to David. After his resurrection, he told his followers to preach the good news of his kingdom after he ascended back to heaven.

The early Christians understood the message of 1 and 2 Samuel. They paraphrased 1 Samuel 13:14 as *"I have found David son of Jesse, a man after my own heart; he will do everything I want him to do"*, and pointed out to one another that David had merely served God's purpose within his own generation.[7] They encouraged one another to be the kind of people God could use in their own generation and to lay foundations for each subsequent generation of believers to be humble, obedient, pure, passionate for God's name and repentant as well. They even embraced the name "Christian" when their enemies used it to taunt them for being "little Christs". Jesus was the ultimate Anointed One – *Messiah* in Hebrew and *Christ* in Greek – and they were happy to embrace his commission to go into all the world as his little anointed ones themselves.[8]

Whenever Christians co-operated with God's programme and became the kind of people he could use, he granted them success and advanced his Kingdom, but whenever they turned to the agenda of Saul and Absalom and Joab, he thwarted them at every turn. Within three centuries the Church conquered the Roman Empire, but in the following centuries the spirit of the Roman Empire reared its ugly head again and again within the Church. Whenever leaders repented, God granted them revival and fresh advance for his Kingdom, but they usually proved as weak as Solomon in continuing along the path of blessing. By the year 1872, a British preacher named Henry Varley was forced

---

[7] Paul says this in Acts 13:22 and 36, revealing the content of much first-century Christian teaching.

[8] Acts 11:26; 1 Peter 4:16. David had hinted at this commission in the song he wrote for the dedication of his Tabernacle. He refers to God's People in 1 Chronicles 16:22 as *"anointed ones"* or *"messiahs"*.

to grieve that *"The world has yet to see what God can do with and for and through a man who is fully and wholly consecrated to him."*

An uneducated American shoe-salesman named Dwight Moody heard Henry Varley's statement and was convicted to the core. *"Varley meant any man! Varley didn't say he had to be educated, or brilliant, or anything else. Just a man! Well, by the Holy Spirit in me, I'll be one of those men,"* he resolved.[9] He went on to persuade hundreds of thousands of people to receive Jesus as their King, and he trained a generation of disciples to be the kind of people God can use.

As we end 1 and 2 Samuel, the writer wants us to be challenged by the successes and failures of Church history as much as Henry Varley and D. L. Moody. He wants us to embrace the message of each of the five sections of his prophetic history book to become humble, obedient, pure, passionate for God's name and repentant, just as David was. He wants us to view it as a description of the character of God's true Messiah, and to treat it as the marching song of those who enlist as soldiers in his Kingdom army.

The Church may appear to be on the run and hidden away in a cave like David and his men at the end of 1 Samuel, but it will advance and conquer the nations for Christ if people like us take our place in Jesus' army and reject the way of Saul, Absalom and Joab in favour of the way of David.

The world has still yet to see what God can do with and for and through a man or woman who is fully and wholly consecrated to him. Put down 1 and 2 Samuel and let the Holy Spirit strengthen you to be that man or woman. As you devote your life to its message for the sake of God's Messiah, you will be the kind of person God can use.

---

[9] John Pollock in *Moody: The Biography* (1963).